CANON

AND

AUTHORITY

Canon
and
Authority

Essays in Old Testament Religion and Theology

edited by

GEORGE W. COATS AND BURKE O. LONG

with contributions by

Peter R. Ackroyd
Bernhard W. Anderson
Ronald E. Clements
George W. Coats
Paul D. Hanson

Rolf P. Knierim
Burke O. Long
James A. Sanders
Wayne Sibley Towner
Gene M. Tucker

FORTRESS PRESS   Philadelphia

Library of Congress Catalog Card Number 76–62614
ISBN 0–8006–0501–2

6199B77   Printed in U.S.A.   1–501

To

WALTHER ZIMMERLI

CONTENTS

PREFACE

The notion of biblical authority points essentially to a way of talking about relationships between the Bible and the individual believer, and by extension, with the Bible, believer, and the church of which he is a part. Seen theologically, biblical authority is based upon God's word given to man; viewed as social reality, biblical authority is a kind of power which is created, legitimated, and actualized in a complex interaction among the believer, his sacred book, and others in his social situation. Implicit is the idea that the Bible is something to which the Christian in some way submits himself.

This component of the life of faith lies behind a great many modern treatments of the Old Testament. This is not surprising, since a large number of such studies have been carried out by persons within the church. That the topic should emerge in modern times as a kind of public issue, however, was probably inevitable. For all its banality nowadays, the observation rings true that biblical authority has gradually become problematical. But the full emotional and cognitive awareness of this state of affairs still comes rather much as a surprise, as though one had been wrenched from inattentive musing to discover a strange landscape, a new interior map, a new language.

Recent social upheavals, so often chronicled by others who are concerned with modernization, need not be rehearsed in detail again. The main point seems to be that traditional repositories of social and religious norms have simply weakened in recent decades, and this change has contributed to the lessening impact of the Bible upon Western society. Many are willing to adopt new foci of religious authority: new relationships, systems of symbols, value orientation and commitments, new modes of being religious. Certainly this spirit of pluralism is not new to our age. But it is perhaps newly esteemed. And in consort with professed toleration for individualism, this new valuation tends to undermine customary pressures toward religious conformity.

Ironically, the fruits of scholarly labors have contributed about as much toward making scriptural authority problematic as have any large social changes. The last one hundred years or so of indefatigable scholarship have produced new and undoubtedly productive methods of biblical study—literary, form, traditio-historical, and redaction criticism.[1] And yet, from one point of view, the results have added up to an overwhelming and undeniable sense of the diversity within the canonical OT. Also, burgeoning exploration of the environment which gave birth to the OT inevitably called into question dogmatic claims about the uniqueness of the Bible in providing norms for belief and practice. Thus what seemed obvious to some was all the more sharply exposed for all: the precritical notion of canon, with its claim to be a unified revelation with primary religious authority—that notion appeared inherently arbitrary, intolerably narrow, and untimely. This was but a statement in new dress of a nineteenth century view which denigrated the notion of canon as simply an ecclesiastical valorization of no real significance for understanding the OT.[2] Even the discernible conservative reaction in wide sectors of the church has had little effect beyond widening the gap between those for whom biblical authority and canon have become problematical and those for whom the times call for renewed affirmation of the Bible's authoritative role in religious life.

In this new context, the issue of biblical authority has become a lively one. The discussion perhaps was not so much initiated as forced upon scholars who were simply doing what they had always done, that is, working out the dimensions of their faith in conversation with themselves, their studies, and their worlds.

A detailed and exhaustive survey of the results of these conversations is out of place in this volume. It is probably impossible to do full justice to the discussion anyway, given the diversity of perspectives and starting points. Nevertheless, a few tendencies may be discerned.[3] Above all, certain scholars have questioned the dominant, negative assessment of canon as it was promulgated by the giants of nineteenth and twentieth century criticism. They have expressed instead a new interest in canon

1. See the series *Guides to Biblical Scholarship* (ed. Gene M. Tucker and Dan O. Via, Jr.; Philadelphia: Fortress, 1970—).

2. See, e.g., W. Robertson Smith, *The Old Testament in the Jewish Church* (2d ed.; London: Black, 1902); Julius Wellhausen, *Prolegomena to the History of Ancient Israel* (Edinburgh: Black, 1885).

3. We acknowledge with gratitude the helpful comments of Brevard Childs, who responded to an earlier draft of this material.

as a subject deserving of serious historical investigation.[4] In addition there have appeared attempts to broaden the notion of canon, and to focus on the *process* by which traditions were transformed into authoritative scriptures. In effect this challenged the consensus. Canon is process, and the results of process; it is not simply a time-bound ecclesiastical pronouncement. Above all, B. S. Childs[5] and J. A. Sanders[6] have opened up the historical and theological dynamics of canonical process—the collection, selection, interpretative sifting and application of traditions, a process which finally produced the body of writings now designated as canonical. This has meant, too, studying with new seriousness the final shape of the OT writings simply because the *textus receptus* represents an important stage in the history of the book.

A kind of secularized, or at least not explicitly theological, form of this newly positive interest in canon may be seen in developments stemming from a general dissatisfaction with classic form criticism. One senses less enthusiasm for the study of small units of tradition and their prewritten history, and more interest in larger components of the actual written text. Thus one thinks of rhetorical criticism[7] and applications of linguistic theory to the OT.[8] Particularly among American form critics an awakened interest in putting traditional form critical questions in new ways to *whole* texts has surfaced.[9] At the very least one may see here a certain resolve to treat the canonical form of the OT as something with integrity and sense, and worthy of fresh study, whether or not the motivations be religious.

One can read much of this concern with the historical dimension of

---

4. See A. C. Sundberg, Jr., *The Old Testament of the Early Church* (HTS 20; Cambridge, Mass.: Harvard, 1964); Sid Leiman, *Canonization of Hebrew Scripture: The Talmudic and Midrashic Evidence* (Hamden, Conn.: Shoestring, 1976); Joseph Blenkinsopp, *Prophecy and Canon: A Contribution to the Study of Jewish Origins* (Notre Dame: University of Notre Dame, 1977).

5. B. S. Childs, *Biblical Theology in Crisis* (Philadelphia: Westminster, 1970).

6. J. A. Sanders, *Torah and Canon* (2d ed.; Philadelphia: Fortress, 1972).

7. E.g., James Muilenburg, "Form Criticism and Beyond," *JBL* 88 (1969) 1–18. J. Jackson and M. Kessler, eds., *Rhetorical Criticism. Essays in Honor of James Muilenburg* (Pittsburgh: Pickwick, 1974).

8. Wolfgang Richter, *Exegese als Literatur Wissenschaft* (Göttingen: Vandenhoeck & Ruprecht, 1971); Erhardt Güttgemanns, *Offene Fragen zur Formgeschichte des Evangeliums: Eine methodologische Skizze der Grundlagenproblematik der Form- und Redaktionsgeschichte* (BEvT 54; 2d ed.; Munich: C. Kaiser, 1971).

9. See Rolf Knierim, "Old Testament Form Criticism Reconsidered," *Int* 27 (1973) 435–67. This attention to the final text is likely to characterize many of the forthcoming commentaries produced by the Claremont Form Critical Project, under the direction of Knierim and Tucker.

canon and the canonical form of the OT as an indirect response to the modern theological issue of biblical authority. The intent does not seem to be directly apologetic. Nevertheless, at least Childs and Sanders join the issue directly. For the latter—and his article in this volume clearly illustrates this—Israel's hermeneutical activity is analogous to contemporary modes of adapting biblical traditions to new situations.[10] For Childs, the final canonical form of the traditions, even though it lives between the rich processes of precanonical and postcanonical developments, does in fact function normatively for the church.[11]

Implicit here, of course, is ultimately a reaffirmation of the OT as a book which is in some way valid for modern faith. The means by which this can be so differ greatly. James Barr, for example, is critical of any notion of canon which tends toward fixity, absolutism, and the like. One detects in his writings a certain acceptance of the Bible's problematic role in modern society, and a full acknowledgment of the fluidity of faith and theology, the diversity within the OT, and an openness to various bases for religious authority.[12] On the other hand, some focus upon a "canon within the Canon," that is, give primacy to a single portion of the scriptures from which one interprets the whole and sees relevant norms for contemporary theology. G. von Rad in effect operated in this fashion with his emphasis upon the pentateuchal traditions as definitively shaped by a "credo."[13] Most recently, Walter Brueggemann has developed the notion that OT wisdom writings speak with particular authority in modern times, and illuminate other portions of the OT.[14] The recent American interest in linking biblical criticism with process theology is in effect another way of interpreting the claims of the biblical text as authoritative.[15]

---

10. Sanders, *Torah and Canon*; see also his "Hermeneutics" (*IDBSup*; Nashville: Abingdon, 1976) 402–7.

11. See especially B. S. Childs, *The Book of Exodus: A Critical Theological Commentary* (Philadelphia: Westminster, 1974).

12. James Barr, *The Bible in the Modern World* (New York: Harper & Row, 1973). See also his "Biblical Theology" and "Scripture, Authority of" (*IDBSup*; Nashville: Abingdon, 1976) 104–11; 794–97.

13. G. von Rad, "The Form Critical Problem of the Hexateuch," *The Problem of the Hexateuch and Other Essays* (New York: McGraw Hill, 1966) 1–78; and his *Old Testament Theology* (2 vols.; New York: Harper & Row 1962–65).

14. Walter Brueggemann, *In Man We Trust: The Neglected Side of Biblical Faith* (Richmond: John Knox, 1973).

15. See, e.g., Lewis Ford, "Biblical Recital and Process Philosophy: Some Whiteheadian Suggestions for Old Testament Hermeneutics," *Int* 26 (1972) 198–209; also the papers by Beardslee, Weeden, Griffin, Janzen, Reitz et al. in a special issue of *Encounter* 36 (1975) 281–432.

The various contributors to this volume of essays represent many of these recent tendencies. Five of the essays raise historical questions. LONG views the religious authority of the prophets from the standpoint of their social interaction and finds that his attempt opens onto questions regarding written prophetic collections for which religious, revelational authority was already being claimed. SANDERS writes that the conflicts between prophets in ancient Israel reveal to us their opposing hermeneutic of religious tradition, and that this shows early impulses toward achieving normative formulation of religious truth. Indeed, CLEMENTS shows how the New Testament claim that the prophets spoke with one voice of the coming of Christ had important precedent in the centuries' older attempts to unify what the Israelite prophets taught, but without reference to a messiah. These impulses toward canonization, or better, toward settling on a generally authoritative body of religious truth, are visible also in the use of superscriptions to the prophetic books, as TUCKER shows. Here at an early stage a crucial element in what was eventually to become canon is present: the claim that a collection of material is unified in its revelational content and authority. Yet so much remains unknown or obscure. And as ACKROYD writes, alternate versions of a prophet's encounter with the king reveal to us the chance factors which went into the evolution of a corpus of authoritative writings. Consistent with the historian's basic effect, he complicates, rather than simplifies, our notions of the process of canonization.

Three other authors, having explicitly or implicitly acknowledged the problematic authority of the Bible, seek ways to recover interpretations of the OT that can speak in a normative way to contemporary faith and theology. COATS touches currents in process theology and develops the canonical image of Moses as a hero of the faith—one who is trusted by a God who persuades rather than coerces his servant, a hero who in turn is set free to persuade God and intercede for the people. On the other hand, HANSON is skeptical of using notions derived from process theology, and looks instead for inner biblical categories. Contradictions within the canonical form of Exodus lead him to an interpretation of biblical authority which stresses the dynamic of divine-human interaction, a dynamic which is creative and liberating, and which transcends all social vehicles within which it is perceived and expressed. TOWNER writes of the shift away from such pentateuchal materials, and chronicles instead the recent attempts to find in the wisdom corpus the scriptural voices which touch and define contemporary experience.

Finally, two essays exemplify the new inclination of biblical scholars to accept the full integrity and value of the canonical form of the OT text. This must be after all one of the important foundations for dealing with the issue of biblical authority. ANDERSON reveals sparkling insight into the theology of Genesis 1 by focusing his attention on the literary style of the priestly account. And KNIERIM aims at a proper understanding of the canonical form of Amos 1–2 by studying closely the Hebrew suffix *nû*.

A collection of essays can hardly touch upon all the issues, and least of all present a systematic discussion of the problem of biblical authority and canon. A volume such as this one can only offer particular and somewhat independent comments. It shows the beginning of the work of synthesis. In that spirit we have dedicated these essays to an esteemed teacher and colleague, Walther Zimmerli, on the occasion of his seventieth birthday and his presidency of the International Organization for the Study of the Old Testament (1977). During his long career Professor Zimmerli has shaped and decisively influenced many areas of OT study. We trust that our concerns have been close to his—hearing the OT with clarity in a world of competing and considerably more strident voices.

GEORGE W. COATS

BURKE O. LONG

CONTRIBUTORS

PETER R. ACKROYD
Samuel Davidson Professor of Old Testament Studies
University of London, King's College

BERNHARD W. ANDERSON
Professor of Old Testament Theology
Princeton Theological Seminary

RONALD E. CLEMENTS
Lecturer in Divinity
Cambridge University

GEORGE W. COATS
Professor of Old Testament
Lexington Theological Seminary

PAUL D. HANSON
Professor of Old Testament
Harvard University

ROLF P. KNIERIM
Professor of Old Testament
School of Theology at Claremont, California,
and Claremont Graduate School

BURKE O. LONG
Associate Professor of Religion
Bowdoin College

JAMES A. SANDERS
*Elizabeth Hay Bechtel Professor of Biblical
and Intertestamental Studies*
School of Theology at Claremont, California
and Claremont Graduate School

WAYNE SIBLEY TOWNER
Professor of Old Testament
Union Theological Seminary in Virginia

GENE M. TUCKER
Associate Professor of Old Testament
Candler School of Theology, Emory University

CANON

AND

AUTHORITY

PART ONE

STAGES IN THE

FORMATION OF CANON

1. PROPHETIC AUTHORITY AS SOCIAL REALITY

BURKE O. LONG

The authority of the OT prophet is not so easy to define and understand as might first appear. When the question is posed at all, it tends to appear in theological dress, heavily dominated by issues of religious truth. The prophet is seen in normative, theological terms, a servant only of God, speaking with divine authority, an exponent of truth in opposition to those who speak falsehood.[1] This perspective, of course, derives in part from the OT itself, which seems concerned to vindicate certain prophets at the expense of others. The theological path is nonetheless a narrow one, and tends to ignore the social dimension of religious authority, as though competing prophetic claims could be issued, evaluated, and decided apart from concrete structures of human community. Whereas the English word "authority" itself is abstract—and the Hebrew language contains little that is really equivalent—the reality must be seen in all its complex concreteness. Authority is a term of relationship, standing for a social reality, and our understanding must be alive to the fluidity of specific situations in which authority may be claimed or exercised.

So far as I am able to judge, the modern sociological discussion of authority is heavily indebted to Max Weber.[2] Authority may refer to a property of person, office, or institution—broadly put, to a property of social order. Or it may describe the relationship between two offices, one superior, the other subordinate. Authority may mean the quality of

1. J. Marsh, "Authority" *IDB* (1962) 1. 319. See Johannes Pedersen, *Israel III–IV* (London: Oxford, 1940) 142. R. B. Y. Scott, *Relevance of the Prophets* (New York: Macmillan, 1968) 100–106; G. von Rad, *OT Theology* (2 vols.; New York: Harper & Row, 1965) 2. 209–10; G. Quell, *Wahre und Falsche Propheten: Versuch einer Interpretation* (Gütersloh: Gütersloher Verlag, 1952) 66.
2. Max Weber, *Economy and Society* (New York: Bedminster, 1956/68). See also J. Wach, *Sociology of Religion* (Chicago: University of Chicago, 1944) who consciously builds upon Weber's earlier work.

3

a communication such that it is accepted as truthful and a basis for action. Or there may be variations of any of these.[3]

Whatever the particular focus, the attribution of legitimacy is fundamental and necessary. Weber thought of authority as "legitimate domination," by which he meant those modes of exercising power that incorporate a sense of rightness, fitness, justification, legitimate order. It is "legitimate power," and while not exclusively a property of institutions, it is most dramatically seen within them.[4]

The attribution of legitimacy means that authority is at least distinct in principle, if not always in practice, from coercion and force on the one hand, and leadership, persuasion, influence on the other. Authority presupposes some degree of willing acceptance. Indeed, it may be based upon the most diverse motives for compliance, in short upon *any* minimum interest which would accord legitimacy to an exercise of power. Thus, authority is fundamentally a *social* reality, having to do with social relationships that are more or less fixed, depending on the circumstances. Authority requires one who dominates and one who accepts domination as legitimate for any number of reasons.[5]

Weber thought of the authority of prophets, magicians, diviners, innovators of various kinds as distinct from other types mainly in the degree to which their authority rested upon devotion to the exceptional character of an individual person and of the normative patterns of order revealed or ordained by him.[6] Naturally this comes closest to the situation of the biblical prophets, who were singularly dependent upon acceptance by others for any measure of authority which they might have exercised. Even though Weber focused on the *person* of the charismatic figure more than on his social context, the fully sociological view was implicit. Authority is real in societal terms only in the interaction between prophet and his public. It is essential to ask about acceptance, about granting legitimacy. What claims are made, *who* accords legit-

3. Peabody, "Authority," *International Encyclopedia of the Social Sciences* (New York: Macmillan, 1968) 1. 473–77.
4. See S. M. Dornbusch and W. R. Scott, *Evaluation and the Exercise of Authority* (San Francisco: Jossey-Bass, 1975); R. Bierstadt "The Problem of Authority" in M. Berger et al., *Freedom and Control in Modern Society* (New York: Octagon, 1954/64); G. Wijeyewardene, ed., *Leadership and Authority: A Symposium* (Singapore, 1968); J. Schütz, *Paul and the Anatomy of Apostolic Authority* (Cambridge: Cambridge University, 1975).
5. Weber, *Economy and Society*, 1. 212.
6. Ibid., 215–16.

imacy, for what reasons, under what conditions? To have answers to these questions is to know something about an act of power, and to know whether it is an act of authority.[7]

This interactionist perspective brings us face to face with a difficult problem in OT studies. One would like to inquire after the prophet's authority in his own situation. But there are only limited and often ambiguous clues as to how a prophet was received, or by whom he was deemed authoritative. Usually we have at our disposal allusions to certain peripheral phenomena. In the midst of conflict, we can see various claims to legitimacy being offered as reasons for according authority; we may observe certain persons appealing to deeds of power as evidence of legitimacy; we are able to envision certain structures of social interaction, and actions which might serve to reinforce or deny claims to authority. But we can glimpse only very imperfectly authority as a mode of exercising legitimate power in biblical times.

There is a second difficulty. We see now through the eyes of tradents and their developed tradition. And here, too, we see imperfectly, supposing at the least that they would have granted authority to the prophet, perhaps while living, certainly after death. But their situations are removed from the immediacy of the prophet's activity. It may well be the case that authority is to be understood differently in such circumstances. At least one would expect that the factors involved would be aligned in new configurations.

My task in this paper, therefore, is to rethink the matter of the prophet's authority within the limits imposed by the textual tradition, and with the use of sociological models as an aid to understanding.[8] As far as possible, I am interested in exploring authority in the immediacy of the prophetic moment, realizing at the outset that most of the data will relate

---

7. Ibid., 242: "What is alone important is how the individual is actually regarded by those subject to charismatic authority, by his 'followers' or 'disciples'. . . . If proof and success elude the leader for long, if he appears deserted by his god or his magical or heroic powers, above all, if his leadership fails to benefit his followers, it is likely that his charismatic authority will disappear." Peter Worsley highlights this social aspect of authority above all in his study of the founders of cargo cults (*The Trumpet Shall Sound: A Study of "Cargo" Cults in Melanesia* [New York: Schocken, 1974], ix–xxi). See Thomas Overholt, "The Ghost Dance of 1890 and the Nature of the Prophetic Process," *Ethnohistory* 21 (1974) 37–63 for a thoroughgoing interactionist study.

8. Weber's "types" are ideal types, of course. Any historical examples therefore can only approximate the analytical category, and we may find that not all of the definitions will stand. Nonetheless, I believe that his questions, his essential way of looking at the elements involved in authority, have stood the test of time. They can aid in our exploration of biblical reality.

to material removed from that. I also wish to capture something of the nuance that occurs when the situation shifts from one of direct inter-action with the prophet to one of interaction with prophetic traditions.

I

The traditions which reflect conflict between the prophets and their opponents frequently appeal to transcendent warrant for prophetic ac-tion. This is in fact such a widely attested theme in the OT and so widely observed in field studies of religious specialists that one cannot doubt that it must have belonged to the real situations in which Israel's prophets sought to support their claims of authority. It is prejudicial to see simply a question of true and false, as the Septuagint and many interpreters have done. Rather, it was a question of contested authority, when truth was rather more difficult to possess than to claim. A Jere-miah or an Isaiah or any of the many unnamed prophets must have in principle faced an identical problem.

When opposed by priests and other prophets, Jeremiah simply cited a specific divine commission: "Yahweh sent me to prophesy against this house and against this city" (Jer 26:12, 15). The same appeal was remembered of Amos (Amos 7:15), and of Micah (Mic 3:8). Implic-itly, a similar appeal informs the argument in Jer 23:16b, 18–22, where it is claimed that the opposition prophets are untrustworthy, illegitimate precisely because they cannot be said to have received such transcendent warrant for their words (cf. Jer 29:9; Ezek 13:2–7).[9] The intent obviously would have been to persuade the audience to accept the proph-et's claim that he speaks legitimately, that is, with a divinely commis-sioned right.

But there is more than religious claim here. Jeremiah also asserts that he is innocent in the matter which so angered his opponents, not because he denies doing what they charge, but because he disclaims ultimate responsibility for his action (26:15). That amounts to claiming, tem-porarily at least, a privileged social status. He is beyond the law, so to speak, acting without guilt when speaking in this instance in a manner that would demand execution for others who might speak with less war-

9. This basic appeal is obviously deeply embedded in the very style of prophetic speech, quite apart from situations of conflict. See, for example, the messenger formula in Israel, and its counterparts in some of the Mari oracles, such as "Dagan sent me . . ." (ARM xiii, 114; ARM iii, 40; ARM ii, 90; cf. *ANET* [3d ed.; 1967] 624 for recent translations).

rant (see 38:4). He claims a status removed from social constraints applicable to other men. When operating as a "man of spirit" (see Hos 9:7; Mic 3:8; 2 Chr 15:1; Ezek 8:1), when speaking the divine word, the prophet is not bound to support the royal city, as presumably other men are.

Such disclaimers are entirely consistent with the theological language of "call," which emphasized the divine prerogative, and set the prophet apart with special protection (Jer 1:4–8; Ezek 2:2–7), powers (2 Kgs 2:9–14), or motivation (Amos 3:8). The stress on lowly origins, with its implicit possibility that the man chosen does not qualify (Amos 7:14–15), underlines the extraordinary circumstances.[10] Even the theme of resistance to the call (Exod 4:1–17; Judg 6:15; Jer 1:6) may in effect reinforce disclaimers of responsibility in prophetic matters. The prophet is not like ordinary men because he acts against his will.

The important step here is to gain some sense of the social reality which accompanied such claims. In this moment of conflict, Jeremiah is in fact excused, is temporarily accorded a special status, but not because of his occupying any formalized social position. The princes may assume that he possesses a certain initial credibility in social convention (he behaves as a prophet), but they specifically cite their acceptance of his claims to speak for the deity (26:16). Nor does this attributed status appear to have anything to do with whether or not Jeremiah was a cult official.[11] The OT nowhere has one prophet citing his position in or outside the cultic establishment as an argument for or against the legitimacy of an opponent. Hence the conflict between prophets must have been one between persons of essentially the same social identity and location. My guess is that Jeremiah and the other so-called classical prophets were exactly like the unnamed *něbî'îm* who, in Johnson's words, "enjoyed a certain official status but not necessarily a very subordinate one."[12] In any case, the social status claimed in Jeremiah 26 is one which is less than formally supported; it is not a question of being in or outside the cult, of being a professional, semiprofessional, or even lay person. The claim to special position rests entirely upon the prior claim

10. Hermann Schult, "Amos 7:15a und die Legitimation des Aussenseiters," *Probleme biblischer Theologie* (ed. Hans W. Wolff; Munich: C. Kaiser, 1971) 462–78.

11. P. Berger, "Charisma and Religious Innovation: The Social Location of Israelite Prophecy," *American Sociological Review* 28 (1963) 940–50; James Williams, "The Social Location of Israelite Prophecy," *JAAR* (1969) 153–65.

12. Aubrey Johnson, *The Cultic Prophet in Ancient Israel* (2d ed.; Cardiff: University of Wales, 1962) 64.

of transcendent commission. And the social realization of that claim depends upon its acceptance by others.

Clearly such a special status was a highly unstable position. It could only exist insofar as particular circumstances might allow. We are in the dark about much of this. Nonetheless, we may observe that Shemaiah, a prophet in Babylon, assumes that Jeremiah, like every other "madman who prophesies" (29:26), operates under the control of Zephaniah, the priest in charge of the temple. Yet, for reasons unknown to us, Zephaniah rejects this claim, allowing Jeremiah to reply to his opponent (29:29–32), implicitly according to Jeremiah some special protection and/or status. In the process, of course, Jeremiah's opponent—who must have been claiming equal authority in the situation—is rejected. Just as easily, the tables could be turned. Pashhur the priest rejects out of hand the authority of Jeremiah (Jeremiah 20), as does King Zedekiah on another occasion (Jer 32:3), and the princes on another (Jer 38:4–5). Earlier, Uriah had been summarily rejected (Jer 26:20–23), and Amos by Amaziah (Amos 7:12).

Hence, Jeremiah's disclaimer of ultimate responsibility for his words, when it meets with acceptance, reflects at the same time a temporary waiver of ordinary convention. Conversely, rejection of Jeremiah's claims would have meant a denial of his special status and claim to speak for Yahweh. Perhaps, but not necessarily, those who spurned the prophet would also have rejected his god.

Owing to its theological interest, however, the tradition has flattened these social ambiguities, and highlighted only the religious issue. The person of Jeremiah matters little; what is at stake for the narrator is the community's response to Yahweh's word (26:17–19). The situation is qualitatively different from withholding legitimacy to one who violates laws, or constitutions, and the like. It is rather a question of relationship to the sacred realm with its fully ambiguous power for good and evil. For the storyteller, who accepts Jeremiah's authority, rejection of the prophet is tantamount to rejection of God, and to bringing about God's calamity (26:19). From the same partisan standpoint, Jer 29:32 terms opposition to Jeremiah as "rebellion against the Lord." In short, appeals for legitimacy in the midst of conflict inevitably go to the heart of a society's attitudes toward the sacred. Undoubtedly the depth of the partisan feelings stirred on such occasions affected the degree of authority granted a particular prophet.

Many scholars presume that just this atmosphere of hostility and rivalry, which was more or less indigenous to prophetism, elicited accounts of a prophet's initial call. G. von Rad expressed a typical opinion when he wrote:

> The men who speak to us in these accounts are men who . . . were faced with the need to justify themselves both in their own and in other people's eyes. . . . The call commissioned the prophet: the act of writing down an account of it was aimed at those sections of the public in whose eyes he had to justify himself.[13]

Recently J. Bright[14] and K. Carley[15] have extended this general view to include much of the autobiographically styled prose in Jeremiah and Ezekiel.

Without doubt, the OT accounts of call claim divinely supported authority. In that sense they seem to present detailed versions of the much simpler appeals found in situations of conflict (Jer 26:12; Amos 7:15). Yet one ought to resist conceiving in too restrictive a way the *Sitz im Leben* for these longer accounts.[16] Nothing in the accounts themselves necessarily suggests that they were created solely for self-justification. Call-like motifs can occur in varied circumstances. Engnell has cited a parallel to Isa 6:8 in Assyrian incantation texts.[17] When routinely speaking oracles, the ecstatics of Mari apparently referred to their divine commission.[18] The Israelite prophets made similar allusions (Jer 3:12). Similarly, diviners from middle India allude to their authority when exorcising evil spirits: "Who binds the spirits? The guru binds, and I the guru's pupil."[19]

---

13. G. von Rad, *Theology*, 2. 54–55. See for example: J. Lindblom, *Prophecy in Ancient Israel* (Philadelphia: Fortress, 1962) 182; J. P. Hyatt, *Prophetic Religion* (Nashville: Abingdon, 1957) 31–49; Th. C. Vriezen, *An Outline of Old Testament Theology* (2d ed.; Oxford: Blackwell, 1970) 234: "the call narrative is considered as a kind of 'letter of credence' . . ."; R. Knierim, "The Vocation of Isaiah," *VT* 18 (1968) 62: "The cause of such a writing is obviously unbelief and opposition to the prophet and his message"; H. Wildberger, *Jesaja* (Neukirchen: Neukirchener, 1965—) 238.

14. John Bright, "The Prophetic Reminiscence," *Die Ou Testamentiese Werkgemeenskap in Suid-Afrika* (Pretoria: Pro Rege-Pers, 1966) 11ff.

15. Keith Carley, *Ezekiel among the Prophets* (SBT 31; Naperville: Allenson, 1975) 67–69. The evidence adduced is hardly persuasive.

16. See B. Long, "Recent Field Studies in Oral Literature and the Question of *Sitz im Leben*," *Semeia* 5 (1976) 35–49.

17. I. Engnell, *The Call of Isaiah* (Uppsala Universitets Arsskrift 4; Uppsala, 1949) 42.

18. See note 9 above.

19. V. Elwin, *The Baiga* (London: Murray, 1939) 391.

Moreover, available data from field studies suggest that accounts of call are rarely recited by charismatic specialists to counter criticism. Such accounts can be elicited (notably by the field anthropologist), but are rarely offered in day-to-day affairs. Of course, respected practitioners are generally known to have established their "call" by means of family ties, claiming stereotyped supernatural experiences, or anomalous behavior before going through whatever process is required for acceptance by their society. But this knowledge amounts to little more than public information possessed by observers external to the process of making a ritual specialist. Traditional societies tend to confirm the charismatic's calling mainly through evaluation of acts—that is, by relying upon external demonstrations rather than subjective claims.[20] Is the prophet, or shaman, or diviner certified in some external way? (Is he from a known line of charismatic specialists?) Does his behavior conform to what is expected? (E.g., was there sickness or vision or deviant behavior interpreted as sign of "call"? Are the reports reliable?) Is the specialist successful at his job? (Does he cure, if that is what is expected? Does he divine workable solutions to problems, if that is what is expected? Does he transmit oracles that conform to community expectations? Is the message relevant to a specific situation?)[21]

Of course, there may be exceptions, and the sources are somewhat

20. T. O. Beidelman ("Priests and Prophets: Charisma, Authority and Power among the Nuer," in T. O. Beidelman, ed., *The Translation of Culture* [London: Tavistock, 1971] 375–415), puts the matter bluntly for the Nuer peoples: "Unlike priests, Nuer prophets must manifest anomalous attributes to demonstrate the validity of their claims to a new and unusual authority. . . . Confirmation of a prophet's calling is mainly through public evaluation of the kinds of acts the nascent prophet claims to have performed after his strange behaviour begins—and by his success in curing, bringing fertility, removing epidemics, divining the future, bringing rain, cursing opponents . . ." (390). Cf. J. Beattie and J. Middleton, eds., *Spirit Mediumship and Society in Africa* (London: Routledge and Kegan Paul, 1969) *passim.*

21. Relevant materials are widely scattered and of varied usefulness. S. M. Shirokogoroff, *Psychomental Complex of the Tungus* (London: Routledge and Kegan Paul, 1935) 344–53, is important for its case histories and careful attention to public evaluation of the would-be shaman's claims. Autobiographical accounts, elicited by the anthropologist, may be found in V. Elwin, *The Baiga* (London: Murray, 1939) 132–38, 158–60; M. A. Czaplicka, *Aboriginal Siberia. A Study in Social Anthropology* (Oxford: Clarendon, 1914) 173–78; W. L. Warner, *A Black Civilization: A Social Study of an Australian Tribe* (2d ed.; New York: Harper, 1958) 210–16; J. Buxton, *Religion and Healing in Mandari* (Oxford: Clarendon, 1973) 275–95; L. Sternberg "Divine Election in Primitive Religion" *Congrès International des Americanistes.* Compte-Rendu de la XXIᵉ Session, I (Göteborg, 1925) 472–512; W. Bogoras, *Chuckchee Mythology* (Jesup North Pacific Expedition, vol. 8, parts 1–2; New York: American Museum of Natural History, 1910) 34–42. A typology of anomalous events associated with "call" of shamans may be found in U. Knoll-Greiling, "Berufung und Berufungserlebnis bei die Schamanen," *Tribus* n.s. 2–3 (1952–53) 227–38.

deficient. But the general point seems assured. In traditional societies, legitimacy, and therefore authority, is evaluated primarily on the basis of behavior. Hence the first line of appeal that a specialist might be expected to take if his authority was contested would be not to recite his "call" but to engage in activities which could concretely demonstrate to others the validity of his claims. This in fact is exactly what happens in some societies in which shamans compete fiercely for supremacy in status and authority.[22] And we see this in Elijah's struggle with the prophets of Baal (1 Kgs 18:20–40).

What then of the biblical accounts of call? They do not seem to me to be directly related to contested authority in the prophet's own situation. Rather, the vocational accounts of Isaiah, Jeremiah, and Ezekiel are balanced presentations of reflected material, far removed from direct conflict and any immediate need to justify. They function most directly in relation to the edited form of the book.

In Jeremiah 1, despite a broad tendency to interpret the text in biographical terms,[23] I remain convinced by E. Nicholson's argument that the chapter forms an editorial unit compiled by later tradents to present an interpretative introduction to the book. Themes that loom large in the material to follow are sounded already at the beginning—in the call sequence, the vision reports, and in the elaborations of vv 15–19.[24] The structure of the material seems carefully planned as well: the reader begins with the call (vv 4–10) and ends with a recapitulation (vv 17–19; cf. v 8); sandwiched between are two vision reports dealing with Jeremianic themes of surety of Yahweh's word, and the destruction to come. And from all this emerges an editorial portrait of Jeremiah—one who has been set apart and will face suffering, but who will prevail (cf. chaps. 26–45). Insofar as this account of call might serve to reinforce authority, it must have done so for a time and situation far removed from Jeremiah himself. It seems a question of vindication for a prophet who "lives" in a tradition, and hence the claims of authority are for a book and perhaps for those who transmit that book as religious truth.

22. See, e.g., Bogoras, *Mythology*, 1–25 and 443. R. M. Berndt, "Wuradjeri Magic and 'Clever Men,' " *Oceania* 17 (1946–47) 327–65, especially 338–44; N. Chadwick, "Shamanism among the Tatars of Central Asia," *Journal of the Royal Anthropological Institute* 66 (1936) 75–112, especially 89–90, and literature cited therein.

23. See the most recent voices in long-standing tradition: W. Rudolph, *Jeremia* (3d ed.; Tübingen: Mohr, 1968) 3–8; A. Weiser, *Das Buch Jeremia* (Göttingen: Vandenhoeck & Ruprecht, 1966) 2, 4–8.

24. E. Nicholson, *Preaching to the Exiles* (New York: Schocken, 1970) 113–15.

Similarly, Isaiah 6 seems removed from the prophet's own situation. The text builds upon the juxtaposition of two traditions—the theophany of God who comes in judgment, and the divine council which selects a messenger to convey the decision.[25] Yet where one expects the actual word of judgment, one hears mysterious, veiled language about the general effect of the prophet's word when he speaks in Yahweh's name (vv 9–10). Elements of the text are very specific, but the total effect is rather more general. The words convey an understanding of Isaiah's overall activity as actually hastening the onset of inevitable destruction. No simple announcement of judgment here, for that could be taken as warning, as occasion for return (see Jonah 3:4–5; Jer 36:2–3). Rather, Isaiah's commission is the functional equivalent of an unalterable decree of punishment. His whole activity—and this could be judged only *ex post facto*—somehow was a part of the action of God working itself out in the catastrophe that befell a people who could not hear. The issue of Isaiah's legitimacy therefore seems secondary to an interest in divine judgment. This is congenial to O. Kaiser's supposition that Isa 6–9:7 formed a complete "roll" aimed at the survivors of catastrophe, and concerning not the call, or the legitimization of the prophet so much as testifying that God's judgment which they had experienced was already decreed.[26] Again, if authority is an issue in this text, it must be viewed in relation to the tradents and the later situation in which they worked, not in relation to Isaiah himself.

Finally, Ezek 1–3:15 offers a carefully shaped, even artistic, account that prefigures much that is to follow in the book of Ezekiel. The reader moves through a kind of visionary tableau that reaches its high point in 1:26–27, and is neatly summarized in v 28: "such was the vision of brightness all about—it was the vision of the image of the glory of Yahweh." Then follows divine address: two nearly identical speeches commissioning the prophet, separated by a brief vision report centering on the prophet's receiving the divine word (2:1–3:11). Then all is concluded with the departure of God's glory, evoking a theme raised at the beginning (2:28 and 3:12). Besides its carefully balanced structure, the text as a whole anticipates important themes to follow: the words of lamentation and woe (2:10; cf. 19:1, 14, et al.); the theme of stubborn

25. See Knierim, "Vocation of Isaiah," 47–68.
26. O. Kaiser, *Isaiah 1–12* (Philadelphia: Westminster, 1972) 73. Cf. N. K. Gottwald, "Immanuel as the Prophet's Son," *VT* 8 (1958) 36–47.

and rebellious Israel (2:3–4; 3:7; 12:1–3), and the glory of Yahweh (2:28; 3:12; 10:3–4; 11:22–33). As in the cases of Jeremiah and Isaiah, this looks like material that is far removed from the life situation of the prophet, and that reflects a more tradition-oriented concern, a concern for introducing and shaping the portrait of Ezekiel, his activity, possibly his vindication.[27] It is again a question of authority of a prophet as he "lives" in tradition.

In sum, I would suggest that the accounts of call have been shaped much more by a later, reflective concern than by the immediacy of the prophetic activity with its potential for contested authority. The accounts reflect a kind of interpretative interest, an interest in shaping a portrait of the prophet and introducing his "book" with a view possibly toward his vindication as a spokesman for truth. It is doubtful that they were ever used in such "full dress" form in the life situation of the prophet. More likely that these accounts might be used to support claims of followers, or successors in a certain prophetic tradition, who, lacking deeds of power, might support their own legitimacy by referring to the transcendent warrant of the master, now of course vindicated by events. In any case, even though we lack detailed information, it seems sufficiently clear that accounts of call relate most directly to problems of authority in the life situation of tradents, persons who looked back on the departed prophet, who were concerned with transmitting a body of vindicated portraits, claims, and exhortations.

II

As important as verbal claims of transcendent warrant and status may have been in the life situation of prophets, an equally important aspect of their authority would have involved actions that could be interpreted by others as demonstrating the prophet's legitimacy. Ezek 13:6 is a case in point: "They [the opposition prophets] have spoken falsehood and divined a lie; they say 'Says the Lord,' when the Lord has not sent them, and yet they expect him to fulfill their word." Explicitly, transcendent warrant and practical demonstration are put together. Implicitly, what is assumed as normal is that the claim of divine commission will be reinforced by an event or events interpreted as proof.

27. See R. Wilson, "An Interpretation of Ezekiel's Dumbness," *VT* 22 (1972) 91–104, who develops the notion that later editors were anxious to defend Ezekiel's standing as a legitimate prophet.

The requisite proof in this case is a prediction which comes true—a very pragmatic test to be applied to claims of authority. The test is widely mentioned in the OT, in early traditions (1 Sam 9:6; 1 Kgs 13:26; 17:8–16; 20:35; 2 Kgs 1:17; 3; 5; 14; 7:16; 9:26; etc.) and in late traditions (Jer 28:9; Deut 18:21). It was also a key perspective in shaping 1 Kings 22 (see v 28 and its "proof" in vv 29–36). The author of Jeremiah 28 made the point elegantly. Following Jeremiah's prediction of Hananiah's death, the narrator notes directly and quietly the latter's death within the month (Jer 28:17). This particular "test" gave rise to a special type of legend that built upon correspondence between oracle and its fulfillment (1 Kgs 17:8–16; 2 Kgs 2:19–22; 4:42–44; 6–7; somewhat 2 Kings 3).[28] A similar perspective became a structural *sine qua non* for the Deuteronomic history. Wherever possible the redactors made the exigencies of the royal affairs correspond to a word spoken by a prophet (1 Kgs 11:31–38; 12:15; 16:12, 34; 2 Kgs 10:17; 14:25; 23:16; 24:2; note especially the didacticism of 2 Kgs 7:16–20 in this regard).[29] Hence oracle and its fulfillment were seen by others in the society, and others who were later transmitting the traditions, as a kind of first order deed of power looked for from the legitimate prophet. It seems entirely typical therefore that Jeremiah's opponents can ridicule a moment of divine silence with the words, "Where is the word of Yahweh? Let it come!" (17:15) At that moment Jeremiah has no authority because he can produce no deed of power, no word to be fulfilled.

Deeds of power beyond words were expected, however. Bystanders could look to prophetic actions as demonstrating legitimacy, and therefore as reinforcing claims of authority. The power of turning away the deity's intended wrath is mentioned in Jer 27:18. More concrete and widely mentioned are "signs" or miracles. Deut 13:1 suggests that "signs and wonders" are to be expected in the normal course of prophets' activities. They were apparently of two kinds: signs interpreted as confirming that a prediction was going to be fulfilled (1 Sam 2:34; 1 Kgs 13:3; 2 Kgs 19:29; Isa 38:7–8) and signs viewed as demonstrating that a prophet's commission came from God (1 Sam 10:1 [LXX]; Judg

28. B. O. Long, "2 Kings iii and Genres of Prophetic Narrative," *VT* 23 (1973) 337–48.

29. See W. Dietrich, *Prophetie und Geschichte. Eine redaktionsgeschichtliche Untersuchung zum deuteronomistischen Geschichtswerk.* (Göttingen: Vandenhoeck & Ruprecht, 1972).

6:14). Both types of signs amount to the same thing: legitimation of the prophet. Moses must receive the power of miraculous deeds before his commission will be accepted by a skeptical public (Exod 4:1–9). Miracle confirms Elijah in his dispute with a distrustful woman (1 Kgs 17:17–24), and in a contest with opposing prophets (1 Kgs 18:36–40), just as it reinforces the authority of his successor, Elisha (2 Kgs 4:8–37). Even events of conspicuous hardship and failure could be interpreted so as to support claims of authority (Jer 1:18–19; 15:19–20).

These matters should not be underestimated. The general situation in ancient Israel seems perfectly consistent with what we know of charismatic specialists in other societies. For example, shamans in Australia, North America, and Asia compete for power and recognition in contests of miracle-making. Almost universally, diviners who show extraordinary knowledge and consistently produce solutions to problems enjoy authority and prestige, often extending far beyond their own village. Conversely, the practitioner who cannot produce convincing deeds of power is usually downgraded, even ignored, by the public. As Weber rightly pointed out, recognition freely given and guaranteed by accepted proof is decisive for the authority of the charismatic individual.[30]

Given this state of affairs, it seems natural enough that the telling of legends about such figures would have something to do with the issue of authority. On the one hand, legends may serve to reinforce authority in settings where the charismatic arts are flourishing. For example, in the course of divinatory rituals, West African Ifa diviners recite thousands of verses, including some narratives about diviners of primordial times. The stories frequently justify certain of the diviners' predictions or some of the sacrificial materials. They also consistently reinforce the clients' belief in the system of divination and the authority of the diviner by holding up examples of belief/disbelief, obedience and disobedience.[31]

On the other hand, when the charismatic arts are on the wane, legends can bolster authority in a slightly different way. In the late 1920s, Rasmussen reported of Eskimo shamanism: "The art rests upon traditions from olden times, and respect for shamanizing is really only created

30. See Weber, *Economy and Society*, 1. 241–42; Worsley, *Trumpet Shall Sound*, xiii; and note 23 above.
31. W. Bascom, *Ifa Divination* (Bloomington: Indiana University, 1969) 122, 129. One striking legend tells of two diviners who oppose one another and the miraculous vindication of the one, along with his materials of sacrifice (484–87).

by what people know from the old tales a shaman *should* be able to perform, if only he is sufficiently up in his art."[32]   The legends thus provide a standard of performance, a measure of evaluation, and presumably a test of legitimacy.   In short, they reinforce the principle while measuring the practice.   Older men among the Azande use tales in exactly this way, criticizing contemporary witch doctors, seeing them as pale and decadent copies of the great doctors known in their tales.   But they simultaneously affirm the efficacy of the art.[33]   The examples of this phenomenon can be multiplied.

Legends can obviously flourish under a variety of conditions, and have a variety of points—when a prophetic movement is youthful, when it is waning, when specialists are established and respected, or when they operate in climates of hostility and contention.   For ancient Israel, it is difficult to gain a clear picture.   It was apparently not unusual for Jeremiah's authority to be contested, and if Jeremiah's then Hananiah's, and if Hananiah's then other prophets unnamed and unknown.   So too Elijah (1 Kgs 18:36) and Ezekiel (Ezek 33:33).[34]   We of course do not see direct narrative evidence of legends about prophets in such situations. But the possibility is a strong one.   For one thing, Jer 26:18–19 notes that certain of the elders cited a precedent from the activities of a bygone prophet precisely in a situation in which Jeremiah's authority was in doubt.   An anecdote about an earlier prophet caught in similar circumstances is preserved as well (26:22–23), as though it were somehow relevant to Jeremiah's situation.   Given the fact that practitioner and laymen alike lived in the midst of conflict, it seems plausible that longer tales of prophets would have been recited in order to support both the claims of the prophets and the belief of their public.[35]

III

Evidently, the prophet, more than any other authority-bearing figure in ancient Israel, was dependent upon acceptance and devotion.   This fact

---

32. K. Rasmussen, *The Netsilik Eskimos* (Copenhagen: Nordisk, 1931) 295.

33. E. Evans-Pritchard, *Witchcraft, Oracles and Magic among the Azande* (Oxford: Clarendon, 1937) 195–99.

34. On prophetic conflict, see also J. L. Crenshaw, *Prophetic Conflict: Its Effect upon Israelite Religion* (Berlin: Walter de Gruyter, 1971); F. Hossfeld and I. Meyer, *Prophet gegen Prophet* (Freiburg: SKB, 1973). G. Münderlein, *Kriterien wahrer und falscher Prophetie* (Bern: Lang, 1974); H. Mottu, "Jeremiah vs. Hananiah: Ideology and Truth in OT Prophecy," *Radical Religion* 2 (1975) 58–67.

35. See B. O. Long, "The Social Setting for Prophetic Miracle Stories," *Semeia* 3 (1975) 46–63.

called forth a number of appeals and actions that were as varied as the particular situations in which the prophet plied his trade. Concrete, impermanent, vulnerable, episodic, are terms that fit the immediacy of the prophet's situation, as well as describe his verbal appeals and deeds of power.

However, this need not blind us to more permanent aspects of the social order which would have reinforced the prophet's position, or maintained conditions supportive of those who accepted his authority. We are in a position to see far less of this than one would wish. Nevertheless, a few suggestions might be made.

Scholars have often noted that prophets associated in groups (1 Sam 19:20; 2 Kgs 2:15; 4:38–41; 6:1), while they also wandered the countryside independent of one another. In addition, Isa 8:16, if the text is trustworthy, mentions "pupils" or "disciples." Jeremiah has his scribe (Jeremiah 36–37; 45). Moreover, the indication that some test of legitimate succession was important to a group of prophets (2 Kgs 2:1–18; Deut 18:15–18) points toward at least rudimentary institutionalization in the early period. The social consequences were likely very important, but we have no way to measure them. Aside from a few scattered references, the social relationships within and without such groups remain virtually unknown to us. Elijah stood at the head of his group (2 Kgs 6:1; cf. 4:38), presiding over a social realm within which his authority could be exercised with very little compromise, and where members of the group would have reinforced each other's beliefs. Probably one important mechanism here would have been the act of preserving and transmitting traditions. These undoubtedly would have been partisan collections, contributing to the cohesiveness of the group, and providing a measure of social control on behavior and attitudes. How the group was seen by outsiders, whether its position was reinforced or not, is completely unknown (cf. 2 Kgs 4:42).

There must have been some form of societal constraints, however, put upon this divine madness. We know that in the vicinity of Mari, for example, ecstatic oracle-givers were routinely subjected to corroboration by more established means of divination.[36] Nothing like this is attested in Israel, but we may assume at the very least that any person claiming to be a *nābî'* would conform to expected patterns of behavior. There may

36. W. L. Moran, "New Evidence from Mari on the History of Prophecy," *Bib* 50 (1969) 21–22.

have been distinctive dress (2 Kgs 1:8; Isa 20:2) or body marks (1 Kgs
20:38–41); certain expected patterns of speech, experiences interpreted
as signs of a "call," such as vision or audition (Isaiah 6; Jeremiah 1;
Ezekiel 1; 2 Kgs 2:11), certain powers of clairvoyance. Certain other
traditions portray the prophet as having private access to the king, and
able to speak at will, quite without flattery (Isa 7:3–9; 38:1–8; 2 Sam
12:1–15; 1 Kgs 20:41–42; Jer 37:16–17; 38:14–16). He is apparently expected to behave deviantly (Hos 1:2–8; Ezekiel 4–5; Isa
20:1–6; Jer 13:1–11), and is looked to for authoritative guidance (1
Kings 22; Ezekiel 8; Jer 37:3–10). Conformity to these role expectations would certainly have played a part in reinforcing claims to authority.

Beyond this, however, the OT adds a more general constraint: legitimacy, and hence authority, can be accorded one who conforms to a
consensual notion of piety, ethics, or demeanor. For example, Jer
29:23 seems to imply that opposition prophets are rejected not only
because their claims of divine warrant are disbelieved, but also because
their actions are contrary to expectations: they commit adultery with
their neighbors' wives. Similarly, Jer 23:11, 13–14, 27 imply that legitimacy may be measured by faithfulness to Yahweh. Indirectly, Micah
offers the same appeal by contrasting his own righteousness to his opponents' abuse of position (Mic 3:5–8). Deut 13:1–5 codifies the
matter. As with any other person (Deut 13:6–18), the prophet who
leads people astray, religiously speaking, shall be put to death, in effect
denying absolutely his authority. We have no way of knowing whether
or how this requirement was actualized in the social realm, or indeed
whether or not the charges of immorality were simple rhetorical gambits.
But at least, we may observe a theoretical formulation in Deuteronomy
13 for a more or less stable constraint upon prophetic action. Claims of
transcendent warrant or a momentary special, responsibility-free status,
or even group-supported legitimacy were not enough. Conformity with
the community's perception of religious decorum was also necessary for
authority to be actualized.

Another glimpse of community expectations appears in Jeremiah 28.
Confronted by Hananiah's oracle promising restoration, Jeremiah is reserved, withholds acceptance, and allows that one who speaks peace is
suspect because his message is out of step with the traditionally pessimis-
tic tone of, one must presume, legitimate prophets (Jer 28:8). Ezek

13:10, 16 presuppose a similar perspective. And "certain of the elders" in Jeremiah 26 cite a precedent for their problem with Jeremiah in an earlier prophet, Micah of Moresheth, who spoke of Jerusalem's demise (26:18). So, too, Jonah about Nineveh, and Amos against Amaziah (Amos 7:17), and Micaiah against Ahab (1 Kings 22). Indeed, the latter story puts the point with extraordinary skill. Ahab is a tragic figure who wishes to rest confidently in the victory-heralding optimism of his four hundred prophets, but who, nevertheless, knows immediately that when Micaiah *also* speaks a word of victory, he has lied—and events prove it.

In all these passages, the appeal clearly is for one to attribute legitimacy to, and hence accept the authority of, those prophets whose particular messages conform to this traditional sense of what is authentic. It is doubtful, however, that this particular appeal belongs to situations of actual conflict between prophets. To judge from our glimpses of such confrontations, words of peace were just as frequent, if not more so, than words of doom (cf. Mic 3:5; Jer 14:13; 6:14). I suspect that it was only in a much later situation, when tradents were looking back on their own history as one of final destruction, that such appeals for legitimacy made much sense. And in fact, the strongest statements of this particular appeal are correlated with obviously partisan traditions that demonstrate how events vindicated the pessimism of one particular prophet at the expense of others (1 Kings 22; Jeremiah 28; Ezekiel 13).

In sum, the authority of a prophet was a vulnerable, shifting social reality—closely tied to acceptance and belief. It was supported by verbal appeals to transcendent commission, and by concrete deeds of power, even momentary claims of special status, removed from bearing ultimate responsibility for one's words. But the authority rested upon acceptance of those appeals. It was reinforced by deeds taken as proof of legitimacy, and by telling legends of such deeds. But it *depended* upon attributing truth to the "sign" or to tales of such signs. The prophet's authority was likely maintained and supported in groups, and reinforced by his conformity with social expectations. But it was made real insofar as his behavior was accepted by others.

Many of the same issues were at work for those who transmitted and redacted the prophetic traditions, although their own times required a different mix of the elements. At the least, we may observe their appeal to elaborate accounts of "call," or to a single-minded focus on the vindication of a prophet in events that bear out his predictions.[37]   At the most, we might see the act of collecting materials into a prophet's book as a kind of final attempt to claim authority—now based in tradition, and no longer in the opening of the heavens or the awesome stroke of the master prophet himself.

37. Amos 7:10–17 has often been taken as undergirding the authority of the prophet. Recently, G. M. Tucker ("Prophetic Authenticity: A Form Critical Study of Amos 7:10–17," *Int* 27 [1973] 423–34) tied this function to controversies "among those who later heard and read the speeches of Amos concerning the authority and validity of those words" (431).   But the text points us to a time considerably later than Tucker envisions.   The narrative has its impact upon those who (1) can accept the claim of divine warrant; (2) can point to a deed of power as demonstration.   In this case, I should think the latter can only be the reality of the exile mentioned or "predicted" in v 17.   Hence we have to do with a question of authority that is argued from tradition, and reinforced by events known to the readers.   I wonder if this very late perspective, namely, that tradents requiring a deed as "proof" settled on the event of exile, explains why the tradition blends together a word of personal doom for Amaziah with the allusion to a general exile for all of Israel.

2. HERMENEUTICS IN TRUE AND FALSE PROPHECY

James A. Sanders

The problem of true and false prophecy in the OT has become a focal point for study of canonical hermeneutics. The thesis of the present study is that prophecy in biblical antiquity, whether "true" or "false," can be more fully understood when studied in the light of three major factors where available: ancient traditions (texts), situations (contexts), and hermeneutics. The following diagram may indicate their interdependence and interrelationship.

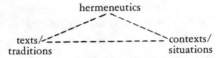

By texts is meant the common authoritative traditions employed and brought forward (re-presented) by the prophet to bear upon the situation to which he or she spoke in antiquity.[1] Such traditions included both the authoritative forms of speech expected of prophets and the authoritative epic-historic traditions to which they appealed to legitimate their messages.[2]

By contexts is meant the historical, cultural, social, political, economic, national and international situations to which prophets applied the "texts." Context here, then, is not solely or even principally a literary reference (though often the literary context is determinative for meaning), but refers primarily to the full, three-dimensional situation in antiquity necessary to understand the significance of the literary record or unit under study.[3]

---

1. The "masculine-neuter" pronouns will be used throughout the essay to refer to both prophets and prophetesses.
2. J. A. Sanders, *Torah and Canon* (2d ed.; Philadelphia: Fortress, 1974) 54–90.
3. See the critical discussion of "situation" by M. Buss in "The Idea of Sitz im Leben —History and Critique," forthcoming in *ZAW*.

By hermeneutics is meant the ancient theological mode, as well as literary technique, by which that application was made by the prophet, true or false, that is, how he read his "texts" *and* "contexts" and how he related them.

I

A review of work done to date on true and false prophecy indicates the importance of attempting to discern the hermeneutics of prophecy, especially in those instances where two or more prophets spoke to the same context, notably the disputations. Focus on these may yield indications for discernment between true and false prophecy not yet fully recognized.

Jeremiah 28, with Deuteronomy 13 and 18, is the *locus classicus* of the problem. G. Quell, in a study published in 1952, is often given credit for liberating study of true and false prophecy from a priori assumptions about Jeremiah's colleague, Hananiah (Jeremiah 28), who had been thought of largely as a cultic, nationalistic pseudoprophet, a fanatic demagogue, a libertine in morals, illiterate of spirit, and, indeed, an offender against the Holy Spirit.[4] He showed, by contrast, that Hananiah subscribed to the same traditions as Jeremiah, employing the same expected forms of both speech and symbolic action as the latter. It was the LXX which introduced the term pseudoprophet; the Hebrew Bible does not have it. Since Quell, intentionality is no longer a criterion for discernment of distinction between Hananiah and Jeremiah, and hence between so-called false and true prophets generally. Not only did Hananiah feel that he was right and Jeremiah wrong, Jeremiah was constrained after their initial encounter to identify with him and his message: "Amen! May the Lord do so!" (Jer 28:6). It is simply not possible to impugn the so-called false prophets with conscious, evil intention. Recognition of this fact in modern study has received broader support from the acknowledgment of pluralism as a factor in research. Unresolved debate at any juncture of history and recognition of the ambiguity of reality are stressed also in the sociology of knowledge.

Gerhard von Rad in 1933 could with some confidence find in his study of Jeremiah 28, and Deuteronomy 13 and 18, confirmation of what he already knew, that history was the vehicle of revelation.[5] And Sigmund Mowinckel in 1934 found that prophecies based on the Word of Yahweh

---

4. G. Quell, *Wahre und falsche Propheten* (Gütersloh: Bertelmann, 1952) 65.
5. G. von Rad, "Die falschen Propheten," *ZAW* 51 (1933) 119–20.

had greater likelihood of being true than those based on the Spirit of Yahweh.[6] Martin Buber in 1947 anticipated Quell's so-called defense of Hananiah in calling him *"ein prinzipientreuer Mann,"* a man true to his principles.[7] But Buber went on to use quite negative epithets: Hananiah was a political ideologue, blind in comparison to Jeremiah, and a successful politician. Although Buber's study of the crucial debate in Jeremiah 28 contains valuable observations for discussion of prophetic hermeneutics, he leaves us with the impression that the passage offers at least functional criteria for distinguishing true and false prophets. All such discussions and suggestions were well received in the neo-orthodox atmosphere of his time.

Since Quell, however, a healthy measure of the ambiguity of reality, and of the thinking of pluralism, has entered into discussions of the problem with sobering effect: so much so, indeed, that skepticism concerning criteria of distinction has been the salient mark of serious work done since 1952. There is no clearly defined criterion to distinguish true and false prophecy, or to identify the true prophet in a debate.[8] Although E. Osswald summarized the thinking of von Rad in her 1962 study, she did so only after careful, critical consideration of all criteria that had been advanced.[9]

J. L. Crenshaw's study (1971) goes the furthest in the direction of skepticism, even to the point of judging that the inevitability of false prophecy, stemming from the lack of criteria to discern it in any given situation, caused the failure and demise of prophecy in the early Exilic Age.[10] His pressing the matter to its logical and realistic conclusion has drawn considerable criticism.[11] And yet Crenshaw himself, following Edmond Jacob,[12] seems to leave us, if not with a criterion of discernment, at least with a clear warning that all true prophets (whoever they

6. S. Mowinckel, "The 'Spirit' and the 'Word' in the Pre-Exilic Reforming Prophets," *JBL* 53 (1934) 206.
7. M. Buber, "Falsche Propheten," *Die Wandlung* 2 (1947) 279.
8. F. L. Hossfeld and I. Meyer, *Prophet gegen Prophet* (BibB 9; Freiburg: Schweizerisches Katholisches Bibelwerk, 1973) 161.
9. E. Osswald, *Falsche Prophetie im Alten Testament* (Tübingen: Mohr, 1962).
10. J. L. Crenshaw, *Prophetic Conflict* (BZAW 124; Berlin: Walter de Gruyter, 1971).
11. See the reviews of Crenshaw by G. Fohrer, *ZAW* 83 (1961) 419; J. G. Williams, *JBL* 91 (1972) 402–4; W. Brueggeman, *Int* 27 (1973) 220–21; M. Bic, *TLZ* 97 (1972) 653–56; F. Dreyfus, *RB* 80 (1973) 443–44; E. Jacob, *Bib* 54 (1973) 135–38.
12. E. Jacob, "Quelques remarques sur les faux prophètes," *TZ* 23 (1957) 47.

might have been) were in constant danger of succumbing to the temptation of confusing the *vox populi* with the *vox dei*. Indeed, Crenshaw
claims, because true prophecy was such a fragile affair and false prophecy so realistically inevitable, that prophecy as a biblical phenomenon
failed and wisdom and apocalyptic took their place in Early Judaism.

L. Ramlot has revived the criterion of the *vox populi* as a positive
factor of discernment by suggesting its role in the later canonical process.[13] It was the *vox* of the later remnant, or surviving Judaism, in
reviewing the pre-exilic and exilic messages of the prophets, true and
false, which found value for survival in those messages which it went on
to preserve for us in the canon. One's own work would underscore such
an observation.[14] But that remnant found itself in a totally different
situation or "context" from that of their predecessors who had actually
heard the canonical prophets and had formed the earlier *vox populi*. It
is in the canonical process that the so-called criterion of "history" (Jer
28:9; Deut 18:22) or fulfillment of prophecy should be understood,
rather than in the simpler sense of specific prediction coming to pass or
not; and it is in this sense that the emphases of von Rad, Buber, and
Osswald on "history" as the vehicle of true revelation can be retained.

Such an observation does not, however, actually contradict Crenshaw's
quite valid view that in their time the *vox populi* was a negative and
powerful pressure on the prophets whose interpretations of their current
history and expectations of their immediate future ran counter to those of
the vast majority of their people, who were well represented by the so-
called false prophets. Numerous passages in the prophets indicate that
they were constrained to indict the people and the so-called false prophets often in the same manner and with the same words (Isa 30:8–14;
Mic 2:6; 3:5, 11; Jer 26:8; Ezekiel 13–14). Their messages simply
were not popular in their time: even the exilic Isaiah challenged his
people in Babylonia (a) not to assimilate to the dominant culture but to
retain their Jewish identity, and (b) to believe that the God who was in
his time redeeming and liberating them was the same who had delivered
Jacob to the despoilers (Isa 42:24, *et passim*). There is no evidence at

13. L. Ramlot, "Les faux prophètes," *DBSup* 8 (fasc. 47, 1971) cols. 1047–48.
14. J. A. Sanders, *Identité de la Bible* (Paris: Cerf, 1975) 153–67; "Adaptable for
Life: The Nature and Function of Canon," *Magnalia Dei: Festschrift G. Ernest Wright*
(ed. Frank M. Cross et al.; Garden City: Doubleday, 1976) 531–60.

all that the great prophet of the exile was the *vox populi* of his day; quite the contrary.

Hence, Osswald designated the criterion of judgment (Jer 28:8) as primary; and it was this aspect which Sheldon Blank and A. Heschel elaborated in their different but equally moving descriptions of prophetic suffering and pathos. Their messages were charges (*maśśā'*; Jer 23:33) which challenged their people's understanding of themselves and their God.[15] Their love for their people was so deep, and their identity with them so complete, that their messages hurt the prophets before and while they delivered them to their people.[16] One's own work also affirms such observations as these, and they touch directly on the question of prophetic hermeneutics.

Apparently following Weber and Jacob, A. van der Woude stresses ancient Zionism or nationalism as a criterion of false prophecy in the pre-exilic situation. In recent work on Micah 4, van der Woude broaches the old problems of so-called post-exilic additions to Micah in a fresh way by the method of identifying *Disputationswörter*.[17] Micah 4 would appear to be a locus of record of debates Micah might have had with contemporary prophetic colleagues who challenged his message of divine judgment in the situation of the eighth century B.C.E. Instead of seeing those passages which appear to contradict Micah's message of chapters 1–3 as later additions, one might view them as quotations of colleagues who held a different theology—that of God as the Holy Warrior who sometimes allows Israel's enemies to encamp at Zion's gates to besiege Jerusalem in order that Israel may the more easily thresh them and destroy them. The enemies outside the gates say, "Let her [daughter of Zion] be profaned, and let our eyes gaze upon Zion" (Mic 4:11). "But they do not know the thoughts of the Lord, they do not understand his plan, that he has gathered them as sheaves to the threshing floor," say Micah's prophetic opponents (v 12). Israel's enemies, if they knew the truth, said the latter, ought better to say, "Come, let us go up to the mountain of the LORD ... that he may teach us his ways" (v 2).

15. S. Blank, *Of a Truth the Lord Hath Sent Me: An Inquiry into the Source of the Prophet's Authority* (Cincinnati: Hebrew Union College, 1955).

16. A. Heschel, *The Prophets* (New York: Harper & Row, 1962) 103–39.

17. A. van der Woude, "Micah in Dispute with the Pseudo-Prophets," *VT* 19 (1969) 244–60; "Micah IV 1–5: An Instance of the Pseudo-Prophets Quoting Isaiah," *Symbolae Biblicae et Mesopotamicae Francisco Mario Theodoro de Liagre Böhl Dedicatae* (ed. M. A. Beek et al.; Leiden: Brill, 1973) 396–402.

These are valuable findings. A review of what earlier scholarship has called secondary passages or exilic additions might indeed yield considerable recovery of such debates between the canonical prophets and their contemporary colleagues. Scholars have struggled with the observation that the judgmental prophets appear to have opposed static application of royalist theology in their day (Jacob) or a simple "parroting of Isaiah" (Buber).

Buber's essay on the encounter between Jeremiah and Hananiah was seminal and is worthy of review. He sought to understand why and how Jeremiah, after saying Amen to Hananiah's message of consolation, could upon reflection return with the strength of his original conviction reinforced, *"Geschichte geschicht."*[18] Time marches on and no one moment can be totally equal to another. The living God is not an automatic machine. God's truth cannot be systematized. Humankind endowed with free will changes to the point that historical reality and the divine will may become quite different in one moment from what they had been in another. Hananiah was the person who had real knowledge but was a prisoner of that knowledge. Parroting Isaiah, he was satisfied to repeat a solution of the past; for with all his knowledge of history he did not know how to listen. He was truly a man of principle who was convinced that God too was a man true to his principles, bound by the promises he had made to Isaiah. Hananiah did not know how to recognize history "becoming." He knew only the eternal return of the wheel, but not the scales of history which tremble like a human heart. He was the typical fanatic patriot who accused Jeremiah of treason. Jeremiah, however, did not think of his homeland as a political ideology but as a colony of people, an assemblage of human living and mortal beings whom the Lord did not want to see perish. In counseling them to submission to Nebuchadnezzar he wished to preserve their life. Despite his grand ideology Hananiah was but a blind man while Jeremiah was a realist. The one, concluded Buber, was but a politician with dazzling illusions, the successful man; the other, in his suffering silence, in the pit, and in failure did not know the intoxication of success.

Ramlot reports that J. Ngally has extrapolated from Buber's essay an affirmation of the sovereign freedom of God and of the politics of the true prophet, which were opposed to the timeless political ideology of the

---

18. Buber, "Falsche Propheten," 277.

false prophet and sought the concrete salvation of flesh and blood people.[19]

II

It would be easy, in using without caution the prism of Buber's moving essay, to draw from it false criteria for discernment of prophecy. Surely one cannot always denounce those who appear to be fanatically patriotic or who strive to live by historically learned principles; that would be but to turn Hananiah, as Buber perceived him, around the other way. But one who has read the Bible in all its pluralism of expression can but affirm Buber's basic observation of the dynamic nature of the divine will, as the Bible expresses it, in ever-changing historical and cultural contexts or situations. Within biblical historical typology there is movement.[20] Although typology appears to be the most fundamental of intra-biblical hermeneutic techniques, especially in the prophets, notably Deutero-Isaiah and the NT, it would be difficult to find a passage where it is applied statically.[21] Although the canonical prophets apparently referred to some form of the Torah story, by citation or subtle allusion, they also stressed listening to the voice of God in their own day.[22]

Crenshaw is right to relate Buber with Osswald's statement: "The true prophet must be able to distinguish whether a historical hour stands under the wrath or the love of God."[23] Such discernment requires both intimate knowledge of the traditions or "texts" of the ways of God in Israel's past (its *mythos* or Torah story) and a dynamic ability to perceive the salient facts of one's own moment in time as they move through the fluidity of history. With apparently no one around after the exile to offer such discernment, history indeed appeared to be static, or worse, to be but some alternating cadence between birth and death, planting and plucking up, breaking down and building up . . . (Qoh 3:2–3).

The student of the history of interpretation well knows how a single text, when stabilized in form and content, scores different points when read in different contexts. Deuteronomy in its original context of sev-

---

19. Ramlot, "Faux prophètes," col. 1042.
20. Cf. H. Gese, "The Idea of History in the Ancient Near East and the Old Testament," *JTC* 1 (1965) 49–64.
21. Cf. H. W. Wolff, "The Hermeneutics of the Old Testament," and "The Understanding of History in the Old Testament Prophets," *Essays on Old Testament Hermeneutics* (Richmond: John Knox, 1963) 160–99 and 336–55.
22. See Sanders, *Torah and Canon.*
23. Crenshaw, *Prophetic Conflict,* 54.

enth century B.C.E. Judah was a challenge to a royalist theology based on unconditioned promises (no matter how much Manasseh had needed the flexibility of domestic policy it offered in the face of Assyrian foreign policy) and the blessed assurance of God's faithfulness. But a stabilized, inflexible text of Deuteronomy (Deut 4:2; 12:32), read unchanged a few decades later in a totally different context, apparently scored a quite different point from that intended by its authors, or heard by Josiah; and the Deuteronomic admonition that disobedience would bring abrogation of the covenant was sometimes read to say, if an individual suffered deprivation and hardship he must have sinned. Deuteronomy did not say that, but Job was surely written in part to record a resounding No to such inversions of the Deuteronomic ethic of election.[24] No one need have changed the text of Deuteronomy for the inverted reading to occur. On the contrary, if one did *not* alter the reading of Deuteronomy dynamically, to adjust its "text" to the new "context," then the inversion was almost bound to occur. Such an observation is common to the student of canonical criticism; it is the nether side of the "stable" aspect of canon.[25]

But it is the very nature of "canon" to be adaptable as well as stable. On this all segments of both Judaism and Christianity—the full spectrum from liberal to conservative—agree: the Bible as canon is relevant to the ongoing believing communities as they pass it on from one generation to the other. They may disagree on its stability, what books are in the canon and in what order (whether the Jewish, the Catholic, or the Coptic canon), but they all agree on its adaptability. Before the triumph of Deuteronomy[26] those authoritative traditions which later came to make up part of the Bible had been quite fluid, largely in oral transmission and subject to many different oral forms, and hence supposedly less subject to the dangers of stability or static application. And yet, as Jacob and Buber stress, the so-called false prophets seemed to tend to employ typology statically.

Hence all scholars since Buber and Quell, as is well attested in the works of Osswald, Crenshaw, and Hossfeld and Meyer, agree that changes in historical-cultural situations indicated that hearing afresh the Word of God and its dynamic message was a mark of the so-called true

24. J. A. Sanders, "The Ethic of Election in Luke's Great Banquet Parable," *Essays in Old Testament Ethics* (ed. J. Crenshaw and J. Willis; New York: KTAV, 1974) 247–71.
25. See Sanders, "Adaptable for Life," 544–52.
26. See Sanders, *Torah and Canon*, 36–53.

prophet, although they do not put it quite this way.   Probably the Reformers had a similar message when, in devaluing the magisterium of the Roman church and its extended traditions, they said that the Bible became the Word of God in new contexts only when interpreted dynamically by the Holy Spirit.

Few would wish to debate the fact that a stable tradition or text may say something different to different situations.   What is difficult for modern heirs of the Enlightenment is determination or definition of what the canonical prophets meant by listening to the voice of God (Jer 7:23, 26), or what the Reformers meant by interpretation by or through the Holy Spirit.   What can be said today about such a factor in the adaptability of the prophetic message to changing historical moments?   What can be said of the prophet's ability "to distinguish whether a historical hour stands under the wrath or the love of God"?

III

Scholarship seems now to be generally in agreement that nothing really critical can be said.   Von Rad and Quell deny that we can establish with clarity or objectivity what the *exousia* of the true prophet at any point was: it simply is not subject to scientific analysis.[27]   Ramlot uses the word *"mystique en un sens large."*[28]   But one wonders if we are reduced entirely to such a judgment.   Partly in response Crenshaw points to what he calls the failure of prophecy and its yielding in the exilic period to wisdom and apocalyptic.

The mid-term between canon's stability and its adaptability is hermeneutics.   The more stabilized a tradition became the more crucial the role hermeneutics played in rendering it relevant to new situations. However, even in pre-exilic times before stabilization of forms had become a dominant feature in the precanonical history of those traditions (the early canonical process), prophets, psalmists, and others frequently made allusion to Israel's *mythos* traditions in order to legitimate their thoughts and messages.   Prophetic literature is replete with such references, as von Rad has shown.[29]   An interesting aspect of study of tradition-criticism today, especially in the prophets, is prophetic her-

---

27. See also Hossfeld and Meyer, *Prophet gegen Prophet*, 160–62.
28. Ramlot, "Faux prophètes," col. 1044.
29. G. von Rad, *Old Testament Theology* (2 vols; New York: Harper & Row, 1962–65).

meneutics. When the ancient biblical thinkers rendered the old traditions relevant to their day, what hermeneutics did they employ?   Such
study is keenly advanced when the hermeneutics of contemporaries can
be compared, for example, if two ancients apply the same epic tradition
to the same contemporary situation but draw quite different conclusions
from it.

Studies in true and false prophecy have to date not taken sufficient
advantage of such comparative study. In the prophetic corpus recognition of disputations between contemporaries centers, of course, in the
encounter between Jeremiah and Hananiah. The work of van der
Woude since 1969 has brought the disputations to the fore, as Crenshaw
recognized.[30] Every study of true and false prophecy since Quell has
attempted, more or less seriously, to discern the theology of the false
prophets. But for the most part scholars have so far seemed satisfied to
give such theologies labels: royal theology (Jacob), establishment theology (Bright), Zionist theology (van der Woude), *vox populi* (Crenshaw), fanatical patriotism and political ideology (Buber), all somehow
voiced at the wrong historical moment. Lacking in the field is a serious
attempt to extrapolate from the disputation passages the hermeneutics of
the debating colleagues.[31] The present paper is a probe in that direction.

Buber's point, followed by Osswald and others, that the historical
context was vastly important in terms of validity of prophetic message,
cannot be gainsaid. Careful study of the Bible in search of what it was
the so-called false prophets actually said and preached yields a number of
passages where such prophets cannot be dismissed facilely in terms of
their theology, or by what little is known of their life-style. All scholars
of the question agree on this. Such agreement permits us to focus on the
form, content, and theology of the "false" prophets. Koch's work, because it is so thorough, permits us to move beyond the question of the
forms they used: they were the same as those used by the so-called true
prophets.[32]

Did they, however, make reference to Israel's ancient epic traditions?
The answer all scholars have given to this is Yes. But it is apparently at

---

30. Crenshaw, *Prophetic Conflict*, 23ff.

31. See J. A. Sanders, "Jeremiah and the Future of Theological Scholarship," *Andover
Newton Quarterly* 13 (1972) 133–45, for a preliminary effort; see also my "Hermeneutics," *IDBSup* 402–7.

32. K. Koch, *The Growth of the Biblical Tradition* (New York: Scribner's, 1969)
200–10.

this point that the question of hermeneutics has failed to arise because thus far it has apparently been sufficient to remark, one way and another, on how the false prophets invoked an otherwise decently good theology but at the wrong time, supporting leaders and people when they needed a challenge. And the right theology at the wrong time is variously described, as we have seen, as royalist, Zionist, and the like, while the so-called true prophets were apparently invoking a right theology at the right time, supposedly a Mosaic view of conditional covenant, or, at least, a different tradition.

If, however, both parties invoked the same theology at the same time addressing the same situation, then hermeneutics would have to enter the picture. Such may or may not be the case in the famous debate between Jeremiah and Hananiah, but we cannot know for certain because the immediate record does not state what "text" or tradition each recited. There are other passages in the prophetic corpus, however, which may assist in this regard.

IV

In order to gain further perspective on the importance of "context" or situation, let us compare Ezek 33:23–29 and Isa 51:1–3. In the first, the situation is 586 B.C.E., or very shortly thereafter, for the pericope is placed just after the report of the message from Palestine to Ezekiel's Babylonian deportee camp that Jerusalem had fallen (Ezek 33:21; cf. 24:26).[33] The historical moment is very clear. Some of the people on that occasion apparently took heart, in a spirit of hope, and cited an authoritative tradition to apply to their situation: "Abraham was only one man, yet he got possession of the land; but we are many; the land is surely given us to possess" (33:24). The hermeneutical techniques employed were typology and *argumentum a fortiori* (or, *qal wa-ḥōmer*). But the central interest of hermeneutics is not in its techniques but in its basic modes and suppositions. In the second passage (Isa 51:1–3), Deutero-Isaiah advances the same argument, in every respect, which the people presented in Ezekiel 33: "Look to Abraham your father and to Sarah who bore you; for when he was but one I called him, and I blessed

---

33. See W. Zimmerli's excellent discussion of the Ezekiel passage in *Ezechiel* (BKAT 13/1, 2; Neukirchen: Neukirchener, 1969) 817–21, being published by Fortress Press in *Hermēneia*; as well as *Ezechiel: Gestalt und Botschaft* (BibSt 62; Neukirchen: Neukirchener, 1972) 35–37.

him and made him many. For the LORD will comfort Zion . . ."
(51:2–3).

And yet in the first passage, Ezekiel rejected the people's argument out
of hand. His response to them was as harshly judgmental as any passage
in the book: God will continue the judgment upon the land until utter
and complete desolation sets in (Ezek 33:25–29). The time or context
was wrong, for the self-same argument was presented some fifty years
later by Deutero-Isaiah as true prophecy. These passages seem not to
have figured so far in any discussions of true and false prophecy, one
supposes, because the Ezekiel text does not specify that the people who
advanced their argument were prophets. And yet, neither does the text
say they were not prophets. But it hardly matters since the form of their
argument is very close to the form or argument of prophecy when it cites
ancient traditions to support its message: it is not, however, in the literary form of *Botspruch*; hence it has been overlooked. Neither, for
that matter, is the form of the passage in Deutero-Isaiah totally con-
formative!

Both the people in Ezekiel 33 and Deutero-Isaiah use the same
hermeneutic techniques of typology and *argumentum a fortiori*. In both
arguments the hermeneutic principle is also the same: the God who
called Abraham and Sarah out of Babylonia will call the exiles out of
Babylonia; he will do the same kind of thing and execute the same kind
of mighty act as he had done in the Bronze Age. The assumption is that
God will be consistent: "the God who brought Abraham out of Babylonia and brought him into the promised land will bring us out of Babylonia into the promised land—all the more so because we outnumber him
by far." Deutero-Isaiah said Yes to what Ezekiel fifty years earlier had
said No. The hermeneutic principle of the "false prophecy" in Ezekiel
and of the true in Isaiah was the same: they both cited the tradition
constitutively, as a support to what the people felt they needed. Those
early moments just after the temple had fallen were not right for such a
message: it would have but increased the people's deception (Ezek
33:30–33). The First Isaiah had had to say No to a similar argument
in a similar situation just after 722 B.C.E. The good folk of Samaria,
with the buoyancy of the human spirit of hope, said: "The bricks have
fallen, but we will build with dressed stones; the sycamores have been cut
down, but we will put cedars in their place" (Isa 9:10). Such un-
daunted spirit all admire and applaud. Who can say it is by principle

wrong? But the First Isaiah, like Ezekiel later, denounced it in as harsh, judgmental terms as may be found in the prophetic corpus. It was apparently the wrong time.

When Jeremiah used the Rechabites as an object lesson for obedience, he did not approve of their static view of it (Jeremiah 35). The Rechabites practiced obedience by attempting to retain earlier nomadic contexts of living: Jeremiah, in contrast, stressed continually listening (Jer 35:14).

When Nebuzaradan had taken Jerusalem and offered Jeremiah a pension in Babylon, the prophet elected to stay in the desolate land (Jer 40:1–6), despite the fact that up to the moment of defeat he had counseled defection to Babylonia (Jeremiah 37–38; cf. 6:16). Jeremiah remained consistent theologically by changing his message when the context changed (cf. Jer 42:10). Context is an important factor. In point of fact, the messages of Hananiah in Jeremiah 28, that of the people in Ezekiel 33, and of Deutero-Isaiah in Isaiah 51 were all similar in announcing restoration. Isaiah 51 is distinct from them only in contextual timing. If restoration had occurred immediately upon destruction, the transformation of the covenantal relation between Israel and God which both Jeremiah and Ezekiel sought could certainly not have taken place (Jeremiah 24; 30–31; Ezek 36:26–28). They both used the great physician metaphor, among others, to speak of that transformation. Divinely inflicted wounds for the purpose of transformation take time to heal properly; otherwise they are but soothed with the ineffectual balm of Gilead (Jer 8:22) or, to use another metaphor, are daubed with whitewash (Ezek 13:10). It would appear that forty to fifty years were needed to let the message sink into the *lēb* of the people: God can abrogate the covenant and act very strangely indeed, all the while pursuing his own agenda which no one generation can verify or falsify.

Actually Deutero-Isaiah faced the opposite problem, it would appear. After a period of time the people would be gravely tempted to abandon their Jewish identity and assimilate to the dominant culture—join the First Church of Marduk, or of Ahura Mazda, so to speak. The challenge they apparently needed to retain their Jewish identity amounted to a symphony of consolation, which Deutero-Isaiah nonetheless intimately related to God's judgments of fifty years earlier.

The importance of context or historical situation can also be seen in tracing in the Bible its most common theologoumenon: *Errore hominum providentia divina*—God's grace works through human sinfulness. This "theology" of prevenient grace can be said to underlie some three-quarters of biblical literature. G. von Rad has brilliantly shown that it is the foundation of the final form of the Genesis text.[34] It is indeed the foundation of Torah. Deuteronomy indicates, however, that Manasseh exploited it and abused it; Jeremiah and Ezekiel agreed, finding abuse of it right up to the destruction of 586. The priestly theologians who shaped the Genesis traditions in the form we have them, as well as the final form of Torah, however, clearly saw that the old theologoumenon was an idea whose time had come once more. Hosea and Jeremiah reflect a minority view that there had been a golden age of obedience and devotion on the part of Israel in the early days before entrance into the land (Hos 2:16–17 [=RSV 2:14–15]; 9:10, 15; 11:1–3; Jer 2:2–3). But the Torah, as well as the other prophets, knows of no such tradition. According to them, although Israel had always been disobedient and recalcitrant, God's grace was not thwarted. Whatever evil Joseph's brothers, Jacob's eponymous sons, "intended" against him, God could and did "intend" it for good to the benefit of all (Gen 50:20). Insistence on the faithfulness of the promiser (Heb 10:23) in some contexts was apparently crucial to survival and continuity, but in other contexts (750–586 B.C.E.?) apparently became deception and falsehood.

In the NT the theme is celebrated decisively in the Gospels and Paul. In the former the ineptitude of the disciples is stressed in the Teachings, while their failure to support Jesus in the Passion Account is woven into the text as integral to his arrest, trial, and crucifixion. In Paul the theme is so central that to comment on it would be to review the Pauline doctrine of grace: God uses human sin and disobedience to effect his plans. Paul celebrates the theme so fully that he had to face the obvious challange to it: shall we sin the more that grace may the more abound? And his answer was a resounding No (Rom 6:15). But very clearly the existential age of the delicate birthing of the early churches required an emphasis on the theme, just as the existential age of the birth of Judaism out of the death of old Israel and Judah in the sixth century B.C.E. required equal emphasis on the same theme in Genesis once the message of divine judgment for disobedience and divine expectation of obedience and right understanding of election expounded by the prophets and Deuteronomy had already been fully expressed (750–586).

34. G. von Rad, *Genesis* (Philadelphia: Westminster, 1961), 13–42.

V

The importance of historical situation and context, therefore, cannot be overstated. In the prophetic disputations, however, the historical situation was always the same for the debating prophets (as ancient biblical theologians): they addressed the same problem but offered totally different suggestions as to what might be expected of God in that context. Even if they simply applied to that situation two different theologoumena, one emphasizing divine grace and faithfulness in and through and despite human sinfulness, and the other stressing divine expectations and obedience of the people in a theology of conditioned grace, the hermeneutical question arises precisely at the point of why they chose the theological theme they did choose.

Did they have a choice, willy-nilly, between a royalist theology of God's unconditioned promises and a Mosaic theology of divine expectation of obedience? Or, more acutely, was the one bound by personal identity to Davidic tradition and the other to the Mosaic, so that they had no such choice?

The case of the first Isaiah would indicate otherwise. The central theological complexity of Isaiah 1–33 is that of its seeming to contain both these theological themes—grace and judgment—both based on authoritative Davidic traditions. Isaiah apparently in his early ministry could base a message of blessed assurance to Ahaz (Isa 7:1–16) on the same Davidic traditions which he later cited in his message of stringent judgment.[35] At some point in his ministry Isaiah perceived that the earlier message had caused deceit and falsehood when carried into the era of the Assyrian threat (7:17–8:8). Upon reflection he perceived that God urged him not to walk any longer in the way of the people in this regard (8:11–15). Such reflection apparently caused him to claim that continuing to rely on the earlier message had caused the people to become deaf, blind, and insensitive to the later message of divine judgment through Assyrian assault upon Judah (6:9–13). God had, in his inscrutable way, poured a spirit of deep sleep upon those prophets who remained true and consistent to the message of divine grace without judgment (29:9–10). Did he include himself in that indictment to the

---

35. Cf. Th. C. Vriezen, "Essentials of the Theology of Isaiah," *Israel's Prophetic Heritage* (ed. B. W. Anderson and W. Harrelson; New York: Harper & Row, 1962) 138–46.

extent that he had been consistent before altering his own hermeneutics?

Isaiah did not change theologies; nor did he shift allegiance from one tradition, the Davidic, to another, the Mosaic. There is simply no textual evidence for such a shift.

Is there, on the other hand, textual indication that he changed hermeneutics, that is, applied Davidic traditions to the new historical context of Assyrian threat *in a different hermeneutic mode?*

Isa 28:21 is a crucial passage in this regard. "For the LORD will rise up as on Mount Perazim, he will be wroth as in the valley of Gibeon; to do his deed—strange is his deed! and to work his work—alien is his work!" The historical references in this remarkable statement are to 2 Sam 5:17–20 (Mount Perazim) and to 2 Sam 5:25 plus 1 Chr 14:10–17 (valley of Gibeon). But in those traditions it was claimed that Yahweh arose to *aid* David against the Philistine threat. Such references, on the face of it, would seem more (theo)logically apt if advanced by those prophets who argued that Jerusalem would be saved from the Assyrian siege, just as David had been saved by Yahweh. And yet Isaiah refers to them to score the opposite point! Yes, indeed, Yahweh *will* act again: he *will* rise up and be wroth as he has done in the past; but this time the Holy Warrior will direct his wrath toward his own people. He will indeed execute another "mighty act" as in the tradition, but this time it will seem strange and alien. Thus, Isa 28:21 seems to be another biblical record of but one side of an ancient debate: in this case, that of Isaiah.

If the self-same authoritative "text" (the tradition in 2 Samuel 5) can be appealed to with such opposing conclusions the difference lies not in theological tradition (Mosaic or Davidic) but in the hermeneutics applied to that tradition. They both referred to the same "gospel" text (of God's past activity) but derived from it totally different messages.

Isa 29:1–8 seems to demonstrate the same point. Again the same historical context or situation is addressed with both parties apparently appealing to the same Davidic tradition. David did indeed encamp in Jerusalem; it is Ariel, the city of the Lion of God. But Ariel is also God's altar where sacrifices are made to him, and Jerusalem will burn like an altar. God will encamp against it and besiege it through the agency of the invader; and the multitude of the foes doing so will be as numerous as the small dust particles Jerusalem experiences in its seasonal *ḥamsin* when heat currents are inverted and the air is polluted so thickly that the city is enveloped in them. It will be like the nightmare of a hungry, thirsty man who awakens to find no relief from his misery. (The metaphor is comparable to that of the Assyrian flood reaching Judah's neck in Isa 8:8).

Isaiah agrees again that Yahweh is a Holy Warrior, but this time he will be at the head of the enemy forces (cf. Isa 1:24). Again each appeals to the same tradition in the same context, but with radically different hermeneutics. And the difference is indicated in Isa 29:15–16. Those who hide deep their counsel and their deeds are those who turn things upside down, that is, those who regard the potter as the clay— those who deny God as creator.

And therein lies the clue to the hermeneutics of those who from 750–586 could apply the ancient traditions of either the Davidic story or the so-called Mosaic Torah story to their contexts or situations and prophesy salvation in and through judgment.[36] To stress the tradition of Yahweh as redeemer, provider, and sustainer and deny Yahweh as creator would be, in that historical context, to engage in "false prophecy." The so-called true prophets never *denied* that God was the God of Israel who had elected Israel and redeemed them from slavery in Egypt, guided them in the desert and given them a home, *and/or* had chosen David and established his throne and city. They referred to those authoritative traditions sufficiently and often enough to be convincing. But in addition to affirming God as redeemer and sustainer, the true prophets stressed that God was also creator of all peoples of all the earth. This would have made a radical difference in hermeneutics.

Amos seems to have been quite clear on this point, but in a different way. "'Are you not like the Ethiopians to me, O people of Israel? says the LORD. 'Did I not bring up Israel from the land of Egypt, and the Philistines from Caphtor and the Syrians from Kir?'" (Amos 9:7). If this sequel of rhetorical questions is viewed in the context of a colleague continually stressing the tradition, or "text," of the Exodus as authority for a message of assurance that the God who brought Israel out of Egypt would not abandon it but would sustain it—it takes on considerable significance. The God who thus redeems and creates Israel also sustains; he is not a whimsical deity who cannot be trusted. His grace would be constant and would indeed function even in the midst of Israel's

36. Cf. W. D. Davies, *The Gospel and the Land* (Berkeley: University of California, 1974) 46 n. 23.

sinfulness. Amos' reply would indicate that he agreed with the "text." Indeed Yahweh *did* bring Israel out of Egypt. But did Israel think it was the only folk who ever had a migration? By no means. If the Philistines and Syrians migrated, as indeed those arch enemies of Israel had done (in their own traditions), then Yahweh as creator of *all* peoples had been their guide (*mōlîk*) as well. But, it was protested, he made a covenant only with us! Yes, indeed, Amos said, but being the creator of all, as well as your redeemer, he is free to "punish you for all your iniquities" (Amos 3:2). Just as being creator of all he was free to judge Israel's neighbors (Amos 1:3–2:3), so he is free as well to judge Israel itself!

The assurance, "disgrace will not overtake us" (Mic 2:6), can indeed be drawn from the Torah story when the hermeneutics of divine grace is applied without reference to divine freedom. "Is not the LORD in the midst of us? No evil shall come upon us" (Mic 3:11; 4:9) is excellent theology in certain situations (Rom 8:31).[37] Deutero-Isaiah could magnificently combine belief in God the creator with belief in God the redeemer[38] when the challenge indicated was Israel's need to maintain its identity, sustain a remnant and resist assimilation to Babylonian and/or Persian cult and culture. Historical moment, or context, as stressed above, is a crucial factor in determining which hermeneutic to apply.

But that alone would be insufficient, for the factor of hermeneutic is equally crucial. *Whenever the freedom of God as creator is forgotten or denied in adapting traditional "text" to a given context, there is the threat of falsehood.* In Deutero-Isaiah's situation, the conjoining of emphasis on God as creator of all the earth with emphasis on God as Israel's particular redeemer in the exodus issued in a powerful *message of retention of identity in the regathering of the people.* He who had used Nebuchadnezzar as instrument of judgment could use Cyrus as instrument of blessing: his was the world and all that was in it.

In Jeremiah's situation, the conjoining of emphasis on God as creator of all the earth with emphasis on God as Israel's particular redeemer in the exodus had issued, on the contrary, in a powerful *message of retention of identity in the scattering of the people.*

If the message of Hananiah as prophet can be viewed also as applying

37. A. van der Woude (see above, note 17) does not seem to recognize this.
38. B. W. Anderson, "Exodus Typology in Second Isaiah," *Israel's Prophetic Heritage* (see above, note 35) 177–95.

authoritative tradition to the context that he and Jeremiah both faced, the debate takes on a dimension beyond what has so far been suggested in studies on it. If he used the traditions of "form" in delivering his message, as has often been noted, might he not also have used the traditions of "text"? Those who transmitted the record of the debate to the literary form we inherit in Jeremiah 28 do not suggest reference to authoritative "text" tradition. But with the constitutive hermeneutic of God as redeemer and sustainer with emphasis on his grace, he might well have preached in the following manner: "Thus says the Lord of hosts, the God of Israel [who brought Israel up out of Egypt, guided it in the wilderness, and brought it into this land]: I have broken the yoke of the king of Babylon. Within two years I will bring back to this place all the . . ." (Jer 28:2–3 with insertion). He might have said, in the debate, "Jeremiah, it is a question of having faith in God that he is powerful enough to keep his promises. He is not whimsical. He who brought us out of Egypt and into this land is strong enough to keep us here. It is a matter of firm belief in his providence and sustaining power." And Jeremiah, upon returning with the iron yoke, might have said, "Hananiah, he who brought us out of Egypt and into this land is strong enough *and free enough* to take us out of here. It is a matter of belief in God not only as redeemer and sustainer, but also as creator of all." As Jeremiah says in 28:14 in reference to Nebuchadnezzar, ". . . I have given to him even the beasts of the field." This is a clear reference to the same God the creator that Jeremiah portrays in 27:5–7:

> It is I who by my great power and my outstretched arm have made the earth, with the men and animals that are on the earth, and I give it to whomever it seems right to me. Now I have given all these lands into the hand of Nebuchadnezzar, the king of Babylon, my servant, and I have given him also the beasts of the field to serve him. All the nations shall serve him and his son and his grandson, until the time of his own land comes; then many nations and great kings shall make him their slave.

There is considerable debate about whether Jeremiah said all that or others later attributed it to him. But as Weippert has indicated with regard to the so-called "C" or Deuteronomistic source in Jeremiah, much of it is in congruity with what the prophet says elsewhere.[39] And cer-

---

39. H. Weippert, *Die Prosareden des Jeremiabuches* (BZAW 132; Berlin: Walter de Gruyter, 1973); cf. W. L. Holladay, "A Fresh Look at 'Source B' and 'Source C' in Jeremiah," *VT* 25 (1975) 394–412.

tainly Jeremiah frequently refers to the freedom of God the creator. "Am I a God at hand, says the Lord, and not a God afar off? Can a person hide himself in secret places so that I cannot see him? [This is a direct reflection of Isa 29:15–16.] Do I not fill heaven and earth? says the Lord" (Jer 23:23–24).

VI

What seems quite clear is that the so-called false prophet did not refer, in times of threat, to God as God also of the enemy. Such an affirmation of God the creator of all peoples is a part of the canonical monotheizing process.[40] It is at one with those struggles elsewhere in the Bible to monotheize in the face of evil, to affirm the oneness or (ontological and ethical) integrity of God in the face of an almost irresistible temptation to polytheize or particularize, and attribute evil to some other god or gods. Because he wanted his people to fall and stumble, or be tested, as a part supposedly of a much larger plan,[41] from the hardening of the heart of Pharaoh all the way to attributing to God the message of false prophets (1 Kings 22; Deut 13:1–5), all was a part of a monotheizing process to which, apparently, the so-called false prophets did not, like the true prophets, consciously contribute.

Within and through the pluralism in the Bible, a basic feature of the canon is its tendency to monotheize. It may be doubted if any large literary unit of the Bible, even Deutero-Isaiah, is thoroughly monotheistic. But there seems to be no literary unit of any size which contradicts the observation that the fundamental canonical thrust of the Bible is its struggle to monotheize.[42] Can it be affirmed that wherever the struggle to monotheize failed "false prophecy" threatened?

Recent study has indicated that no single criterion of distinction between true and false prophecy can be emphasized, whether judgment (Jer 28:8), "fulfillment" (Jer 28:9; Deut 18:22; cf. Deut 12:2), or any other criterion or combination of such. But surely to polytheize (Deut 13:2; 18:20) in any form whatever (including particularizing God without affirming his ontological *and* ethical integrity) is in canonical terms falsehood. Conversely, to adapt any "text" or tradition to any "context"

---

40. See above, notes 14 and 31.
41. Crenshaw here is especially perceptive; see his *Prophetic Conflict*, 77–90.
42. M. Smith (*Palestinian Parties and Politics that Shaped the Old Testament* [New York: Columbia University, 1971]) confirms this observation by a quite different method of approach to the canonization of the OT.

without employing the fundamental hermeneutic of monotheizing within the dynamics of that situation is in canonical terms falsehood.

Under that fundamental hermeneutic rubric, a given context or situation may indicate adapting the "text" in a constitutive mode—to organize and lead a program of obedience by seeking supportive guidance in the "texts," and in the manner of Deutero-Isaiah; or in a prophetic mode—to challenge an established program of obedience by seeking corrective guidance in the "texts," in the manner of Jeremiah. The impulse to monotheize must affirm the possibility that the creator was fashioning a new thing, a new heart, a new spirit in his people, indeed was transforming his people, by wounding and healing, into a new Israel.

3. PATTERNS IN THE PROPHETIC CANON

RONALD E. CLEMENTS

In his book entitled *The Law and the Prophets*[1] Professor Zimmerli raised afresh the question of the mutual relationships of law and prophecy in the OT in the light of modern critical research. Since the issue is of fundamental importance to the respective hermeneutical traditions of both Judaism and Christianity, it must undoubtedly continue to elicit the attention of scholars, and can bear a good deal of further inquiry. The extent to which the preaching of the prophets can be shown to be dependent on specific traditions of Israelite law, of a developed social and clan ethic, and of the older cultic election traditions of the people, is a significant part of this inquiry which has received considerable attention. However, in its basic formulation and in the manner in which it has been most keenly felt in Jewish and Christian traditions of interpretation, the question of the relationship of law to prophecy is only a part of the wider issue concerning the law and the prophets. This is essentially a question about the canon of the OT, and of the way in which its two basic parts are to be understood in their mutual interrelationships. What light does the law shed upon the prophets, and, conversely, what light is shed by the prophets back upon the first section of the canon? Growing awareness of the hermeneutical significance of the interpretation of the first part of the canon as Torah[2] and of the complex history of the way in which this term was understood in its application to the OT writings has highlighted the problem still further. If so basic a hermeneutical feature can be seen to be present in the categorization of the first part of the canon, what significance attaches to the canonical form and structure of the second part of the canon, the prophets?

1. W. Zimmerli, *The Law and the Prophets. A Study of the Meaning of the Old Testament* (New York: Harper & Row, 1965).
2. J. A. Sanders, *Torah and Canon* (Philadelphia: Fortress, 1972).

As soon as we formulate the issue in this way we encounter some striking features which have a considerable bearing on the understanding of prophecy in its written form. When we turn to the NT, for example, we find some valuable guidelines to the way in which prophecy was being interpreted in the first Christian century. In Peter's speech, as it is reported in Acts 3, we are presented with an illuminating picture of the way in which the prophetic corpus of the canon was conceived to present a unified and coherent message: "And all the prophets who have spoken, from Samuel and those who came afterwards, also proclaimed these days" (Acts 3:24; cf. also Acts 3:18; 1 Pet 1:10–12). Two things are immediately striking in this summary of OT prophecy; the prophets are regarded as having proclaimed a unified message, and this message is regarded as one concerning the era of salvation which the NT writers now regard as having dawned. These two features—the unity of the prophetic message and its concern with the age of salvation—provide a basic pattern of interpretation for the NT understanding of prophecy. Yet it leads us immediately to face the fact that it is precisely these features which modern literary-critical scholarship has found most difficult to accept in its own study of the prophetic literature. The great pre-exilic prophets who stand at the fountainhead of the Israelite prophetic achievement have been primarily, although not entirely uniformly, regarded as *Unheilspropheten*—prophets of doom and destruction. Furthermore, far from regarding the prophets as having spoken with one voice, the interest of scholarship has been to identify the many voices which lie behind the prophetic writings and to relate these many voices, so far as is possible, to individual flesh and blood personalities. The result undoubtedly is that the early Christian regard for Jesus as the one whom all the prophets foretold stands at a considerable distance from the way in which modern critical scholarship has endeavored to show a development and continuity between the OT prophets and Jesus' preaching of the Kingdom of God. How are we to bridge this gap, and how are we to relate the extant prophetic writings of the OT with the way in which the NT, and the main lines of Christian hermeneutical tradition afterward, have interpreted them? Nor is this solely a concern for Christian theological scholarship, since we find too that Jewish understanding of prophecy has been deeply affected in the same way.

The answer is to be found, at least in an important part, by devoting more attention than has usually been given to the literary structure and "patterns" of the written prophetic collections. It is this canonical form of prophecy which brings together the various sayings and messages of individual prophets and co-ordinates them into a unified "message." Likewise it is this same canonical form and structure which make prophecy as a whole a message of coming salvation. Even a prophet such as Amos, with his dire warnings of coming judgment and disaster, is, in the canonical form in which his prophecies have now been given, a prophet of coming salvation for Israel (Amos 9:11–15).[3] Our concern here is not to reopen the much discussed question whether such a promise of salvation can be regarded as authentic to the original prophet or not, but simply to note that the form in which his prophecies have been remembered and reaffirmed in Jewish and Christian tradition is how he has been understood. From Ben Sira we obtain a further important clue to the way in which the written canonical form of prophecy has contributed to the establishing of this interpretation. In Sir 49:10 we read: "May the bones of the twelve prophets revive from where they lie, for they comforted the people of Jacob, and delivered them with confident hope." Here we find the same essential element of concern with salvation— "confident hope"—as we have already noted to be present later in the interpretation of prophecy in the NT. Here, however, it is not all the prophetic writings, but simply the twelve, which are characterized in this way. Nevertheless, Ben Sira leaves little doubt that this is how he understood all the OT prophets (cf. Sir 48:17–25), and it becomes plain that it is the canonical written collection of prophecies which has helped to make this interpretation possible.

The tradition that prophecy is to be understood in this way can be traced back still further, for we find in the important *Prophetenaussage* of 2 Kgs 17:13–15 that prophecy could be viewed as possessing some kind of uniform message, and one that held out hope for Israel. In this case the evidence is all the more noteworthy because it must refer to only a part of the canonical corpus of prophecy. "Yet the Lord warned Israel and Judah by every prophet and every seer, saying, 'Turn from your evil ways and keep my commandments and my statutes in accordance with all the law which I commanded your fathers, and which I sent to you by my servants the prophets.'" I have already argued elsewhere that this statement has a significant bearing on the development of a conception of

3. Cf. the interpretation of Amos 9:11–12 in Acts 15:16–18.

canonical prophecy.[4]   There are therefore good reasons for recognizing that the basic features of the interpretation of OT prophecy which are evident by NT times do not represent a hermeneutic imposed upon the prophetic witings entirely from outside, but rather must be seen as an extension of patterns of interpretation which are woven into the literary structure of the prophetic corpus.   When we turn to look at the main features of the interpretation of prophecy to be found in the Qumran literature, most especially 1QHab, we find that this also falls within the categorization that we have outlined.   We may conclude this brief outline of the way in which prophecy was being understood by the close of the OT period by summarizing three of its salient features:

1. The prophets were interpreted in relation to their message, not the special experiences of God which they encountered.   Hence it was the message that was regarded as inspired, and the inspiration of the prophet was inferred from this.

2. This message concerned the destruction and restoration of Israel, but special emphasis was attached to the latter.   This was because this restoration was still looked for in the future, while the destruction was believed to have already taken place.   The prophets therefore were felt to have foretold the future, but in certain very broad categories.

3. This message of restoration allowed great flexibility of interpretation as regards time, circumstances, and the particular form which Israel would assume in the time of its salvation.   The great variety of ways in which Jewish messianism has been expressed and understood is a consequence and expression of this.

That the problem of identifying and tracing the development of an eschatological hope in the prophets is a complex one is so self-evident as to need no separate explanation here.[5]   Increasingly scholarship has sought to bring light to this problem by its examination of tradition-elements within the individual prophetic books.   This concern with the traditions which lie behind the preaching of the prophets, however important they have been, has not been able to resolve the peculiar difficulties which attend the emergence of a prophetic eschatology.   On the other hand, the attempts to regard the growth of a prophetic eschatology as a

---

4. See my *Prophecy and Tradition* (Oxford: Blackwell, 1975) 41–57.
5. See my *Prophecy and Covenant* (SBT 43; London: SCM, 1965) 103–18.   See now also H. P. Müller, *Ursprünge und Strukturen alttestamentlicher Eschatologie* (BZAW 109; Berlin: Walter de Gruyter, 1969).

purely post-exilic phenomenon have not been altogether successful in relating the pre- and post-exilic elements of prophecy to each other.[6] We can at least see now that a part of the reason for this lies in the fact that it is the literary shaping of the prophetic material into a canon which has contributed to this difficulty, and that it was at this stage that sayings and utterances took on a significance which can properly be described as eschatological. As a result, sayings and prophecies which possessed a relatively straightforward historical interpretation in the situations in which they were originally given can be seen to have acquired further meanings in the extended context which the canonical collection provided. This is not to claim that we must make an artificial distinction between an "original" and a "canonical" meaning, but rather to argue that the original meaning took on a certain extension and development once it was allied to other prophecies in a written collection which held a proto-canonical status.

A single example of this may be sufficient for our immediate purpose, although examples could easily be multiplied. In Ezek 7:1–4 we find a prophetic pronouncement given by Ezekiel upon the theme that "the end" is about to come upon Israel, which harks back to the prophecy of "the end" in Amos 8:2. Thus a prophecy which originally applied to the downfall of the Northern Kingdom of Israel has been carried forward into a later situation and made applicable to the threatened fall of the surviving kingdom of Judah more than a century later. By such a development the earlier prophecy of Amos is certainly affected, in its written form, since this too acquired new meaning in relation to the new context. The theme of the end and destruction of Israel, which is to be found extensively throughout the pre-exilic prophets in the very center of their preaching, becomes supremely related to the debacle of 587 B.C., with its fateful consequences for Israel-Judah. That a very extended sequence of disasters and political misfortunes led up to this tragic climax provides one clue to the way in which the various prophetic messages have been coordinated so that they point to a unified message. The message is the destruction of Israel, although the separate pronouncements and warnings given by the prophets refer more directly to specific situations and

6. This seems to me an important weakness in the otherwise fresh and valuable treatment by G. Fohrer, *History of Israelite Religion* (New York: Nashville: Abingdon, 1973) 316–29. Cf. also his "Die Struktur der alttestamentlichen Eschatologie," *Studien zur alttestamentlichen Prophetie* (BZAW 99; Berlin: Walter de Gruyter, 1967) 32–58.

dangers in which first Israel and then Judah were threatened. In this way the individual threats became a part of a greater threat—the threat of all Israel's destruction. It is this larger threat which properly deserves the description eschatological, if that term is to be employed at all in relation to pre-exilic prophecy. Events which historically spanned a long period, from the mid-eighth century to the first quarter of the sixth century B.C., have been linked together and viewed connectedly as an expression of divine judgment upon Israel. In this process the formation of written collections of prophecies has contributed to such a connected pattern of interpretation.

If this process of connecting separate prophecies together and of viewing them collectively is evident in regard to the message of doom and destruction, even more prominent is its effect in regard to the message of hope and salvation. It is impossible to deny the fundamental soundness of scholars who have seen that it is only toward the end of the Babylonian exile, in the second half of the sixth century B.C., that a truly "eschatological" message of hope was delivered to Israel.[7] This sounded forth with the preaching of Deutero-Isaiah, who must be reckoned above all other prophets as the herald of salvation for Israel. Yet it is certainly wrong to regard his preaching as coming from an isolated voice, bereft of any antecedents and sounding an entirely new note of hope and comfort for a suffering nation. We cannot justifiably deny to Ezekiel his rightful place as "the watchman of Israel," assuring the Jews who had survived in Babylon that there was hope for them, and the promise of a restored nation. Similarly we must also accept as certain that Jeremiah was a true comforter of Israel by his proclamation of a message of hope and reassurance to Judah in its darkest hour.[8] Admittedly this original Jeremianic word of hope has been much elaborated and expanded at the hands of a Deuteronomistic preaching circle, but its roots in the authentic words and actions of Jeremiah remain secure. Furthermore, it is unlikely that this Deuteronomistic expansion of the Jeremianic prophecies stems from a period as late as that to which we must ascribe the beginning of Deutero-Isaiah's activity. The latter's preaching therefore does not mark the first emergence of a prophetic

7. Beside the work of G. Fohrer referred to above, see S. Mowinckel, *He That Cometh* (Nashville: Abingdon, 1956) 125–86.
8. See especially Jer 32:6–15, which bears all the circumstantial marks of its authenticity in itself, but which has been further expanded by a Deuteronomistic circle. See P. Diepold, *Israels Land* (BWANT 5/15; Stuttgart: Kohlhammer, 1972) 129ff.

promise of restoration for Israel, even though it gives to it an immediacy and an attachment to political and historical realities which is of the utmost importance. The hope of Israel's restoration is therefore a message which was given over a wide period of time, through more than one prophetic voice, and clearly looked for the reversal of Israel's fortunes after the catastrophe of 587 B.C. As in the case of the message of judgment, so also with that of the hope of restoration, there is a broad thematic unity linking together prophecies which display a great deal of variety and individual expression.

To view the question of the message of restoration in the prophetic literature of the OT in this way, however, is to consider only a part of the difficulty which it has provided for the critical scholar. Were we to restrict the question of the authenticity and meaning of the message of hope to the post-587 situation there would be no great literary and theological problem for scholarship to unravel. This is not the case, however, for all of the prophets, even Amos, the earliest and most threatening of them all, are presented in the extant prophetic books as heralds of salvation. How can this have been the case, if the hope which they are reported to have foretold was only to be realized, or even capable of being realized, after 587 B.C., approximately two centuries after the earliest of these prophecies was given? As a consequence there has grown up the observation, familiar enough to commentators, that we are dealing here with post-exilic additions. To some extent this is undoubtedly the case, and there can be little opposition to the claim that such passages as Amos 9:13–15 and Hos 14:4–9 derive from the sixth century or later.

What we must endeavor to understand is how such additions have come to be made. That it was purely for liturgical purposes, to alleviate an excessively somber note when the prophetic writings were read in worship, is quite inadequate.[9] It is rather precisely the element of connectedness between the prophets, and the conviction that they were all referring to a single theme of Israel's destruction and renewal, which has facilitated the ascription to each of them of the message of hope which some of their number had proclaimed after 587 B.C. In this way the collection of the various prophetic sayings into books, and of these books into collections, has been a process which was concerned to present the

9. Such a view has most recently been put forward by O. Kaiser, *Introduction to the Old Testament. A Presentation of Its Results and Problems* (Minneapolis: Augsburg, 1975) 224.

wholeness of the prophetic message, not an attempt to preserve separately the *ipsissima verba* of individual prophetic personalities. The canonical interest lies in the message, not in witness to the prophetic personalities as such, even though this cannot remain altogether hidden. The formation of a canonical corpus of prophetic literature therefore has not felt any element of impropriety in affirming the message of the hope of coming salvation in relation to all of the forewarnings of doom which individual prophets made. So far as the redactors and scribes were concerned, who must be postulated as the agents of this activity, they were simply expressing a feature which they regarded as authentic to the message, even though a modern critic would have to admit that it was not necessarily authentic to each particular prophet's lips.

In such fashion we can at least come to understand the value and meaning of the way in which distinctive patterns have been imposed upon the prophetic collections of the canon so that warnings of doom and disaster are always followed by promises of hope and restoration. By such means all the prophets have been presented, in the canonical testimony to their preaching, as prophets of salvation. They are *Heilspropheten*, as the concerted witness of early Jewish and Christian interpretation has understood them to be. They spoke with one voice of the salvation that was to come. Yet, just as in the case with the message of doom and judgment, so also with that of coming salvation, a process of telescoping, and of the reinterpretation of prophecies to meet the exigencies of later situations, can be seen to have occurred. Already this is evident in the case of Amos, for, as it has been argued by G. von Rad,[10] the hope of the restoration of Israel under a Davidic kingship expressed in Amos 9:11–12 is best understood as originally applicable to a situation in the eighth century. It is not necessarily therefore to be regarded as a post-exilic addition, but may be understood as a part of the hope that Israel would once again become a single united nation under a Davidic ruler, a hope which is entirely credible and appropriate in this century. Particularly is this hope understandable after the fall of Samaria in 722 B.C., but there is no need to restrict its setting to such a time. Whether or not such a saying can then be ascribed to Amos personally remains a matter of doubt, but this is in any case not our present concern, and is scarcely capable of being resolved with any cer-

10. G. von Rad, *Old Testament Theology* (2 vols. New York: Harper & Row, 1962–65) 2. 138.

tainty. What concerns us here is that it provides an interesting example of how a prophecy which makes perfectly good sense if it is regarded as deriving from the eighth century B.C. would have taken on a much wider meaning in the sixth.[11]

As with the message of doom, the hope of national restoration after 587 B.C. gave to earlier prophets of hope an "eschatological" dimension, and greatly extended the range of meaning which was found in them. There is certainly no necessity therefore for restricting the emergence of a message of hope for Israel entirely to the post-587 situation, or for insisting that all the canonical prophets before this time were exclusively prophets of doom. On the contrary, the more carefully the actual expressions of hope ascribed to the pre-exilic prophets are examined, the more apparent does it become that many of them can be perfectly well understood in a pre-exilic context. This does not mean that all such prophecies are to be regarded in this way, but rather that the message of hope which emerged during the Babylonian exile had an important basis in prophetic tradition.

When we look at the various prophecies which make up the OT collection of the prophets we find that three particular historical events provide basic points of reference. These are 1) the fall of the Northern Kingdom of Israel, epitomized in the fall of Samaria to the Assyrians in 722 B.C.; 2) the fall of Jerusalem and Judah, visibly attested in the collapse of Judean power after the siege and fall of Jerusalem in 587 B.C.; 3) the restoration of political and religious life in Jerusalem after the advent of Persian power in 538 B.C. Each of these events provided a point of focus for political changes and threats which extended over a lengthy period, so that the activities of prophets, and individual prophetic sayings, range over a wide span of time. Nevertheless, it was these events which provided a series of catalysts, relating prophecies firmly to political realities and giving to them a basis of "fulfillment."

So far as the emergence of a message of hope is concerned, there are good reasons for recognizing that the downfall of Israel and Samaria in 722 was followed by a period of hope centered upon Judah. The role of Jerusalem as Yahweh's chosen sanctuary and of the Davidic dynasty in the divine purpose for Israel are firmly stressed in the Deuteronomic

11. We should then add that such a meaning has been still further enlarged by the first century A.D., as shown in Acts 15:16–18, noted above.

literature, especially the history from Joshua to 2 Kings.[12] The problem of the message of hope in the eighth century prophets is well exemplified in the case of Hosea. The undoubted relevance of his warnings of judgment to the final collapse of the Northern Kingdom of Israel in 722 B.C., poses a major hurdle to understanding how any message of hope that he gave may have been expected to be realized. At the same time the importance of the element of hope in his preaching is so strong that few scholars have been willing to deny that it has an authentic place among Hosea's prophecies.[13] What is certain is, that whenever it may originally have been proclaimed, in the form in which it is now preserved, it has meaning for the situation which came into being after the fall of Samaria in 722.[14] From this time the hope of Israel's restoration was closely linked with the political fortunes of Judah and of the reestablishment of a united Israel under a Davidic head. In this way the very foundations were laid for the essential features of the hope of restoration which took on a far wider significance after 587. Old prophecies, expressing a message of hope, could be reapplied to subsequent situations as the political possibilities underwent change.

When we turn to Isaiah, the greatest of the eighth century prophets, we find something of the same dilemma regarding the presence in Isaiah 1–39 of very prominent expressions of hope for Israel's future salvation, linked especially with the Davidic kingship and the traditions regarding the role of Mount Zion. Very frequently scholars have relegated such hopes to an origin in the post-exilic age, at times to a surprisingly late date. Yet they possess a perfectly credible setting in the eighth century in regard to the role of Judah after most of Israel had been lost to the ravages of Assyrian expansion in the west. While the Northern Kingdom disappeared, the inheritance of all Israel had not been lost. Yet, as we now know, such hopes proved abortive, in the form in which they had originally been nurtured, for eventually Judah also suffered a similar fate, and only an exiled community in Babylon remained as the main bearer of

12. Cf. P. Diepold, *Israels Land*, 140ff.

13. That Hosea was exclusively a prophet of doom is argued by W. F. Stinespring, "A Problem of Theological Ethics in Hosea," *Essays in Old Testament Ethics* [J. Philip Hyatt, in Memoriam], (ed. J. Crenshaw and J. T. Willis; New York: KTAV, 1974) 131–44. The question is dealt with further in my essay "Understanding the Book of Hosea," *RevExp* 2 (1975), 405–23.

14. The strongest point of anchorage for such a message of hope in Hosea is to be found in Hos 11:8–9. See W. Rudolph, *Hosea* (KAT 13/1; Gütersloh: Gerd Mohn, 1966) 217–18.

such a hope after 587. When this happened, it is once again clear that earlier prophecies expressing such hope came to be seen in an entirely new light. In the form in which the collections of the prophecies of such men as Hosea and Isaiah are now preserved, there are good grounds for recognizing that it is to the post-587 situation that their affirmations of hope are intended to be referred, although this is not the situation to which they were originally addressed. New events have created the need for new interpretations of old prophecies, and this process had already been firmly established by the time an exilic, or post-exilic, collection of such prophecies came to be assembled together, as is presupposed by 2 Kgs 17:13–15. This is not in any way an attempt to argue that all the prophecies of hope to be found in the eighth century prophets are authentic to them. Such is certainly not the case, but we may at least recognize some of them as quite correctly emanating from the period to which the editorial structure of the separate books now ascribes them.

What has happened is that quite disparate prophecies, expressing greater or lesser possibilities of hope for Israel's future, have acquired a relatively uniform pattern of interpretation in the light of the situation which arose after 587. The process of collecting and editing, leading to the canonization of prophecy came to be invested with a number of basic guidelines as to its meaning, especially its spelling out of hope for the restoration and salvation of Israel. In this process we can see that the broad features which prophecy had drawn to itself by the end of the OT era, namely, that it was a message, given with one voice concerning the future salvation of Israel, came to be firmly established.

That prophecy was regarded as a mysterious and enigmatic phenomenon, capable of bearing more than one meaning, is well attested from the way in which the prophetic writings of the OT show the application of more than one interpretation to specific prophecies. An excellent illustration is provided by the three sign-names given to Hosea's three children (Hos 1:4–5, 6, 9), where each is given two further, and radically different, interpretations (Hos 2:2, 3, 24–25 [=RSV 1:11; 2:1, 22–23]). What we are concerned to argue in the present context is that this same process of reinterpreting prophecy has taken place in the stage of the formation of a canonical collection of prophecies. By such a process of hermeneutical development, a much more markedly "eschatological" character has been given to the whole, and the element of hope has been much more emphatically brought into the forefront. What has so often been dismissed as "secondary" material in the various prophetic writings must be recognized as contributing a vital stage, or series of stages, in fixing a pattern of how earlier prophecies are to be understood.[15]

No one has demonstrated this principle of exegesis more ably and convincingly than has Walther Zimmerli in his masterly commentary on Ezekiel.[16] By conjoining words of hope to threats of doom, the original threats take on a more timeless significance and are set in a new perspective. As Zimmerli has argued, this process of developing a prophetic saying may, in a number of instances, go back to the original prophet himself. What we are concerned to argue here is that this process of development cannot be restricted to the separate prophetic books, so that each of them can be treated in relative isolation from the rest as a self-contained entity. Rather we must see that prophecy is a collection of collections, and that ultimately the final result in the prophetic corpus of the canon formed a recognizable unity not entirely dissimilar from that of the Pentateuch. As this was made up from various sources and collections, so also the Former and Latter Prophets, comprising the various preserved prophecies of a whole series of inspired individuals, acquired an overarching thematic unity. This centered on the death and rebirth of Israel, interpreted theologically as acts of divine judgment and salvation.

In such judgment and salvation the events of 587 B.C. marked a vital turning point, establishing the dividing line between them. However, as later Jewish and Christian interpretations of prophecy make abundantly clear, the salvation was not regarded as realized through the early returns from exile and the restoration of political and religious life in Jerusalem. This brings us to another feature concerning the way in which the overall pattern provided by the canonical collection served to heighten and intensify the eschatological element in prophecy. The saving events for which the exilic prophets Jeremiah, Ezekiel, and Deutero-Isaiah looked were primarily pointed in the direction of a return from Babylon

---

15. Much useful material in this regard is to be found in Ina Willi-Plein, *Vorformen der Schriftexegese innerhalb des Alten Testaments* (BZAW 123; Berlin: Walter de Gruyter, 1971). Her treatment, however, appears to me to be defective precisely because she has dealt with "secondary" material as made up of independent units and not as supplements to extant material, with which it must be read. The addition gives further direction to that which is there, and cannot be properly understood independently of this.

16. Cf. W. Zimmerli, *Ezechiel* (BKAT 13; Neukirchen: Neukirchener, 1956–69) 367–71, 388–90, and 450–52.

and the rebuilding of the temple in Jerusalem. These were to be central aspects of the restoration of Israel to a full and independent national life. The actual restoration which was achieved under Persian domination fell far short of this expectation, and so we find the prophetic voices of this period pointing increasingly toward a more remote and transcendent salvation, ultimately bordering on the frontiers of apocalyptic vision. In this respect also we may discern an important consequence of the way in which the compilation of a canonical collection has affected the interpretation of its parts. Where we might easily have looked back upon the promise of salvation given by the exilic prophets as one that was realized under the years of Persian rule, we find that this was not how later ages of Jews regarded it. It was a promise that still awaited fulfillment, and this was in many ways regarded as the most central of all the features of prophecy. It was a message of the salvation that was to come.

This directs our attention to those prophets of the fifth and fourth centuries B.C., whose preaching provides for the interpreter a host of problems. Where the background of such men as Haggai and Zechariah is firmly attested, so that their preaching can be readily related to historical events, that of Isaiah 56–66, of Malachi, and Zechariah 9–14 are obscure in the extreme, to say nothing of the problems attendant upon understanding Isaiah 24–27 and Joel. The very character of prophecy has evidently undergone a change, so that it has become more concerned with themes, and religious institutions such as the temple and the priesthood, and less directly related to events. It has taken on a more explicitly eschatological and supra-historical character. Yet this is not simply true for these prophets only, as separate contributors to the prophetic corpus of the Old Testament, for it is their preaching which has established the guidelines by which the earlier prophets came to be understood. Their preaching also was invested with the same eschatological reference which colored the preaching of the prophets of the Persian era. Once again, as in the case of the proclamation of doom, the process of forming a canonical collection has carried with it a tendency toward establishing a uniformity of interpretation. In consequence, all the prophetic assurances about a future salvation have been affected by the predominantly eschatological character which the latest parts of the prophetic corpus attest.

If our contention is correct, that the formation of a canonical corpus of prophecy has served to encourage the development of a unifying frame of reference by which each of them has been affected, then we cannot leave this layer of interpretation out of account in understanding them. The way in which prophecy was understood in the Judaism of the first century B.C., and by the Jews and Christians of the ensuing century, does have a very significant basis in the patterns woven into the prophetic collections. It has naturally and rightly been the aim of critical scholarship to pay every possible attention to the elements of diversity within the prophetic collections, since these offer an invaluable guide toward rediscovering the origin and setting of each of its constituent parts. Yet we must also note that the ancient hermeneutical traditions of both Jews and Christians have rather contrarily stressed the unity of the message which they proclaimed. It is evident that a comprehensive exegesis of the OT must pay attention to both, for only so can the wholeness of the divine word be properly grasped. Not only is this required by a truly "historical" exegesis, but it is of very special importance for the study of the prophetic books, if the literary-critical and theological aspects of the task are not to fall apart into two irreconcilable compartments of scholarship.

We have already pointed out that it is fundamental to the hermeneutical traditions of both Jews and Christians that the prophets spoke of a coming salvation for Israel. On the other hand, critical scholarship has consistently found the most challenging feature of prophecy to lie in its threats and denunciations, warning of the coming of judgment upon a godless people. The place where both aspects are brought together is to be found in the structure of the canonical collection of prophecy. The threat of doom is followed by the word of salvation, which does not evade the judgment but looks beyond it. By holding these two things together in this way, the prophetic part of the OT canon witnesses to the wholeness of the Word of God.

4. PROPHETIC SUPERSCRIPTIONS AND THE GROWTH OF A CANON

GENE M. TUCKER

At first glance it is not surprising that the superscriptions to the prophetic books have attracted very little scholarly attention. They appear to be innocuous and uninteresting notations concerning the book, the prophet, and his date. They are widely recognized as later than the work of the original figures who uttered the prophecies themselves. These texts have received their due consideration by commentators on the individual books, attention focusing primarily—at least until recently—on the reliability of the information in them for writing the biographies of the prophets. But few scholars have investigated the superscriptions as a whole or as a genre.[1] Surely the time is past when secondary material can be regarded *ipso facto* as less significant than the "authentic" sayings of a prophet, and when biographical considerations should necessarily predominate.

The superscriptions to the prophetic books pose a number of interesting and potentially important issues. What, indeed, is in a name, the name of a book? What are the meaning and purpose of these headings? When, in what institutional context, and why did they originate? What is the relationship between the superscriptions and the words of the prophets? Are there ancient Near Eastern parallels which shed light on our texts?

Most of these questions may be pursued by means of form critical and redaction critical methods, but not all of them can be answered with equal confidence. Furthermore, the pursuit of these issues, and the reso-

1. The exceptions are two impressive recent studies: H. M. I. Gevaryahu, "Biblical colophons: a source for the 'biography' of authors, texts, and books" (VTSup 28; Leiden: Brill, 1975) 42–59; and Th. Leskow, "Redaktionsgeschichtliche Analyse von Micha 1–5," *ZAW* 84 (1972) 61–64.

lution of some of them, can lead in the direction of what James Sanders has called "canonical criticism."[2]   He calls for an approach which "takes the measure of the authority that the ancient tradition exercised in the context of its use.   To what use did the biblical writer put the story of the exodus when he cited it?   How did he use it?   What were his hermeneutical rules?"[3]   One need not await a full-blown and refined definition of the methodology and hermeneutic of canonical criticism before pursuing Sanders's questions.

These questions turn out to be particularly appropriate with regard to the superscriptions of the prophetic books.   If indeed these texts are secondary, then they represent stages in the transmission and interpretation of the prophetic traditions.   Certainly the authors or redactors of the superscriptions did more than pass on the material which they had received.   That it was considered worthy of transmission is obvious, but why?   Brevard Childs's generalizations concerning the historical superscriptions to the Psalms apply as well to the headings of the prophetic books: "The titles represent an early reflection of how the Psalms as a collection of sacred literature were understood.   The titles established a secondary setting which became normative for the canonical tradition.   In this sense the titles form an important link in the history of exegesis."[4]

The prophetic superscriptions form not only a link in the history of exegesis, but also a significant chapter in the history of the biblical canon.   At the very least, a canon as an official list of sacred books presupposes that those books have names.   Titles may be incipits, taken from the first words of the book itself, or they may be substantive, as in the prophetic superscriptions.   It is the substance of these titles and the accompanying data which reveal that the creation and growth of these headings were decisive stages along the road to a formal collection and list of authoritative scriptures in Judaism.

I

Before turning directly to a form critical analysis of the headings of the prophetic books, we should define some terms.   The first of these is superscription.   A superscription is, quite simply, a statement prefixed to

2. James A. Sanders, *Torah and Canon* (Philadelphia: Fortress, 1972), especially xv–xviii.
3. Ibid., xvii.
4. Brevard S. Childs, "Psalm Titles and Midrashic Exegesis," *JSS* 16 (1971) 137.

a written work, such as a book, a song, a collection, or individual prophetic sayings. The term refers to the place of this statement in relationship to the structure of a work, namely, preceding and standing outside
the body of the work itself. Superscriptions are different from introduc-
tions in that where the latter occur they are integral to the body itself as
its opening part.

Superscriptions abound in the OT before books of all types: narratives
("The words of Nehemiah the son of Hacaliah" Neh 1:1), poetry ("The
song of songs, which is Solomon's" Cant 1:1), wisdom books ("The
proverbs of Solomon son of David, king of Israel" Prov 1:1; cf. Eccl
1:1), as well as all but three of the prophetic books. They also occur
frequently within books as the headings of individual parts; in addition to
the Psalm superscriptions note these examples: Hab 3:1 ("A prayer of
Habakkuk the prophet, according to Shigionoth"); Prov 10:1 ("The
proverbs of Solomon"); 30:1; 31:1; Jer 48:1 ("Concerning Moab");
49:1, 7, 23, 28; 50:1; Gen 5:1 ("This is the book of the generations of
Adam"). In some cases, such as Gen 5:1, superscriptions serve as
chapter headings in larger works. In other instances, it is not easy to
distinguish between superscriptions and narrative or interpretive pref-
aces. Jer 29:1–3, standing before Jeremiah's letter to the exiles, is a
case in point. This unit occurs outside the work itself (the letter), and
begins like many superscriptions: "These are the words of the letter
which Jeremiah the prophet sent from Jerusalem to the elders of the
exiles. . . ." It goes on to give the date and circumstances of the letter as
well as the names of the messengers who carried it. Whether it is a
superscription or a narrative introduction need not be resolved here.

The form and content of the OT superscriptions vary considerably,
although they ordinarily present information about the works they pre-
cede. This information may characterize the work in terms of itself
(what it is, e.g., *mišlê šĕlōmōh*), in terms of its origin (authorship and
date), or the use to be made of it. Therefore the superscription may
consist of a variety of elements, such as author, addressee, title, date,
location. While the composition of most of these elements can vary
between texts, superscriptions in the OT ordinarily indicate the character
of the work, either in the concise, definitional form of a title ("A Psalm
of David," Ps 101:1) or in a more elaborate form (as in some of the
prophetic superscriptions, e.g., Jer 1:1).

Titles should be distinguished from superscriptions. A title is a word or concise phrase that constitutes the name of a particular literary work (book, song, chapter, collection, etc.). A title ordinarily characterizes the work in terms of itself ("A Psalm," Ps 98:1) and/or its (supposed) author ("The proverbs of Solomon," Prov 10:1). But both in Judaism and in the literature of the ancient Near East titles could consist of the first word or words of the composition, for example, Enuma Elish, *běrē'šît*, whether or not this title characterized the contents. (It is only coincidental that the two examples cited suggest the nature or contents of the compositions.) Titles in the OT typically occur as superscriptions or as elements of them, although one occasionally finds titles mentioned in narrative contexts, for example, "the book of Jashar" (Josh 10:13; 2 Sam 1:18), "the Book of the Chronicles of the Kings of Israel" (1 Kgs 16:14), and perhaps "the book of the covenant" (Exod 24:7).

Of the fourteen prophetic books,[5] eleven are prefixed with superscriptions.[6] The form critical analysis and description of these texts should proceed on the basis of the final form; hypotheses concerning any prior written or oral stages should await the results of that investigation. It may be noted at the outset that, with a single possible exception, the superscriptions are not in any way grammatically attached to what follows; the body of the book simply begins after the superscriptions. Thus it is likely that what now are counted as the initial verses of the first chapters were understood to be as detached from the books as the present titles in large type above the works in the Masoretic Text. Furthermore, this detachment shows that while the superscriptions clearly presuppose the existence of the books, the reverse is by no means the case. The only possible connected superscription is Amos 1:1–2, in which v 1 is linked to the "motto" in v 2 by means of the transitional *wayyō'mer*.[7] However, this transition is not a part of the superscription, or of the body of the book, but of the "motto," which probably is even later than at least the original superscription.[8]

The analysis of the structure of the prophetic superscriptions may begin with a consideration of Amos 1:1 as a point of departure for

---

5. Jonah is not counted since it is a story about a prophet. Note, however, that its narrative beginning, while not a superscription, is similar to certain superscriptions, and may in fact be dependent on them.

6. The exceptions are Ezekiel, Haggai, and Zechariah.

7. Cf. Gene M. Tucker, *Form Criticism of the Old Testament* (*Guides to Biblical Scholarship*; Philadelphia: Fortress, 1971) 71–74.

8. Cf. Werner H. Schmidt, "Die deuteronomistische Redaktion des Amosbuches," *ZAW* 77 (1965) 168–93.

comparison and contrast, since it is attached to the earliest prophetic book and is the most extensive, in terms of formal elements, if not the longest (cf. Jer 1:1–3). The structure of Amos 1:1 may be outlined as follows:[9]

I. Title of the book ("The words of Amos . . .")
II. Elaboration of the title
    A. Concerning the prophet ("who was among the shepherds of Tekoa. . .")
    B. Concerning the words ("which he saw [*ḥāzāh*] concerning ['*al*] Israel. . .")
    C. Concerning the date
       1. Synchronistic royal date ("in the days of Uzziah king of Judah and in the days of Jeroboam the son of Joash, king of Israel. . .")
       2. Specific date ("two years before the earthquake.")

This superscription, as all the others,[10] is not a complete sentence but a phrase with a series of relative clauses appended. The title itself identifies the book in terms of both its contents and its authorship. The first relative clause depends upon the proper name, identifying the prophet in terms of occupation and homeland; the second relative clause ("which he saw concerning Israel") on the other hand depends upon "words,"[11] identifying them both in terms of source—they were revealed —and addressee—they were for the Northern Kingdom. The two temporal clauses do not go back to the title itself, but depend upon the verb in the second relative clause, specifying in two ways when the words were "seen" (*ḥzh*). This syntax leaves us with a title elaborated in three ways, concerning the prophet, the words (or the book), and the date, the last given in two ways.

How typical is this particular superscription? It has already been indicated that it is the fullest of the headings to the prophetic books, and that none of them is a complete sentence. Which formal elements, or other features, are constant and which are variable? The most common element of the superscriptions is the occurrence of a title, and always at the same location, the very beginning. All the superscriptions

9. Cf. Tucker, *Form Criticism*, 71–73.
10. The exception is Jer 1:3, in which a complete sentence follows, and probably expands, the original superscription.
11. Cf. Schmidt, "Die deuteronomistische Redaktion," 169.

include at least a title which invariably mentions the name of the prophet
and characterizes the book; only one of them (Obadiah) *consists* of a
title: "The vision (*ḥāzôn*) of Obadiah." But in this respect two others
are noteworthy. The heading of Nahum includes two distinct titles
which are simply juxtaposed: "An oracle (*maśśā'*) concerning Nineveh.
The book of the vision (*ḥāzôn*) of Nahum of Elkosh." Mal 1:1 likewise
may consist of two titles, "An oracle" (*maśśā'*) and "The word of the
LORD . . . ," but that is by no means certain.

In every case except Obadiah the title is elaborated in one or more of
the respects seen in Amos 1:1. Only Amos, Isaiah, and Micah contain
all three elaborations, in terms of the prophet, the words (or book), and
the date. The most common elaboration of the title is in terms of the
prophet, found in nine instances (Jeremiah, Hosea, Zephaniah, Joel,
Habakkuk, Nahum, in addition to the three just cited), but there are
variations here in terms of content. Only one (Jeremiah) identifies the
prophet's parentage, home, and the occupation of his father. The most
common note concerning the prophet specifies his parentage (Jeremiah,
Isaiah, Hosea, Zephaniah, Joel); Zephaniah gives a four-generation
genealogy. Four give the prophet's home or place of origin (Amos,
Jeremiah, Micah, Nahum), and two (Amos, Habakkuk) mention his
occupation. Here Habakkuk is noteworthy as the only superscription
which identifies the prophet as such (*hannābî'*); and that superscription
is followed immediately, not by a prophetic address, but by an address *to*
God.

Almost as frequent as the elaborations concerning the prophet are
those concerning the date, occurring in six cases (Amos, Hosea, Micah,
Isaiah, Jeremiah, Zephaniah). All these give at least a royal date; only
Amos and Hosea give synchronistic royal dates. Only Amos and Jeremiah include specific dates, the one in Amos being distinct from the royal
chronology, and the one in Jeremiah giving the specific regnal years.
Jeremiah also extends the original date to encompass the (supposed)
completion of the prophet's work, again in terms of a regnal calendar.
Only Amos, Micah, Isaiah, and Nahum contain elaborations concerning
the addressees.

II

Before moving to conclusions concerning the setting and intention of
the superscriptions, we should examine more closely the form and con-

tent of the titles themselves. In terms of form, the titles may be divided into three categories.[12] They are:

1. The word identifying the book in the construct followed by the name of the prophet. There are two variations of this pattern; Amos and Jeremiah are entitled "The words of (*dibrê*) . . . , " while Isaiah and Obadiah are called "The vision of (*ḥăzôn*). . . ." Compare here also the second title to Nahum.

2. The title as the phrase "The word of the LORD" (*dĕbar Yhwh*) followed by the relative clause "that came to . . ." (*'ăšer hāyāh 'el*). It seems clear that the initial phrase alone cannot be taken as the title, but requires the prophet's name in the relative clause. This pattern is found without variation in Hosea, Zephaniah, Micah, and Joel.

3. Titles beginning "An oracle" (*maśśā'*) or "The oracle" (*hammaśśā'*), but not following regular syntactical patterns. In Habakkuk the term is in the construct and the title is followed by a relative clause: "The oracle of God which Habakkuk the prophet saw." In Nahum it is a construct, "An oracle concerning Nineveh" (*maśśā' nînĕwēh*), and the second title follows. Whether the word is a separate title or a construct in Malachi cannot be determined.

It is probably going too far to suggest that these different categories represent clearly identifiable "superscription traditions," and to draw firm conclusions concerning their relative ages. However, a few generalizations about the background of these titles seem warranted. At least the second and third types seem to derive from headings which originally stood over individual prophetic addresses. Concerning the third form, while two of the books where it is employed probably stem from the seventh century (Nahum, Habakkuk), the title *maśśā'* occurs elsewhere with units which derive from the exile and much later (cf. especially Zech 9:1; 12:1; Isa 13:1; 21:1). The second type is similar to and likely dependent upon the prophetic word formula (*Wortereignisformel*).[13] This formula with some variations ordinarily provides the narrative introduction to a prophet's reception of revelation: "The word that came to Jeremiah from the LORD" (*haddābār 'ăšer hāyāh 'el yirmĕyāhû* Jer 11:1). According to Wolff, the expression occurs twelve times in the

12. Lescow ("Redaktionsgeschichtliche Analyse," 61–64) recognizes three different pre-exilic *"Grundformen"* and then a fourth which he considers (post) exilic.
13. Cf. H. Wildberger, "Jahwewort und prophetische Rede" (Dissertation, Zurich, 1942); and W. Zimmerli, *Ezechiel* 1–24 (BKAT 13/1; Neukirchen-Vluyn: Neukirchener, 1969) 89.

Deuteronomistic history work, thirty times in Jeremiah, and fifty times in Ezekiel.[14] As a title and an element in the superscriptions, the phrase may very well be Deuteronomistic, as Lescow suggests.[15]

But more enlightening with regard to the setting and intention of the superscriptions than the formal features of the titles is the investigation of their content. Alongside the names of the prophets themselves, we find a limited number of substantives characterizing what follows. They are called "the words" of the prophet, "the vision" of the prophet, "the word of Yahweh," or "the oracle." All these terms amount to a technical vocabulary which should be investigated.

It is clear that, at least in its context in Amos and Jeremiah, the plural *dibrê*, "words," refers to more than individual vocables. It is used, as Mays indicates, "in the technical sense of 'saying,' what is spoken by a prophet in one oracle; as elsewhere in the OT the plural is simply a title for a collection of sayings, e.g., Eccl 1:1; Prov 30:1; 31:1; Neh 1:1; Job 31:40."[16] That is, the expression is a broad classification, which may refer to various kinds of literature—wisdom sayings, wisdom literature, prophecies and even narratives—and therefore probably is not a technical term for prophetic speeches as such. Nevertheless, one recognizes in the use of the term a certain reflection on the contents of the book, and an attempt to classify the literature properly.

While the precise meanings of the other three terms are not equally transparent, it is clear that they are technical expressions referring to prophetic activity and/or experience. The "word of the LORD" (*děbar Yhwh*) is used almost exclusively in the OT for the revelation received by a prophet, or for the oral communication of that revelation as a speech of Yahweh. Those two occasions (revelation and communication) cannot always or easily be separated from one another. "It is of the very nature of a revelation that it should be made known to others.... Every revelation is at the same time a message."[17] But it seems clear that when this expression occurs in the superscriptions it is used in a derivative and a special sense. It no longer refers to a particular revelation or a specific oral address, but to the words of the prophet as a whole,

14. H. W. Wolff, *Hosea: A Commentary on the Book of the Prophet Hosea* (Hermeneia; Philadelphia: Fortress, 1974) 4; cf. Lescow, "Redaktionsgechichtliche Analyse," 62.

15. Lescow, "Redaktionsgechichtliche Analyse," 62.

16. James L. Mays, *Amos: A Commentary* (Philadelphia: Westminster, 1969) 19.

17. J. Lindblom, *Prophecy in Ancient Israel* (Philadelphia: Fortress, 1962) 220.

as committed to writing. Some of James Mays's conclusions concerning this phrase in Hos 1:1 can be extended to include the other instances of the title as well: "The book as a whole is 'the word of Yahweh,' the message of the God of Israel. The category of 'word' (*dābār*) is extended to include the total tradition deriving from a prophet, all his oracles and the narratives which tell of his activity (cf. 1:2–9 and chap. 3)."[18] However, Mays probably goes too far in concluding that the phrase interprets the prophetic tradition as "the one unified 'word of the LORD,' "[19] although it is significant that the singular is employed.

It is not certain, on the other hand, whether "vision" (*ḥāzôn*) is to be taken as singular or collective. The form is singular, and it frequently refers to individual revelatory experiences and the reports of them (cf. Dan 8:15; 1:17; Ezek 12:26; Jer 14:14), but it also has an abstract connotation (cf. Mic 3:6; Ezek 12:26; Isa 29:7), and in at least a few instances clearly serves as a collective or plural (Hos 12:11; 1 Sam 3:1) since a plural form does not occur.[20] The term probably derives from the reports of the individual visions of prophets and seers, but later becomes very popular as a designation for apocalyptic visions (cf. its frequent use in Daniel). In the superscriptions it certainly corresponds to the prophetic self-understanding (cf. Isa 22:1, 5; 30:10; Hos 12:11) that their words were revealed,[21] but not necessarily in the narrow sense that each address was the result of a visionary experience.

The least understood of our terms is *maśśā'*, ordinarily translated "oracle," or "burden," depending primarily on how the question of its etymology is resolved. The results of an examination of its usage are equally indecisive, since it most commonly occurs detached as a superscription or part of a title. Most—but not all—units with this heading are announcements of judgment, usually against Israel's neighbors. Whatever its precise original meaning was, the word probably connoted a unit—and as a title in the superscriptions, a collection—of prophetic address, and was roughly synonymous with *dābār*.[22] It is a technical

18. James L. Mays, *Hosea: A Commentary* (Philadelphia: Westminster, 1969) 20; cf. Wolff, *Hosea*, 4, 6.

19. Mays, *Hosea*, 20; cf. Wolff, *Hosea*, 4, 6.

20. H. Wildberger, *Jesaja 1–12* (BKAT 10/1; Neukirchen-Vluyn: Neukirchener, 1972) 6.

21. Cf. ibid., 5

22. Cf. S. Erlandsson, *The Burden of Babylon: A Study of Isaiah 13:2–14:23* (ConB, OT Series 4; Lund: CWK Gleerup, 1970) 64ff., where the recent literature is cited, and O. Kaiser, *Isaiah 13–39: A Commentary* (Philadelphia: Westminster, 1974) 1.

term for addresses by a prophet taken to be communicated to him by Yahweh.

Thus for the most part the key vocabulary in the titles to the prophetic books is theological language which designates them as divine revelation. The one apparent exception to this rule is the title "the words of Amos/Jeremiah," which is neutral concerning the (ultimate) source of the book. However, in both appearances of this title the superscriptions modify "the words" or describe the prophet in such a way that there can be no doubt about this matter: "The words of Amos . . . which he saw. . . ."[23] "The words of Jeremiah . . . to whom the word of the LORD came. . . ." These relative clauses convey the meaning of the other titles, namely, that the book, as a collection of utterances, stems from revelatory experiences. Furthermore, other superscriptions which had already employed the technical language of revelation in the titles reiterate the point, often in different words, in relative clauses (cf. Isa 1:1; Mic 1:1; Hab 1:1).

To summarize: the most consistent formal element in the prophetic superscriptions is a title, which is structured according to a limited number of patterns. The titles consist of the name of the prophet and—with the two exceptions noted—technical terminology which interprets the book as divine revelation.

III

The questions of the setting of the prophetic superscriptions as a genre and their intention must be considered together. In what institutional context did they arise, and why? It is all but self-evident that the superscriptions were not created by the prophets themselves. They refer in the third person, and retrospectively, to the activity of the prophet, and to the books which contain the prophetic words. Thus the superscriptions, if not necessarily the headings of individual units, tend to presuppose that the work of the prophet has ended,[24] whether or not it actually had (cf. Jer 1:1–3). Furthermore, by describing the book which follows they presuppose that the words of the prophet have already been committed to

---

Unfortunately the etymology of the term cannot be determined on the basis of Jer 23:33–40.

23. Note that the term is used in Amos 1:1 although it does not appear in the vision reports; cf. Schmidt, "Die deuteronomistische Redaktion," 170.

24. Cf. Wildberger, *Jesaja 1–12*, 3.

writing. Finally, source and redaction critical analysis (see below) have shown that at least the final form of most of the superscriptions is considerably later than the work of the prophets.

Leaving aside for the moment the question of the group or groups responsible for the prophetic superscriptions, we should investigate the issue of the background of superscriptions in general. The view has become widespread that superscriptions arose in the context of wisdom thought, being first used for the writings of the wise men and then providing the model for the headings of the prophetic books.[25]   But that conclusion should be reexamined and at the very least refined. The main evidence for this view is twofold: the regular appearance of superscriptions as titles for wisdom books and for presumably earlier collections of wisdom sayings (e.g., Prov 1:1; 10:1; 25:1; 30:1; 31:1; Eccl 1:1; Cant 1:1), and the parallels in ancient Near Eastern—and particularly Egyptian—wisdom literature.

Are there, in fact, significant ancient Near Eastern parallels to the superscriptions which might help resolve not only the question of their original setting but also the question of their intention?   Gevaryahu has called our attention to a number of possible parallels and advanced several theses concerning the origin and history of the prophetic superscriptions.   He finds the closest connections with the Akkadian colophons, and argues that the superscriptions once stood at the end of the prophetic books and only later were transferred to the beginning.[26]   But there is no direct evidence that the prophetic superscriptions originally were colophons at the end of the books.   What the colophons and the superscriptions have in common is the fact that they stand outside the body of the composition and provide information about it.   But from this point the differences are more striking than the similarities.   The Akkadian colophons most frequently provide data concerning the scribe who copied it and its sponsor or owner, less frequently facts concerning the date, contents, or title of the work, and almost never present the name of an author.[27]   Interesting are quite a number of Sumerian texts (mainly hymns) in which the colophons characterize the composition in terms of its genre and/or its use.[28]   More important still is a text which Lambert

25. Ibid., 2; H. W. Wolff, *Dodekapropheton 2: Joel, Amos* (BKAT 14/2; Neukirchen-Vluyn: Neukirchener, 1969) 149.
26. Gevaryahu, "Biblical colophons," 42–43.
27. W. G. Lambert, "Ancestors, Authors, and Canonicity," *JCS* 11 (1957) 1.
28. Cf. *ANET*[3] (1967), 577ff., 583, 591.

has identified as "a catalogue of texts and authors" which he dates to the first quarter of the first millennium. The catalogue does not consist of superscriptions or colophons, but of a list of titles, some of which are substantive while others are taken from the first lines of the texts, followed by the names of the supposed authors.[29]　In many cases the authors are identified in terms of vocation; the parentage of some is given. There is little reliable information here concerning the authorship of Babylonian texts. "The importance of this catalogue lies in its manifestation of critical scholarship. The over-whelming majority of Babylonian texts circulated anonymously."[30] Thus this catalogue, the linking of titles with authors, is the work of critical and scribal activity.

In fact, the closest parallels to the OT superscriptions—prophetic and others—appear to be the ones ordinarily adduced by scholars who argue for a wisdom setting, namely, the superscriptions of Egyptian "wisdom" texts. For example: "The Instruction of the Mayor and Vizier Ptah-Hotep, under the majesty of the King of Upper and Lower Egypt; Izezi, living forever and ever."[31] The work is identified in terms of itself and its author, whose occupation and date are provided. So there are real parallels—if not necessarily connections—between the prophetic superscriptions and wisdom literature. However, to call the setting of the genre "wisdom" is too broad and vague. It is probably more accurate to say that the genre resides in scribal activity. This conclusion is supported by the appearance of the superscription as a literary genre, the Egyptian parallels, and the interest of scribes in titles and authorship as reflected in Lambert's catalogue.

Whether the prophetic superscriptions were the work of scribal circles in some formal sense or of others who were influenced by their practices cannot be known for sure. But scribal and scholarly interests are reflected in these headings in several ways. To name a book is at least to make it available for cataloguing and future reference; to give it a substantive name entails an act of classification. To identify the author and to provide data concerning him and his time involve investigation of one kind or another. In fact, there is very little information in the superscriptions which could not have been derived from a study of the contents of the books themselves. This is not to deny that those who passed

---

29. W. G. Lambert, "A Catalogue of Texts and Authors," *JCS* 16 (1962) 76.
30. Ibid., 59.
31. *ANET*[3], 412; cf. also 414, 418, 419, 421.

on the prophetic words and added superscriptions were, as is usually suggested,[32] followers of the prophets, whether the original disciples or later interpreters. It is only to suggest that, whatever else they were, they were also scribes, so it is not surprising that some of their "scholarly" interests would surface in the texts.[33]

The specific intentions of the prophetic superscriptions are reflected above all in the particular vocabularly used to classify the books. The basic concern behind this language is the theological problem of authority and revelation. Thus the fundamental intention of the superscriptions is to identify the prophetic books as the word of God.[34] What had originally been claimed by the prophets for their individual oral addresses is now claimed for words written down, to be copied, read, and therefore to live in future generations.[35] But this claim is qualified in several ways in most of the superscriptions. In no sense is this revelation seen as handed down directly from heaven, but always through a specific human individual. With this in view, it is remarkable that hardly any "biographical" interest is shown in the prophets, here or elsewhere.[36] What does develop along with the theological interest is an historical concern. At least in the superscriptions which include dates, "the sayings are to be read and understood as words for a particular time and place through one individual man. Rather than an embarrassment, their historicality is a key to their meaning."[37]

IV

When did the theological and historical interest reflected in the superscriptions arise? The answer to that question is at least potentially different with regard to every individual prophetic book, and to explore each of the works would go far beyond the scope of this essay. But at

---

32. Cf. Lindblom, *Prophecy in Ancient Israel*, 241–42, 279ff.

33. Cf. E. Jacob, "Principe canonique et formation de l'Ancien Testament" (VTSup 28; Leiden: Brill, 1975) 112ff., 116.

34. Cf. Wildberger, *Jesaja 1–12*, 6; Mays, *Hosea*, 20; Mays, *Amos*, 20.

35. The purpose of the superscriptions is not necessarily the same as that of the original written collections of prophetic words. On the reasons for writing the prophetic words down in the first place, cf. Douglas Jones, "The Traditio of the Oracles of Isaiah of Jerusalem," *ZAW* 67 (1955) 229–37, and Jacob, "Principe canonique et formation de l'Ancien Testament," 113–14.

36. Most prophetic stories were told in order to present a message rather than to convey information concerning the life of the prophet. Cf. Gene M. Tucker, "Prophetic Authenticity: A Form-Critical Study of Amos 7:10–17," *Int* 27 (1973) 423–34.

37. Mays, *Amos*, 20.

least two discernible stages in development can be recognized and should be discussed.

First, it has long been recognized that there is evidence of Deuteronomistic editing in several of the superscriptions. In fact, it is tempting to attribute the superscriptions themselves and the theological perspective on the prophetic books described above to the Deuteronomistic editors, but this would go far beyond the evidence. Nevertheless, there are relatively clear traces of the work of these editors, particularly in the pre-exilic books.[38] Perhaps the strongest evidence of such redactional work is found in the chronological data in some of the headings, particularly the synchronistic royal dates in Amos 1:1 and Hos 1:1. These clauses probably stem from the chronological framework of the Deuteronomistic history work with its use of the "chronicles of the kings of Israel and Judah."[39] The fact that the Judean kings are listed first usually is taken to reflect a Judean point of view.[40] That there are no synchronistic royal dates for the remainder of the prophetic books poses a question only with regard to Isaiah and Micah, but the chronological notations there, as well as those in Jeremiah and Zephaniah may very well be Deuteronomistic also. Another likely Deuteronomistic expression is "Judah and Jerusalem" in Isa 1:1, which reverses the usual order in Isaiah's speeches (cf. 5:3; 3:1, 8; 22:21), occurs frequently in the Deuteronomistic history work, and is common in the Chronicler's work.[41] Furthermore, the possibility that the titles "The word of the LORD that came to . . ." are Deuteronomistic has been raised earlier.

So there was a Deuteronomistic redaction of at least some of the prophetic superscriptions, probably in the mid-sixth century B.C. or shortly thereafter. Is there any evidence for an earlier superscription tradition, particularly for one which interpreted the books as divine revelations? That is unlikely but possible in the case of Hosea, Micah,[42] and Isa 1:1, which is probably later than the superscription in Isa 2:1.[43] But, on the other hand, it is all but certain that there was an old, pre-Deuteronomistic superscription in Amos 1:1 which read, "The words of

38. Schmidt, "Die deuteronomistische Redaktion des Amosbuches," 168.

39. Ibid., 170.

40. Mays, *Amos*, 18; Mays, *Hosea*, 21; Wolff, *Hosea*, 3; Wolff, *Joel, Amos*, 150–51.

41. Jones, "The Traditio of the Oracles of Isaiah of Jerusalem," 239.

42. Lescow, "Redaktionsgechichtliche Analyse," 62.

43. G. Fohrer, "Entstehung, Komposition und Überlieferung von Jesaja 1–39 (BZAW 99; Berlin: A. Töpelmann, 1967) 115–16, 149.

Amos of Tekoa, which he saw concerning Israel, two years before the earthquake." The evidence for this widely accepted conclusion[44] is the redactional duplication in the verse, and the specific date which would make sense only for a relatively limited time. This superscription probably stems from the early collectors of the words and traditions of Amos.[45] And at least in this case the pre-Deuteronomistic redactors have presented the view that the collected and written prophetic words are to be handed on as revelation.

The collectors and redactors of the prophetic tradition—early and late—began to interpret the words attributed to the prophets as a written form of divine revelation. With the superscriptions to these books they advanced ideas of authority which would eventually surface in the form of the biblical canon. But they did not have, nor is there evidence that they believed in, a prophetic canon. Here the distinctions proposed by Sundberg are important. He argues wisely that a history of the canon cannot be written so long as the terms "scripture" and "canon" are used synonymously. "My proposal is that the term 'scripture' should be used to designate writings that are regarded as in some sense authoritative, and the term 'canon' used to designate a closed collection of scripture to which nothing can be added, nothing subtracted."[46] While the superscriptions to the prophetic books do not represent the stage of canonization, they do reveal the decisive turning point when—at least for certain circles in Israel—the spoken prophetic words had become scripture.

44. Schmidt, "Die deuteronomistische Redaktion des Amosbuches," 170; Mays, *Amos*, 18.
45. Lindblom, *Prophecy in Ancient Israel*, 241–42, 279–80.
46. Albert C. Sundberg, Jr., "The Bible Canon and the Christian Doctrine of Inspiration," *Int* 29 (1975) 356.

5. A JUDGMENT NARRATIVE BETWEEN KINGS AND CHRONICLES? AN APPROACH TO AMOS 7:9–17

PETER R. ACKROYD

In the present form of the book of Amos, 7:9–17 is set within the group of four visions gathered in 7:1–8; 8:1–2(3). The section is clearly marked off from what precedes and follows. The vision sequence is clearly interrupted by this, the only narrative passage in the book.

Apart from the strikingly different book of Jeremiah, the prophetic books of the OT contain few actual narratives. The Jeremiah case is so different, and the relationship of the narratives to the Deuteronomic "school" of writing raises such complex questions, that it is clear that it must be treated as in many ways a quite distinct problem.[1] Prophetic narratives are not uncommon in the books of Samuel and Kings. Of these, one series, 2 Kgs 18:13–20:19, reappears with some significant differences in Isaiah 36–39.[2] Some others of them, together with new ones, appear in the books of Chronicles. The difference between this type of prophetic material and that which is found in the prophetic books may be roughly stated: the former present stories about prophets in which their utterances are incorporated, usually briefly; the latter provide primarily collections of oracular and other such material, attached at some few points to brief narrative or annalistic (chronological) statements.[3]

---

1. For some observations of my own, see "Historians and Prophets," *SEÅ* 33 (1968) 18–54, especially 37–54; and "Aspects of the Jeremiah Tradition," *Indian JT* 20 (1971) 1–12.

2. For comments on some aspects of this, cf. my "An Interpretation of the Babylonian Exile: A Study of 2 Kings 20; Isaiah 38–39" *SJT* 27 (1974) 329–52.

3. Isaiah 7 has an example in which the annalistic material corresponds to 2 Kings 16. But where the latter has no mention of the prophet, the former subordinates the narrative content to the prophetic message. See my "Historians and Prophets," 22–27.

Apart from these narratives in Jeremiah and Isaiah, there are only four passages in the prophets which can properly be described as narratives. (I would exclude here, because of their different character, the accounts of call experiences or of visions [e.g., Isaiah 6; Jer 1:4–10], in which such narrative as is present is limited to the sphere of relationship between prophet and deity, and involves no other human participant.) One of the four is the book of Jonah, clearly *sui generis*; the second is Ezek 11:1–13, a remarkable and in many respects unique passage, in which, however, the narrative element is really only in vv 1 and 13, the theme of Pelatiah's death being thus subordinated to the oracular material.[4] The third appears in Hag 1:12–14 where the narrative describes the response to the prophetic word; it forms part of the framework to the oracles, and the structure of this book is again, with Zechariah 1–8, *sui generis*.[5] The fourth is the Amos passage with which we are concerned.

STRUCTURE AND MAIN FEATURES

G. M. Tucker has presented a form-critical study of vv 10–17[6] and a number of the points which he makes, in relation to form and purpose, will need further comment. He does not discuss whether the passage really begins at v 10 or whether v 9 ought to be included with it, but for the most part assumes, although the point is made explicit once,[7] that v 9 is either a comment on the preceding vision or visions[8] or a link verse designed to connect the narrative passage with the preceding visions.[9]

---

4. Were it not for v 13 with its unusual indication of the direct sequel to an oracle (cf. Jer 28:17), this passage could as well be classified with other examples of oracles attached to a brief narrative or annalistic statement. The presentation of symbolic actions in the book of Ezekiel, as in Jeremiah, provides another genre, in which the narrative is purely in terms of the word of instruction to the prophet and the carrying out of that word, together with its interpretation (cf. also Hosea 1 and 3).

5. See W. A. M. Beuken, *Haggai-Sacharja 1–8* (Stud. Sem. Neerl. 101; Assen: Gorcum, 1967) for a full discussion, and R. A. Mason, "The Purpose of the 'Editorial Framework' of the Book of Haggai," *VT* 27 (1977).

6. G. M. Tucker, "Prophetic Authenticity. A Form-Critical Study of Amos 7:10–17," *Int* 27 (1973) 423–34; see 426–27 for a schematic presentation of the structure.

7. Ibid., 425.

8. So e.g., W. Rudolph, *Joel. Amos. Obadja. Jona* (KAT 13/2; Gütersloh: Gütersloher, 1971) 236–37, who treats it as an explanation of vv 7–8, which then provides a link to what follows. Cf. S. Amsler, *Amos* (CAT 11; Neuchatel, 1965) 227; J. L. Mays, *Amos* (OTL; Philadelphia: Westminster, 1969) 133.

9. So e.g., H. W. Wolff, *Dodekapropheton Amos* (BK 14/2; Neukirchen: Neukirchener, 1969) 348. So also V. Maag, *Text, Wortschatz und Begriffswelt des*

We may observe that, while this fragment could have been added to the third vision to clarify its meaning, it is certainly not part of the vision series, nor is it at all clear that it does really provide a clarification of v 8. The four visions of Amos 7–8 form a perfectly balanced and structured unit: visions 1 and 2 (7:1–3, 4–6) form a matched pair, and so do visions 3 and 4 (7:7–8; 8:1–2). It is true that 8:3 is an addition standing outside the series,[10] and this might suggest that 7:9 is comparable, but against this may be set the close relationship between v 9 and vv 11 and 16. V 9 may in some measure be seen as the "text" upon which that which follows is a narrative "exegesis" (see below). A near parallel is to be found in Jer 26:18–19, where the citation of Mic 3:12 provides the introduction to the interpretative narrative comment.[11] We may observe that Jer 26:18 introduces the prophetic citation with a statement of the name of the prophet Micah and the occasion of his utterance; the relevance of this to the Amos passage will be suggested below.

Vv 10–17 contain, briefly outlined, the report to Jeroboam (10–11), the command to Amos (12–13), and the prophetic response (14–17). Tucker, after a full discussion of alternatives, stresses the element of "authentication" in the narrative. Near parallels may be seen in what we may term "prophetic conflict" material, such as Jeremiah 28, where the element of authentication may be held to be significant, perhaps even primary. But to this we shall return.

We may also observe the degree to which word play enters into the passage. One element of such word play turns on the use of *gālāh*; this appears first in v 11 in an oracular utterance which partly overlaps v 9, but introduces the new motif of the exile. This may be seen as a first stage in the exposition of v 9, for the phrase *wĕqamtî 'al-bêt yorobĕ'am behāreb* becomes *bahereb yāmût yorobĕ'am*, and is then elaborated with *wĕyiśrā'ēl gālōh yigleh mē'al 'admātô*. This theme is picked up further in v 17, where the judgment by the sword is applied to the priest's sons

---

Buches Amos (Leiden: Brill, 1951) 47–48, who describes it as *"Splitter eines Amoswortes,"* owing its position to the compiler of the book. His proposed addition of an extra clause is unwarranted.

10. Note especially the application to the "day" in clause *b*. The fifth vision, 9:1a, is quite different in structure from the other four, and it is difficult to see how it can be held to belong to an originally coherent series with them (*contra* Tucker "Prophetic Authenticity," 425, who cites the support of "most commentators").

11. Cf. H. Graf Reventlow, "Gattung und Überlieferung in der 'Tempelrede Jeremias,'" *ZAW* 81 (1969) 342 n. 118.

and daughters, the theme of *'ădāmāh* is developed in terms of disinheritance (*tĕḥullāq*), of exile (*'ădāmāh ṭĕmē'āh*), of death (*tāmût*), applied to Amaziah. The passage is rounded off by the repetition of the exile clause of v 11. We may further ask whether there is intended to be a play upon the exile theme in that Amaziah may be held to be attempting to "exile" Amos from the Northern Kingdom, and this is countered by Amos' pronouncement of exile for Amaziah and Israel; but this is more remote and there is no verbal link.

LANGUAGE AND THOUGHT

The examination of the language of 7:9–17 reveals a small number of suggestive points:

1. The proper name *yiśḥāq* (vv 9, 16) occurs only here and in Jer 33:26 and Ps 105:9; elsewhere it is always written *yiṣḥāq*. In the Jeremiah passage it appears in a formulaic reference to the patriarchs of a kind which is probably a late feature both in the Deuteronomic writings and in Jeremiah;[12] dating a psalm is notoriously uncertain, but it is unlikely that Psalm 105 is early. No other reference to Isaac appears in Amos; such references are limited in the OT to the narratives in Genesis, to the patriarchal threefold formula (in Exodus to Numbers), to the corresponding formula which appears as a probably late amplification in the Deuteronomic writings,[13] and six times in the Chronicles, of which three are in lists, one is in the citation of Psalm 105 (*yiṣḥāq*), and two are in prayers using the formulaic threefold phrase. The general lack of patriarchal references in the prophetic writings makes any conclusions unsatisfactory, but we may note that a reference to Isaac stands out as unexpected in Amos, and that the spelling variant may be late.[14]

2. Whereas in the oracles cited in vv 9 and 11 Jeroboam is referred to

12. Cf. J. van Seters, "Confessional Reformulation in the Exilic Period," *VT* 22 (1972) 448–59.

13. Only Josh 24:3–4 is nonformulaic, in a brief statement of patriarchal genealogy.

14. S. Terrien, "Amos and Wisdom," *Israel's Prophetic Heritage* (*Festschrift J. Muilenburg*; ed. B. W. Anderson and W. Harrelson; New York: Harper & Row, 1962) 108–15, see 113–14, and Wolff, *Amos*, 356, suggest a link to the Beersheba references in 5:5 and 8:14, but this seems very farfetched. Equally improbable is the suggestion of A. van Selms, "Isaac in Amos," *Studies on the Books of Hosea and Amos* (Ou-Testamentiese Werkgemeenskap in Suid-Afrika, 1964–65) 157–66, that Isaac here indicates Transjordan, with particular reference to "the temple complex of Penuel-Mahanaim" (164). Van Selms offeres useful comments on the probability that the *śin* forms of name and verb (*śḥq*) are late.

simply by name, in v 10 he is described as *melek yiśrā'ēl.* Such a specification is natural in a narrative context, and particularly appropriate in narratives in which both kingdoms are mentioned; in this context, within the book of Amos, it is odd.[15] The name occurs otherwise only in the heading in 1:1.

3. The verb and noun from the root *qšr* occur frequently in the books of Samuel, Kings, and Chronicles.[16] It is also found in Jer 11:9 and in Isa 8:12, although its precise sense in the latter is problematic; indeed, the context in Isaiah presents difficulties of both text and interpretation.[17] In the sense of "conspiracy," which is appropriate to both the Amos and the Jeremiah passages, it finds its clear parallel in a variety of narratives, especially in Kings.[18]

4. *kûl* (hiph.) in v 10 occurs otherwise in Kings, Jeremiah, Ezekiel, Joel, Chronicles.[19]

5. *nāṭap* (hiph.) in v 16 appears literally of liquid in the late 9:13.[20] Of prophetic speech, as here, it is found in Ezek 21:2, 7, parallel with *nibbā'*, and in the difficult passage Mic 2:6, 11.

6. The usage of *ḥōzeh* (v 12) is most frequent in the Chronicler,[21] although there are occurrences also in 2 Sam 24:11; in Isa 29:10 (probably a gloss); 30:10; 28:15 (probably a textual error); in Mic 3:7, parallel to *qōsěmîm.* The verb appears in Amos 1:1, but is not otherwise used in the book; in the visions the verb is always *rā'āh.*

7. To these we may add a number of smaller points. The use of *bāmôt* for "sanctuaries" in v 9 is discussed below; the only other occurrence in 4:13 is quite distinct. *bôqēr* (v 14) is a *hapax legomenon*; the often proposed emendation to *nôqēd*, to conform with 1:1 and to fit more properly with *ṣō'n*, can hardly be regarded as necessary, but would still leave us with a word not used in the oracles. *bôlēs* (v 14) is also a *hapax legomenon*, and *šiqmîm* (v 14) is unique here in Amos; their

---

15. Wolff, *Amos*, 355, explains it as due to the narrative having been composed in Judah after Amos' return. But this makes assumptions about the material which need examination (see below).

16. See also note 23.

17. Cf. N. Lohfink, "Isaias 8:12–14," *BZ* 7 (1963) 98–104.

18. *qšr* in the sense of "bind" occurs elsewhere, but this is not relevant here. Ezek 22:25 may well be corrupt, but if correct may stand with Jer 11:9 alongside the narrative books.

19. Of other forms of this root, only *pilpel* occurs in early material.

20. This sense belongs also to the *qal*, and some occurrences are probably early.

21. Cf. Wolff, *Amos*, 358; the use is mainly exilic and post-exilic.

technical use, like that of *bôqēr*, sets them somewhat on one side as evidence. More significant may be the occurrence only in this passage in Amos of *znh* (v 17); *ṭāmē'* (v 17), the nearest parallel to "unclean land," here is in Josh 22:19 (*'ereṣ*) of the land beyond Jordan remote from the tabernacle, probably a late passage; *miqdāš* (vv 9, 13); *ḥlq* (v 17), only here of the division of land. But the usage of these words elsewhere is very wide, and their absence from the remainder of Amos may or may not be important. Less significant too, because of their very common use, are *brḥ* (v 12), *ḥebel* (v 17), *yākôl* (v 10), *'ānāh* (v 14).

In addition we may note that *šlḥ* (qal) occurs only in v 10, elsewhere in Amos in pi. (7) and hiph. (1); *ysp* occurs in v 13 with *l* and inf.; elsewhere with inf. alone.

8. We must also note that other vocabulary in this passage is found, with greater or less frequency, in other parts of the book of Amos. It may be doubted if there is any other sufficiently clear difference of usage to warrant a distinction being made.[22] Similarly, it may be noted that some words which occur quite frequently elsewhere in Amos are not found in 7:9–17: thus *'ădônāy* (25), *'ĕlōhîm* (15), *hinnēh* (14), *yôm* (wide use, especially of the day of Yahweh), *ya'ăqôb* (6), *ṣĕbā'ôt* (9), *šûb* (13).

It is clear that such linguistic evidence is insufficient to suggest any conclusions in other than tentative terms; the most that it may allow is that, if there are other indicators, the narrative is less close to Amos than it is to narratives in the historical books, and it might be designated as later than Amos.

So far as the content of the message is concerned, as it is here ascribed to the prophet, we may observe that the theme of judgment on the royal house is not found elsewhere in Amos; the theme of the exile (vv 11, 17) occurs in a number of other passages (with *gālāh*—5:5, 5:27, with specific reference to "beyond Damascus"; 6:7; 9:4 has *šĕbî*; cf. also the picture of driven cattle in 4:2–3). Doubt has been expressed about the genuineness of some of these passages, in particular those that use *gālāh*. It may be noted that other judgment themes in Amos are in terms of destruction rather than of exile. The point may be left open, with the

---

22. I have examined all the evidence set out by Maag, *Wortschatz*, much of which contributes very little to our understanding of Amos. It could be argued that the sense of *lqḥ* (v 15) is different from that appearing elsewhere; so too for *npl* (v 17), but perhaps for this cf. 5:2; 8:14.

recognition that there is a possible linkage here of both thought and language. The theme of destruction of sanctuaries is also to be found elsewhere in Amos: so 5:5 with its word play *gālāh*/Gilgal, where there is also the implied transformation of Bethel to Beth-awen (more characteristic of Hosea; cf. 4:15; 5:5; 10:5); and 9:1 with its theme of judgment on the temple buildings. Such themes in Amos are, however, more related to doom for the worshipers (e.g., 8:14) than specifically to downfall of the shrines.

We may summarize this very limited evidence by saying that the words attributed to Amos in 7:9–17 are not unrelated to what we may observe more generally in the Amos tradition, but that on balance they are not quite what we should expect. If we were looking for "genuine" sayings, it is more probable that we should find them elsewhere. This might suggest that what we have here is nearer to what a narrator might tell *about* the message of Amos, rather than oracles directly attributable to him. It is more or less what we might regard as a summary of his message, but less clear that it is really couched in words that he would have used.

A CONJECTURAL RECONSTRUCTION

The theme of conspiracy (*qšr*) already noted is particularly characteristic of the narratives of the books of Kings, and it appears in certain blocks of material.[23] Of these blocks, the most distinctive is that which appears in relation to the Northern Kingdom from Jehu (2 Kings 9) to Hoshea (2 Kgs 15:30). But we may observe that the theme is also used of Judean events; and further extended in 2 Chronicles 24–25.

What is noteworthy in the narratives of 2 Kings 9–15, insofar as they concern the Northern Kingdom, is that they show the origins of the dynasty of Jehu/Jeroboam II in a prophetic narrative which utilizes the

23. 1 Sam 22:8, 13 (Saul. On the use of *qšr* as a theme word in 1 Sam 18:1; 22:8, 13, see my "The Verb Love—*'āhēb* in the David-Jonathan Narratives," *VT* 25 [1975] 213–14). 2 Sam 15:12, 31 (Absalom). I Kgs 15:27; 16:9, 16, 20 (Baasha, Zimri). 2 Kgs 9:14; 10:9 (Jehu); 11:14 (2 Chr 23:13, against Athaliah); 12:20 (cf. 2 Chr 24:25–26, against Joash). 14:19 (against Amaziah of Judah, son of Joash; cf. 2 Chr 25:27; and see below); 15:10, 15 (Shallum); 15:25 (Pekah); 15:30 (Hoshea); 17:4 (with *māṣā'*; cf. Jer 11:9, of Hoshea in relation to Assyria); 21:23, 24 (=2 Chr 33:24–25, against Amon). Also Neh 4:2 (RSV=4:8) of opponents to Nehemiah. Cf. further 2 Chr 24:21, of conspiracy against Zechariah son of Jehoiada the priest, in the context of the Joash conspiracy noted above, and cf. T. Willi, *Die Chronik als Auslegung* (FRLANT 106; Göttingen: Vandenhoeck & Ruprecht, 1972) 220 n. 20 on *qšr* as *Leitbegriff*.

qṣr motif, together with a precise promise of four generations (10:30), and that this is echoed in 15:12 in the sequel to the *qṣr* of Shallum which marks the end of that dynasty (15:10). The *qṣr* theme is then taken two stages further in the Pekah and Hoshea material in 15:25, 30. Remarkably, we have a positive prophecy, attributed to Jonah ben Amittai, for the reign of Jeroboam II (14:25), and the narrator offers a theological appraisal of this in 14:26–27.[24] The absence of a prophetic judgment on the dynasty of Jeroboam at this point is noteworthy. It is, of course, exactly comparable with what we observe in 2 Kings 24–25 where we should expect at least an allusion to Jeremiah. We may, however, see in Jeremiah 37–44 a form of the narrative which incorporates Jeremiah material and relates his message explicitly to the fall of Jerusalem.[25] Is it possible, in view of the use of the *qṣr* motif in Amos 7:10, that 7:9–17 is a relic of such a judgment narrative? This would argue for the existence of two forms of the Kings material: the one (as we know it) not including any reference to Amos,[26] the other (as here postulated) presenting Amos as the prophet of judgment on the dynasty of Jehu/Jeroboam.[27]

It would go considerably beyond the scope of this study to examine fully the vexed problems of 1 Kings 13,[28] but its possible relationship to the Amos narrative must be considered. The views in which a link is entertained cover a wide range.[29] That there is some relationship ap-

24. F. Crüsemann, "Kritik an Amos im Deuteronomistischen Geschichtswerk," *Probleme biblisher Theologie* (*Festschrift G. von Rad*) ed. H. W. Wolff (Munich: C. Kaiser, 1971) 57–63, argues that 2 Kgs 14:27 is deliberately directed *against* the message of Amos. But it must be observed that there is nothing in the wording which corresponds precisely. Cf. further below.

25. On this, cf. Ackroyd, "Historians," 37–54.

26. Or even critical of him, if Crüsemann, "Kritik an Amos," is right.

27. H. Schmid, "Nicht Prophet bin ich, nicht bin ich Prophetensohn," *Judaica* 23 (1967) 68–74 observes the possible relationship between Amos 7 and the Jehu narrative of 2 Kings 9, particularly in the use of *qṣr*. But he argues that the accusation of Amaziah derives from the supposition that Amos is just such another as Elisha, initiating rebellion, and that Amos' reply (see below) is directed toward denying such a view. In my view, Schmid is right in seeing a connection, but wrong in his interpretation of its nature.

28. There is a considerable literature on 1 Kings 13. The recent study by E. Würthwein, "Die Erzählung vom Gottesmann aus Juda in Bethel. Zur Komposition von 1 Kön 13," *Wort und Geschichte* (*Festschrift K. Elliger*; ed. H. Gese and H. P. Rüger; AOAT 18; Kevelaer: Butzon und Bercker, Neukirchener, 1973) 181–90, provides both sufficient bibliography and a useful analysis of the divergent traditions within this complex.

29. Cf. J. Bleek, *Einleitung in das AT*, 4th ed., ed. J. Wellhausen (Berlin: Reimer, 1878) 244; O. Eissfeldt, *Kleine Schriften* (Tübingen: Mohr, 1968) 4. 137–42; especially 138–39 and bibliography, 138 n. 2. So too W. Rudolph, *Amos*, 100.

pears inherently probable. It is clear that the oracle put in the mouth of the unnamed prophet in 1 Kings 13 is a prophecy *ex eventu*, designed to be specifically linked to the Josiah narrative. Does it perhaps replace a different judgment oracle?[30] The theme of judgment on the altar is reminiscent of Amos 9:1, although the wording is different. There are two verbal links with Amos 8—the phrase *'ākal leḥem* (1 Kgs 13:8–9 [16, 19]; Amos 7:12), a crucial theme in 1 Kings 13, subordinate but not unimportant in Amos 7; and the use of *bāmôt* (1 Kgs 13:2; Amos 7:9), a term not otherwise found in Amos in this sense (see above).

Is it possible that there were in existence two forms of the story, associated either with Amos or with an unnamed prophet? The one, in which there is conflict between prophet and king (Jeroboam), was utilized in 1 Kings 13,[31] and attached to a complex of other prophetic legends, in particular to a prophetic grave tradition (1 Kgs 13:30–31; cf. 2 Kgs 23:17–18),[32] a tradition comparable in some degree to that associated with Elisha (2 Kgs 13:21). We may note that the shift of this narrative, in which judgment is pronounced upon Jeroboam and his dynasty, from Jeroboam II to Jeroboam I would be not simply the result of a confusion between two rulers of the same name, but rather an expression of the desire of the eventual compiler of Kings to correlate his view of the apostasy of the North, especially as associated with Bethel, with his view of Josiah as the instrument of divine judgment upon it.[33] It is thus an expression of the overall pattern in which the kings of the North are throughout condemned for their adherence to the apostasy of Jeroboam ben Nebat. The other form of the story, in which there is conflict between prophet and priest (Amaziah), although behind the priest stands the king (Jeroboam), has come to us inserted into the vision material of Amos, interrupting the sequence but providing an authentication of Amos' status in that it incorporates elements suggestive

---

J. L. Crenshaw, *Prophetic Conflict* (BZAW 124; Berlin: Walter de Gruyter, 1971) 41–42, argues for general influence from Amos on 1 Kings 13, though noting important points of difference. The link has recently been denied by such scholars as M. Noth, *Könige* (BK 9; Neukirchen: Neukirchener, 1968) 295; and H. Jepsen, "Gottesmann und Prophet," *Probleme biblischer Theologie* 171–82; see 180 n. 15.

30. So Würthwein, "Komposition," 184.
31. Ibid., 182–85, who does not, however, discuss any possible source for the narrative.
32. Ibid., 185–87.
33. On Bethel and its significance, cf. Würthwein, "Komposition," especially 188–89, and Jepsen, "Gottesmann," 174.

of the call motif.[34]   What has already been said about the linkages and
non-linkages of thought and language with Amos would suggest that we
leave open the question whether the narrative was originally associated
with Amos or not.   Clearly it was believed to be so when it was inserted
in Amos 7.   On the other hand, it is easier to see an anonymous narrative coming to be attached to a known prophet (cf. 1 Samuel 9), than to
suppose that an Amos narrative lost its identity.

A further line of investigation emerges when we consider 2 Chr
25:14–16.   As a preliminary we may recall that this too is in a context
which utilizes the *qṣr* motif.[35]   For Athaliah (2 Chronicles 23), Joash
(2 Chronicles 24), and in relation to the latter, Zechariah the son of
Jehoiada the priest (24:21), and again for Amaziah (25:27), this motif
is either taken over from the Kings narratives or is added by the Chronicler.   It is within this context that we are told of an act of apostasy by
Amaziah, king of Judah.   A prophet, unnamed, is sent to him by God to
accuse him: "Why have you directed inquiry to the gods of a people
when they could not deliver their own people from your power?"
Amaziah's reply runs: "Have you been appointed King's counselor?
Hold your tongue (*ḥdl*)!   Why should you be put to death?"   Significantly, the sequel runs: "So the prophet did hold his tongue, but he said:
'I know that God (thus) counseled to destroy you, because you have
done this thing and have not heeded my counsel.' "[36]   It is noteworthy
that there is a word play on the root *y'ṣ*, picked up also at the beginning
of v 17 in the next section of narrative.   More significant is the content
and character of these verses.

There is no parallel to 2 Chr 25:14–16 in the Kings material.   Should
we suppose pure invention, or can we deduce whence the Chronicler
derived it?   The former is not likely in view of the Amos/Amaziah
narrative and also that of 1 Kings 13.   We may observe three forms of
comparable material: a narrative of prophet (unnamed) and king
(Jeroboam) in 1 Kings 13, which concerns apostasy; a narrative of
prophet (Amos) and priest (Amaziah) who reports to the king (Jeroboam), in which the primary theme is judgment for religious failure
(explicitly in Amos 7:9); and a narrative of prophet (unnamed) and
king (Amaziah) in 2 Chronicles 25, which concerns apostasy.   We may

34. Cf. Tucker, "Prophetic Authenticity," 430, and see also below.
35. See note 23.
36. The free translation is my own.

note further that in each case there is an attempt at silencing the prophet which fails. In particular there is a degree of correspondence between 2 Chr 25:16 "the prophet ceased (*ḥdl*)" but nevertheless is shown to have had the last word, and the Amos narrative in which the prophet is commanded to stop prophesying (*lō' tôsîp 'ôd lĕhinnābē'*) in the North, but goes on to make a dire pronouncement against the one who dares to infringe the divine prerogative of commanding the prophet to speak. The natural inference is that the Chronicler was making use of a form of the same tradition which we have in the other two passages; this tradition preserved the name of Amaziah, and so the Chronicler attached it in a suitable position to his account of the king of that name. It provides a good example of the Chronicler's exegetical method.

SOME POSSIBLE CONSEQUENCES

That Amos 7:9–17 may be a tradition about the prophet (or about a prophet) independent of the other material in the book appears clear enough.[37] That it is part of a larger unit would also seem quite possible.[38] Its function is not biographical,[39] nor does it set out to relate how Amos' work in the North came to an end.[40] May it not simply be that the basic purpose of this narrative is to pronounce doom on the dynasty of Jehu, within the larger theme of the apostasy of the Northern Kingdom, and in the context of this, equally to pronounce doom on the one who, like Jeroboam in 1 Kings 13, Jehoiakim in Jeremiah 36, and Amaziah in 2 Chronicles 25, endeavors to deflect the true will of the deity and the mediation of his word?

If it is proper to regard the passage as a fragment, extracted from a narrative source, then can we suggest a reconstruction of at least its

---

37. Cf. Tucker, "Prophetic Authenticity," 425.

38. Ibid., 426, citing T. H. Robinson, *Amos* (HAT 14; 3d ed.; Tübingen: Mohr, 1964) 99; H. Grosch, *Der Prophet Amos* (Gütersloh: Mohn, 1969) 19.

39. Ibid., 429, citing T. H. Robinson *Amos*, 99; J. D. W. Watts, *Vision and Prophecy in Amos* (Leiden: Brill, 1958) 2, 31; E. Hammershaimb, *The Book of Amos* (Oxford: Blackwell, 1970) 15, as upholders of the biographical view (cf. also A. Weiser, *Das Buch der Zwölf Kleinen Propheten I* (ATD 24; Göttingen: Vandenhoeck & Ruprecht, 1959) 165; J. L. Mays, *Amos*, 134); see E. Würthwein, "Amos-Studien" *ZAW* 62 (1950) 10–52, especially 23–24, for criticism of it.

40. Many popular textbooks (and some more sophisticated commentaries) assume that Amos returned at this point to Judah, and, being unable to prophesy further in the North, gathered his message into written form there (see below). One might gain a little support for this view by adducing the 2 Chr 25:16 statement that "the prophet ceased," but this would be somewhat hazardous.

opening? It is clear that it would not open with a bald oracle of doom. There are various possibilities. We may follow the wording of Jer 26:18 and suggest: "Amos of Tekoa prophesied at that time (or in the days of Jeroboam king of Israel) and said: Thus says Yahweh of hosts. . . ." Another possibility would be to follow 1 Kings 13: "And behold a man of God (Amos) came from Judah at the behest of Yahweh to Bethel and said. . . ." A third would be to follow 2 Chr 25:14: "So Yahweh sent a prophet (Amos of Tekoa) to him. . . ." Comparison might also be made with such forms as occur in 1 Kgs 14:7–11 and 16:1–4.

Within this judgment narrative, the purpose of the appeal to prophetic authority in vv 14–15 may be seen as undergirding the prophetic word with a claim to divine commission. This is of particular interest if we associate the narrative in the overall pattern with 2 Kings 9. The dynasty of Jehu was divinely appointed by Elisha, and the stress on divine authority is underlined in the account in 9:1–10. The designation of Jeroboam in 2 Kgs 14:27 as savior of Israel makes his position appear secure. By what right then can a prophet from Judah pronounce doom on this royal figure and royal house? The credentials of the prophet must be challenged. The narrative of 1 Kings 13 has the king endeavor to have the prophet arrested. Amos 7 presents the attempt at frustrating the divine will by having Amaziah order the prophet out of the country.[41] The response in each case is catastrophic. In 1 Kgs 13:4, the king's outstretched arm is withered so that he cannot withdraw it. In Amos 7, the priest's attempt is countered by the appeal to a divine commission which is ineluctable, and the priest who dares to counter that commission himself falls under judgment (vv 16–17). The attack on a true prophet is an attack on God himself. The same point is implicitly made in 2 Chr 25:14–16 and also in Jeremiah 28.

Insofar as the prophetic word in Amos 7:9–17 can be seen to counter that of Elisha in 2 Kings 9 and also the more immediate word of blessing on Jeroboam in 2 Kgs 14:27, there is implicit a contribution to the wider theme of the validity of the prophetic word. A valid word of prophetic promise may be seen to be overtaken by a further word of doom.

---

41. We may note that the study of the nature of this passage and of the parallels to it lends no support to the supposition that Amaziah was giving Amos a kindly warning to escape before any word came back from Jeroboam. (So Wolff, *Amos*, 358 tentatively; Würthwein, "Amos-Studien," 19–24. Cf. the sensible strictures of Tucker, "Prophetic Authenticity," 427). Such a view depends in any case upon a very simplistic reading of the text.

Similarly (as for example in Jer 33:10–11 and other passages in Jeremiah 32 and 33) a word of doom may be overtaken by a further word of blessing. If we may postulate that this Amos passage stood in a larger narrative context, we may see it as saying, for example to the exilic or post-exilic community, that prophetic messages may be updated, their terms modified, their full significance understood only when they are seen in a larger context.

The question: "Was Amos a prophet?" has bedeviled a great deal of the discussion of 7:14–15. From one point of view, the question may be simply answered. The claim to a commissioning from God in v 15 underlines the authority of the prophet's word which follows in vv 16–17, countering the attempted prohibition of his activity in Bethel. We may observe also the use here of a familiar form, found particularly clearly paralleled in 2 Sam 7:8: *'ănî lĕqaḥtîkā min-hannāweh mē'aḥar haṣṣō'n*,[42] stressing both the legitimation of one who is exalted to high office with a convention of lowly origin. By that very emphasis on origin, and by implication on the lack of qualification for office, the motif underlines the divine prerogative, just as this is done in other call material by stressing unwillingness (so Moses, Jeremiah) or unfitness (so Isaiah, Ezekiel).

Some of the wider problems of interpreting the response of Amos in v 14 need not here detain us. The present writer's preference is for the interpretation of the negatives as interrogative: "Am I not a prophet?"[43] Alternatively we may suppose emphatic *l/lû/lā*.[44] The meanings of *nābî'* and *ben-nābî'* may then most naturally be understood as parallel.[45] If the latter is held to denote "member of a prophetic guild," then we must see Amos as claiming such guild membership, too.[46] This is a

42. So Hermann Schult, "Amos 7:15a und die Legitimation des Aussenseiters," *Probleme biblischer Theologie* (ed. Hans W. Wolff; Munich: C. Kaiser, 1971) 462–78; especially 476, adducing a wide range of comparative material for this form.
43. Cf. the discussion with examples, by G. R. Driver, "Affirmation by Exclamatory Negation," *JANESCU* 5 (1973) 107–14 (*Festschrift M. Gaster*).
44. Cf. H. N. Richardson, "A Critical Note on Amos 7, 14," *JBL* 85 (1966) 89. Also J. Crenshaw, *Prophetic Conflict*, 67, and G. Ahlström, *Joel and the Temple Cult of Jerusalem* (VTSup 21; Leiden: Brill, 1971) 21 n. 2 and 96 n. 2 for further literature.
45. So Amsler, *Amos*, 230.
46. Richardson, "Amos 7:14"; S. Cohen, "Amos Was a Navi," *HUCA* 32 (1961) 175–78, especially 177; Schmid, "Nicht Prophet," 73, and Crenshaw (in an oral comment) would all maintain that the first phrase is emphatic: "I certainly am a prophet," but that the second is negative: "but not a member of a guild." This shift is extremely awkward. It is impossible here to attempt a discussion of the problematic

much more natural interpretation than to suppose that the statements of v 14 are in contrast with those of v 15: the latter explicates the basis of the prophetic status, and more specifically the basis of the commission to the North which has been called in question.

Two further possible consequences may be briefly adduced. 1) The recognition of the nature of this narrative passage and of its possible original place outside the book of Amos makes it particularly important that we should not conflate evidence from it with evidence from the oracular material, without very careful prior consideration of the kind of information which may be legitimately extracted from each. This is a basic principle of biblical (and other) interpretation, too often honored in theory and ignored in practice.

2) If this is an Amos tradition, can we deduce what became of the prophet? Did Amos, like the unnamed prophet in 2 Chr 25:16, "hold his tongue," though not without having the last word?[47] Can we infer anything further from that passage? The king threatens death to the unacceptable prophet: are we to suppose that he overlooked the final relentless word and let the prophet go unharmed? That prophets could be put to death, even extradited for that purpose, is clear from Jer 26:20–23. We are not even told that Amos accepted the orders of Amaziah, although it may be proper here, as with the absence of any reply from Jeroboam, to draw no deductions from the silence of the narrative, which has presumably no concern with this point. But we cannot simply draw the conclusion that Amos went back to Judah and wrote down his prophecies. The arguments for that depend solely on suppositions regarding the making of the book of Amos; it does not follow, because we see Amos only alone and only confronted by an opponent, that there were none in the Northern Kingdom to hear and

---

passage in Zech 13:5, with its apparent citation of the words of Amos: *lō' nābî' 'ānōkî.* The coincidence of the words cannot prove citation, although the degree to which earlier material is used in Zechariah 9–14 must make this probable. (Cf. R. A. Mason, "The Use of Earlier Biblical Material in Zechariah IX–XIV: A Study in Inner Biblical Exegesis," Ph.D. Dissertation, London, 1973). We cannot, however, argue from the meaning given to the words in their present context to their meaning in Amos, and the difficulty of their present context makes any firm decision impossible. Cf. Mason, *Zechariah,* 251–52; also P. D. Hanson, *The Dawn of Apocalyptic* (Philadelphia: Fortress, 1975) 367, and Crenshaw, *Prophetic Conflict,* 105–6.

47. Crenshaw, *Prophetic Conflict,* 59, seems to miss the point when he describes this prophet as "immoral," "expediently silent," although he admits that the prophet does have the last word.

heed his words and none associated with him to preserve the tradition of what he said.

From this discussion, we may perhaps add a slender piece of evidence for an alternative view of what became of Amos. If we see a possible relation to the other prophetic narrative of 1 Kings 13 (2 Kings 23), that of the grave tradition, then we may ask: Was there a tradition of a grave of Amos at Bethel?[48] Admittedly, it is more proper to treat the two main themes of 1 Kings 13 as originally separate, but perhaps there is here a clue, if not to historic truth, at least to a possible source of origin for the much later tradition that Amos had a martyr's death, a tradition which may be said to have at least as much basis, if not more, than the supposed "martyrdom of Isaiah" under Manasseh.[49]

The tentative result of this inquiry is to look behind the present position of Amos 7:9–17 to consider its original nature and function. The passage may then be considered at two levels rather than one.

In its present position, set in the context of Amos' visions, it serves, like other call narratives and other conflict narratives,[50] to indicate to those who gathered and to those who heard the prophetic words, the authority of the prophetic message. An appeal is made to the reality of his commission by God, and the validity of that commission is under-girded by the prophetic word of doom to Amaziah and his family and of exile for Israel. The fulfillment, and therefore the validation, of that word belongs to history. The whole message of the prophet is thereby validated and its continuing function as the Word of God assured for a later generation.

Its position, as postulated by this discussion, was originally as part of a narrative concerned with judgment on the Northern Kingdom, and as such stood in a form of the Kings material which, like Jeremiah 37–44, elaborates the function of the prophets in the period of the monarchy, thus underlining still further the theme of prophecy and fulfillment al-

48. For this, cf. also Eissfeldt, *Kleine Schriften* 4. 139.
49. Cf. the comments of Crenshaw, *Prophetic Conflict*, 95. For the "martyrdom of Amos," cf. T. Schermann, *Prophetarum Vitae* (Leipzig: Teubner, 1907) and *Propheten—und Apostellegenden* (TU 31/3; Leipzig: Hinrichs, 1907) 51–53; C. C. Torrey, *The Lives of the Prophets* (SBLMS 1; Philadelphia, 1946) 26, 41. Cf the wider discussion of this whole theme in O. H. Steck, *Israel und das gewaltsame Geschick der Propheten* (WMANT 23; Neukirchen: Neukirchener, 1967), especially 249–50 on Amos.
50. E.g., Jeremiah 1, Isaiah 6, Ezekiel 1–3 for the former, and Jeremiah 20, 26, 28 for the latter.

ready present in the familiar form of the text. It serves more particularly to authenticate the judgment on the Northern Kingdom in the period of Jeroboam II, delivered by a prophet in the face of opposition, with the opposing functionary himself caught up in the doom he seeks to evade. As a further element within this, we may see that the exiling of Amaziah to an "unclean land" is correlated with the exiling of Israel, and the figure of the priest becomes, as it were, a type for the subsequent fortunes of the people—the more significant reference of the passage being then beyond the doom of the North to the eventual doom of Judah in 587.[51]

The existence of such alternative forms of the text is already demonstrated by the presentation of Samuel-Kings in the books of Chronicles, which offer a highly homiletic version of the earlier material.[52] Other clues may be seen in the LXX form of the Kings text. The recognition of such alternatives, deducible often only from fragmentary information, does not of itself actually increase our direct knowledge of the wider range of literature available in ancient Israel, but it does enable us to get a fuller picture of the complex processes of the evolution of that literature toward what eventually comes to be fixed in a canonical form. It is a pointer to the degree to which canonical fixation of particular texts is the result of what must be regarded as chance factors, although we may always endeavor to discover reasons for the choice of one particular text-form rather than another. The inclusion of the Isaiah material in the familiar form of 2 Kings (chaps. 18–20), with the possibility that behind that too lies a "non-Isaiah" form of the Hezekiah narrative,[53] is a further reminder of that chance element, here illuminated by the fact that Isaiah 36–39 offers yet another alternative text. These points are important in the consideration of the canon and a warning against too narrow a view of canonicity and canonical authority, for the texts that have come down to us, when considered in all their various forms and presentations, do not in fact provide a basis for a simplistic view of biblical authority.[54] They demand a careful consideration of the signifi-

---

51. For a comparable instance, see my "Babylonian Exile" (see note 2), and observe a possible link with the theme of "unclean" in Ezek 4:13.

52. Cf. my forthcoming "The Chronicler as Exegete" in *Journal for the Study of the Old Testament* 2 (1977) 2–32.

53. Cf. Ackroyd, "Babylonian Exile," 350.

54. For some further comments on this theme, see my "The Open Canon," *Colloquium. The Australian and New Zealand Theological Review* 3 (1970) 279–91.

cance of all the forms in which materials appear, and an endeavor to discover, within those forms, clues to the circumstances and beliefs of the communities in which the literature was brought into being. It is out of such a richness of tradition that the subsequent interpretations of both Judaism and Christianity can grow.[55]

55. I am indebted to colleagues and others who have commented on the material for this discussion in earlier forms, and in particular to Burke O. Long for his discerning notes on an earlier draft of the text. Two articles by T. J. Wright, ("Amos and the 'Sycomore fig,'" *VT* 26 [1976] 362–68 and "Did Amos Inspect Livers?" *ABR* 23 [1975] 3–11), were available to me only after the completion of this article. They do not affect the issues considered here.

PART TWO

ASPECTS OF

CANONICAL HERMENEUTICS

6. THE KING'S LOYAL OPPOSITION: OBEDIENCE AND AUTHORITY IN EXODUS 32-34

GEORGE W. COATS

To obey or not to obey seems an uncomplicated choice, at least for the framework of the Sinai traditions. In Exod 19:5, the appeal is clear. "Now therefore, if you will obey my voice and keep my covenant, you shall be my own possession among all peoples." Moreover, the content of the obedience Yahweh expects from his possession is flagged by the introductory formula in v 6b. "These are the words which you shall speak to the children of Israel." Yet, the choice is not always a simple one, as the traditio-historical layers in the law would suggest. It must have been necessary always to reconsider what the content of obedience might be. Indeed, the choice can raise a pressing problem. Is it not necessary on occasion to resist a command, to appeal for some new formulation of the law?[1]

The question is sharpened by the work of Lewis S. Ford.[2] It is of central importance to affirm that God does not coerce his creatures, but rather strives to persuade them to obey his aims for their future.[3] Yet, that image could emerge as a rather weak and inadequate tool for expressing the breadth of thought about God. In an effort to do justice to facets of theology concerned with God's sovereignty, Ford suggests appropriating imagery of God as King. It is clear that the suggestion is rooted deeply in biblical tradition.[4] But the pattern calls for some de-

1. George W. Coats, "Abraham's Sacrifice of Faith: A Form-Critical Analysis of Genesis 22," *Int* 27 (1975) 389–400.
2. Lewis S. Ford, "Biblical Recital and Process Philosophy: Some Whiteheadian Suggestions for Old Testament Hermeneutics," *Int* 26 (1972) 198–209.
3. Lewis S. Ford, "The Logic of Divine Power: God as King and the Kingdom of God," MS presented to a symposium on biblical theology and process philosophy, Indianapolis, February 28–March 1, 1974.
4. See particularly Norman Perrin, "The Interpretation of a Biblical Symbol," *JR* 55 (1975) 348–70.

liberation about royal "persuasion." In what manner can a king tolerate opposition? Everyone knows the kind of conformity that can be expected by the pope, the president, the bishop, or the dean. The image of the king, though not a part of our society's categories for power structure, surely evokes an equal if not a greater response of awe and obedience, that is, conformity to the norm recognized as the king's will. And so, if we speak of God as King, do we not commit ourselves unconditionally to a stance of obedience to his demands? Does the king not persuade with force? What sense, then, is talk of opposition, particularly when the "opposition" is qualified by the term "loyal"? In Isa 45:9, the prophet makes the point: "Woe to him who strives with his Maker, an earthen vessel with the potter! Does the clay say to him who fashions it, 'What are you making?' or 'Your work has no handles!'?" For Second Isaiah, opposition to the king is not loyal. It is only opposition. In the Kingdom of God, is not loyalty to be understood as automatic, unquestioning obedience to the God who calls for response?

Yet, remarkably, the pious faith of Israel allows for struggle with God to work out the meaning of loyal obedience. For Israel obedience to the King was not the obedience of an automaton. Jeremiah's opposition to the King (Jer 12:1) illustrates the point: "Righteous art thou, O Lord, when I complain to thee; yet I would plead my case before thee." The collocation is different here from the one in Isa 45:9. Here the preposition following the verb is *'el*; God would, in that case, be the judge for the case. Isa 45:9, on the other hand, employs the preposition *'et*, suggesting that God is a litigant. Yet, the content of the case in Jeremiah is formulated in terms identical to those in Isaiah. In both cases, an accusing question is addressed directly to God (cf. Jer 12:2).[5] Yet, Jeremiah is not dismissed as a rank rebel. Thus, the hermeneutical problem: What distinguishes a question of accusation addressed to God, or the King, as an act of loyal trust and faith from one that can be taken only as revolution or apostasy?

The problem relates to a broad range of biblical tradition. Thus, for example, in the murmuring traditions of the wilderness theme it is crucial

5. On the question as accusation in a lament, see Claus Westermann, "The Role of the Lament in the Thelogy of the Old Testament," *Int* 28 (1974) 27–28. It seems significant to me, in this context, that Genesis 32 can develop an etiology for the name "Israel" out of a story that depicts the eponymic father struggling with God. Regardless of the original character of the story, or the original meaning of the crucial verb, the point of the etiology is that Israel is in essence, i.e., in name, the one who struggles with God.

to ask in each instance whether key questions addressed by the Israelites to Moses constitute matters consistent with faithful obedience or matters that spell revolution.   Norbert Lohfink is correct particularly in his observation that the pericope in Exod 15:22–27 does not describe a rebellion.[6]   The question in v 24 involves no breach of faith; one must therefore consider whether the verb *lûn* properly connotes such a question of faith *as well as* clear acts of rebellion, or whether in v 24 the verb wrenches the content of the story out of its original lines and forces a reinterpretation of a story originally cast as an account of a faithful request for water.   If some such reinterpretation has occurred, it in itself would reflect the hermeneutical problem at stake.   A thin line divides a faithful and obedient request from one that implies rejection of the status quo and revolution.

The issue is more sharply focused in Exod 17:1–7, since here the verbs *lûn* and *rîb* are closely associated.   I have argued that the question with the verb *rîb*, structured like the question in Exod 15:24, does not imply revolution but can be understood as neutral, whereas the question with the verb *lûn* implies revolution, rejection of Moses' authority and leadership.[7]   But the two acts are not always distinguishable.   What appears at one point to be loyal opposition, consistent with behavior one might expect from a faithful disciple, becomes at another point disloyal rebellion.   Claus Westermann has captured the same problem by suggesting that the murmuring pattern reflects the influence of the lament.[8]   The lament question and the murmuring accusation appear in the same mold. But the one is an act of faith, the other rebellion.   Must the lamenter not always be cautious, lest his lament pass over into revolution?[9]

6. Norbert Lohfink, "Die Ursünden in der priesterlichen Geschichtserzählung," *Die Zeit Jesu* (ed. G. Bornkamm, K. Rahner; Freiburg: Herder, 1970) 46 n. 32.

7. George W. Coats, *Rebellion in the Wilderness: The Murmuring Motif in the Wilderness Traditions of the Old Testament* (Nashville: Abingdon, 1968) 53–62. Lohfink, *Ursünden*, 46 n. 32, sees rebellion more readily connoted by the verb *rîb*. Yet, for both *lûn* and *rîb*, patterns of rebellion must be defined on the basis of evidence derived from the context, not imposed on, or developed from a reconstruction of, the context.   Lawrence Dunlop develops a similar point in his "The Intercessions of Moses: A Study of the Pentateuchal Traditions" (Dissertation; Rome: Pontifical Biblical Institute, 1970) 171.   Dunlop, however, reconstructs the key text, placing the neutral question with the verb *lûn* and the question of revolution with the verb *rîb*. (See p. 176.)

8. Westermann, "Lament," 29–31.

9. Walter Brueggemann, "From Hurt to Joy, from Death to Life," *Int* 28 (1974) 3–19.

EXEGETICAL FOCUS

In order to focus on the problem in a limited context, I shall confine detailed discussion to the pericope in Exodus 32–34.[10] The golden calf episode provides a completion of the call for obedience in Exodus 19, not only in clearly picturing a people's revolution and subsequent restoration to covenant, but also in the representation of Moses. It is my conviction that a model for a genuinely loyal obedience emerges from the interaction of the two facets.

THE REVOLUTION

There can be no doubt about the fact that the pericope begins with an account of gross apostasy. In the first panel of the unit, 32:1–6, construction of the golden calf is represented as the creation of gods for the people. In the opening imperative addressed by the people to Aaron, the point is explicit not only in the collocation, *'ăśēh-lānû 'ĕlōhîm* (v 1), but also in the formula *'ēlleh 'ĕlōhêkā yiśrā'ēl 'ăšer he'ĕlûkā mē'ereṣ miṣrāyim* (v 4). Thus not only by the act of creating the images, but even more by the act of creating *multiple* images, the people revolt against the loyalty they should owe to Yahweh. Moreover, they assign to those images the credit for the exodus. The act is, therefore, relatively clear. To ascribe the exodus to golden calves is revolution.

Yet, the act is *relatively* clear because the report represents a point of view which, in all probability, sets the golden calves over against the cultic center in Jerusalem (cf. 1 Kgs 12:26–33). Insofar as the present form of the text is concerned, the hermeneutical question is no problem. To go to Dan and Bethel instead of Jerusalem, to revere the golden calves instead of Yahweh, is by definition revolution.[11] But, if the history of the tradition does reveal a stage behind the pro-Jerusalem polemic, then the construction of golden calves may not have been so clearly an act of apostasy![12] And the appeal to the populace in 1 Kgs 12:28 would set out the weight of the question. How should the people

10. For a review of the literary critical problems in this text, see Brevard S. Childs, *The Book of Exodus: A Critical Theological Commentary* (Philadelphia: Westminster, 1974) 553–624, as well as the literature cited there.

11. On this stage, see Childs, *Exodus*, 560–61.

12. So Murray Newman, *The People of the Covenant: A Study of Israel from Moses to the Monarchy* (Nashville: Abingdon, 1962) 179–82. See also Jan Dus, "Ein richterzeitliches Stierbildheiligtum zu Bethel? Die Aufeinanderfolge der frühisraelitischen Zentralkultstätten," *ZAW* 77 (1965) 268–86.

know whether worshiping God at Dan or Bethel is better than worshiping God at Jerusalem? Perhaps the innovation of Jeroboam is a reformation promoted by genuine faith, a desire to correct the abuses in the cult in Jerusalem and thus return the people to a proper, obedient relationship with God. Must we not be cautious in concluding too quickly, with Dtr, that the innovation is in reality the nauseous and perverse crime of apostasy?

Exod 32:1 is, however, still more subtle in its depiction of the revolution. The initial imperative to Aaron, calling for construction of the calves, casts the act as an effort to replace *Moses* rather than a direct act of rebellion against Yahweh. "This Moses, the man who brought us up from the land of Egypt, we do not know what has become of him."[13] One might conclude that revolution against a particular administration can be separated from loyalty to the state only with great difficulty. Refusing belief in Moses is tantamount to refusing belief in Yahweh. And apostasy is to replace one administration with another, at least from the point of view of the displaced administration. For this text, moreover, the revolution against Moses focuses attention on the office of Moses. What authority does Moses have to lead the people further when the people have found new modes of leadership? Thus, one might anticipate by the tension established in the first panel not only a fitting response to the apostasy from God, but also some confirmation of Mosaic authority within the operation of the people.

The second panel of narrative (32:7–35) develops these two points. An initial movement carries Yahweh's response to the revolution, first as a report to Moses of the people's apostasy (v 8), and then as a judgment speech. The judgment spells the dissolution of the covenant and the destruction of the people. Moreover, Moses' authority is elevated in v 10b by virtue of Yahweh's designation of Moses as the new elect. Thus, in contrast to the people's move to desert Moses and build new leaders out of gold, here God deserts the people and announces his

---

13. For a different position, see Jack M. Sasson, "Bovine Symbolism in the Exodus Narrative," *VT* 18 (1968) 384. Sasson concludes: "These repeated equations between Moses, *the man who brought the Hebrews out of Egypt*, and the calf, symbol of the *deity that brought the people of Israel from bondage*, render it plausible to assume that, to the newly-freed slaves, the molten calf was a substitute for Moses. . . . In the ancient Near East it was not uncommon for certain animals . . . to represent deities and highly esteemed personalities." Yet, the narrative context does not suggest that the calf is considered a representative for Moses. The calf substitutes for Moses by replacing him.

plan to build a new people out of Moses. And it is only the virtue of Moses' intercession that stays the total tragedy. Significantly, in the intercession no reference to the plan for Moses as founder of a new people appears. The brief allusion is simply dropped.

The double pattern of the panel is nonetheless present in the execution of the judgment. Moses responds in anger to the festival of the golden calf by breaking the tables, an act that represents the dissolution of the covenant.[14] And the destruction of the calf, with the people sentenced to drink the remains, is at least an act of hostile coercion, if not a trial by ordeal, to determine loyalty or revolution in the bowels of the people. Moreover, Moses' involvement in the ordination of the Levites also shows his authority to respond in kind to the apostasy of the people. The penalty for the crime of innovation in electing new leaders in the place of Moses is thus severe and, in a manner that stands in tension with Moses' intercession on the people's behalf, reminds any revolutionaries that one objects to the King only with fear and trembling.[15] The double motif is completed when, following a new intercession, Yahweh refuses to reinstate the people, reminds Moses that the guilty must suffer the consequences of their rebellion, and promises the judgment. The one amelioration for the judgment is a reconfirmation of Moses' task in leading the people. The promise for an angel does, to be sure, suggest some degree of divine presence. But it does not renew the covenant with the people or point to any stage along the way. The angel confirms the authority of *Moses* in v 34: "Now go, lead the people to the place of which I have spoken to you [sing.]; behold, my angel shall go before you [sing.]. Nevertheless, in the day when I visit, I will visit their sin [plur.] upon *them*." And the judgment follows in v 35. Thus, despite the continuation of the journey, despite the reconfirmation of Moses as the leader of the people, the covenant is broken. God is not with his people. If the story to this point represents the interests of Jerusalem as polemic against the North, then the impact of the polemic is clear. The covenant is broken. And there stand the pieces. The picture is unfortunately all too sharp.

14. Childs, *Exodus*, 569.
15. See the treatment of these aspects as narrative style in ibid., 563.

INTERCESSION

The pericope in Exodus 32 develops a polar motif as a point of tension with the major focus on the revolution of the people. And the polar motif, namely, the intercession of Moses, opens a narrative line that is not completed in chap. 32. Yet, precisely in the intercession of Moses the problematic quality of the loyal subject's obedience to the King emerges.

Exodus 32

Moses' intercession on behalf of his people appears twice in 32:11–13 and 32:30–32. In both cases the intercession represents a polar contrast with the context. The first intercession follows two of Yahweh's speeches to Moses, the second of which announces the divine intention to destroy Israel and replace it with a nation drawn from the seed of Moses. The intention to destroy is expressed by reference to the hot wrath of God burning against the people (*wĕyiḥar-'appî bāhem wa'ăkallēm*, v 10). Moses' intercession (v 11) opens with an explicit reference to that hot wrath (*lāmāh yhwh yeḥĕreh 'appĕkā bĕ'ammekā*). It thus connects clearly with the preceding context.[16] Moreover, this opening question appears in the form of an accusation, like the accusation of the lament or the murmuring rebellion. With second person suffixes it addresses God directly and calls into question the legitimacy of the divine act. "O Lord, why does thy wrath burn hot against thy people?" The question alone is enough to raise the specter of rebellion around the head of the servant of the Lord, since the clay ought not to say to him who fashions it, "What are you making?" But the specter grows in the continuation. Moses argues by citing a hypothetical response from the Egyptians, should Israel die at the hands of God in the wilderness: "With evil intent did he bring them forth, to slay them in the mountains, and to consume them from the face of the earth" (v 12).

The development of the argument is crucial. It is not that the Egyptians would attribute an evil intention to God, and thus in order to protect his reputation he should desist. Rather, it corresponds to similar arguments in intercession (Num 14:13–19); to pursue the intention to destroy the people would violate the previous promise to establish a

16. The intercession reflects heavy influence from Dtr. See ibid., 559, as well as Childs's comparison with the Dtr parallel, 567–68.

covenant of loyalty with the people. It is on the basis of an appeal precisely to that promise that Moses himself labels God's intention to destroy as an evil (*hārāʾāh*). The point of the argument is that, even for God, violation of the initial aim in the relationship between God and people is evil. And the intercession attempts to persuade God to pursue the initial aim, to act in consistency with his own promise. For this tradition, even God must live in the tension of the hermeneutical problem. Where is the line that distinguishes justifiable innovation from unjust rebellion against loyalty to the covenant? Thus, God does not impose the lure of loyalty as a tyrant unbound by a reciprocal commitment of loyalty. Rather, he enters a mutual commitment without appropriating his creatures as instruments of his pleasure dangling on his string. On the basis of the intercession, God is persuaded. He repents and reassesses his announced goal. But also of significance here, the tradition shows Moses as a servant who can intercede boldly for his people without himself falling under divine wrath as a rebel. Moses' intercession saves the day. It persuades God. And his persuasion, even with threats of coercion, is his responsibility as an obedient servant of God.

The polar tension between intercession and revolution continues in the following panel. In a report of Moses' descent to the people with the tables of God in his hand, the text shows no clear indication of impact from the Mosaic intercession or the divine repentance. Indeed, it has long been recognized that the report apparently presupposes that in the descent, Moses had no prior knowledge of the rebellion. And when he discovers the apostasy of the people, he responds in a fit of wrath that rivals the previous intention of God to destroy his people. He breaks the covenant, forces the people into a trial by ordeal, summons Aaron to account for the crime, and finally condemns at least a portion of the people to destruction. Where is the appeal to mercy now? To be sure, the destruction scene incorporates an ancient tradition of ordination for the Levites. But in its present form, the scene can only be taken as the occasion of Moses' wrath. Moreover, the occasion leaves the people without covenantal commitment. And without covenantal commitment, the consequence of God's concession to the intercession in v 14 is not very clear.

The same point can be made in reference to the intercession and concession of Num 14:13–25. Following a divine announcement of intention to destroy the whole people and establish a new people through the seed of Moses, Moses intercedes. And the basis of the intercession is the prior promise. To destroy the people would destroy the promise. V 20 marks the concession. But then follows a sentence that reduces the impact of the concession. If the people must die in the wilderness, with only Caleb or Caleb and Joshua heirs to the promised land, where is the impact of the concession? Yet, the display of wrath does not appear to be disruptive in the narrative. It is, on the contrary, a narrative style built from interplay of polar tensions.[17] And the polar tensions create the essential movement in this story.

The continued crisis in Exodus 32 is captured by a renewal of the intercession in vv 31–32. In this case the intercession begins with confession. The people are, in fact, rebels. But the appeal that might correspond to the accusation in the previous intercession is broken, with only a protasis suggesting the formal structure it might have carried. The weight of the intercession is, however, carried by a contrasting protasis and its completion. "Now, if thou wilt forgive their sin—and if not [if you will not forgive them], blot me, I pray thee, out of thy book which thou hast written." The appeal is now a threat. And the serious quality of the appeal is clear (cf. Num 11:11–15).

Contrary to the previous intercession, in this case the appeal of the intercession, or at least the threat, is not heeded. In a direct rejection of the threat, the response to the intercession notes that only the guilty will be blotted out. The innocent may not stand in the place of the guilty. Moses will not die. But the negotiation is stalemated. The impact of that point is made quite clear in v 34b. The day will come when the guilty will stand their sentence (cf. Num 14:21). Thus, the commitment is not renewed. The presence of God that defines Israel as distinctive from all people is not returned. V 34a emphasizes this point. Moses, not God, must lead the people. And the angel goes before Moses, the seal of his leadership. Yet, a crucial point of the pericope seems to be that Moses can oppose the divine intention and not himself be counted as a rebel. In an audacious threat, Moses submits his resignation. And the divine response affirms the legitimacy of Moses' office, his struggle for his people. He has not yet persuaded God to complete the restoration. But his efforts to persuade have not been met with

17. So ibid., 567.

rejection. The future is open for Moses to continue his struggle, for the
shape of the mutual commitment to be hammered out in a mutual exchange of aims between God and his servant. In this case to contend
with God is the mark of the obedient servant.

Exodus 33–34

The concluding comment in 32:35 leaves the goal of the intercession
unfulfilled. The covenant is broken, the people punished. And so, in a
sense, the pericope is complete. Rebels will be plagued. Yet, the appeal
to the prior promise, already a part of the narrative in chap. 32, remains
at center stage in chap. 33. The transition to the first panel in chap. 33
is somewhat rough, pointing to the tension between the broken covenant
and the intercession. Vv 1–6 repeat the movement of 32:33–34.
Yahweh directs continuation of the move toward the land, and the
foundation of the direction is the promise. But the movement must
occur without God's presence. An angel will lead the way. But there is
no indication that the angel alleviates the threat posed by God's absence.
The suffixes here are still singular, as in the parallel section of chap.
32. It is not so clear here, however, that the singular suffixes refer to
Moses in contrast to the people (cf. v 3). The angel represents leadership in some degree for all the people. But even with this concession,
the angel's leadership is a step removed from God's presence. Moreover, God will himself dispel the occupants of the land. But even that
promise does not reduce the judgment in the directive. "But I will not
go up among you, lest I consume you in the way, for you are a stiff-
necked people." The goal of the intercession is thus as yet unfulfilled.
The role of Moses vis-à-vis the people demands some attention here.
In 32:33–34 the judgment stood against the people, with Moses distinct,
not guilty of his people's sin. And the angel functioned in some manner
as an affirmation of his leadership. Here, there is some confusion. In v
1 Moses receives the directive to lead the people to the land of the
promise. V 2 might be taken as a parallel to the promise for an angel in
chap. 32 since the suffixes in the judgment sentence of v 3 as well as the
central pronoun are also second person singular (contrast 32:34b).
Yet, the people, not Moses alone, are intended. "You [sing.] are a stiff-
necked *people*." Thus, the distinctive function of the angel in chap. 32

to confirm Mosaic leadership fades, and the focus falls on the punishment. The movement is repeated in vv 4–6 with a narrative report to
the people of the *bad* news (*haddābār hārā'*). The report includes in v
5 a citation of the judgment. But in this case the division between
Moses and people, apparent in 32:33–34, again emerges. The citation,
a speech addressed to Moses, is introduced with a message commission
formula. Thus, Moses is to address his people with an oracle of God.
And the message defines the people as stiff-necked with a second person
plural pronoun. "You [pl.] are a stiff-necked people" (v 5). The
people stand under the judgment, whether addressed in plural or singular
forms. And Moses mediates between the condemned people and the
judge.[18]

With the repetition of the judgment as denial of presence for the
people in their move to the land, the narrative shifts to the intercession.
Vv 7–11 set the stage by describing Moses' regular office as mediator,
associated intimately with the tent of meeting.[19]   And central to the
description is the symbol for divine presence. When anyone would seek
Yahweh, he would approach the tent. Then Moses would enter the tent
and the pillar of cloud would descend on it. And the conclusion stipu-
lates Moses' unique position. "Thus, the LORD used to speak to Moses
face to face, as a man speaks to his friend" (v 11). In the face of such a
general introduction to Moses' role as intercessor, the intercession in vv
12–13 is doubly poignant. For the crisis provoking the intercession is
the threat of divine absence.

The intercession begins in v 12 with a citation. God had instructed
Moses to bring the people up. "Thou sayest to me, 'Bring up this
people.'" The issue is thus personal, not *simply* on behalf of the people.
V 12 a[b] would then appear to contradict the promise for an angel to
lead the way: "Thou hast not let me know whom thou wilt send with
me." But the issue cannot be resolved by such a circumlocution. The
promise for an angel is not the same as the promise for God's own
presence. And it is that promise which is at stake. Thus, with another
citation, Moses develops the argument out of personal position. "Thou
hast said, 'I know you by name, and you have also found favor in my
sight.'" Significantly, it is out of that personal favor that the point of

18. Various layers in the history of tradition may well account for the rough quality
of this narrative element, rather than redaction of literary sources. See ibid., 584–86.
19. Ibid., 592.

the argument appears in v 13: "Now . . . if I have found favor in thy sight, show me now thy ways, that I may know thee, and find favor in thy sight." But the appeal is general. It is only in the final touch of the storyteller's hand that the argument suggests the particular content of the intercession. "Consider that this nation is *thy* people." That point demands careful attention. It refers to the people as "thy people" (*'amměkā*), a point which may imply the covenantal promise. But the reference does not ground the appeal Moses makes to God, at least not in the same sense as the promise tradition in 32:13.[20] The argument is not that because these people are God's people, God should show Moses his way. The argument is that because Moses enjoys favor in the sight of God, God should show his way, that is, see that the people are his people. Thus, an appeal that appears general has a subtle particularity. It is a call for a reformation of the covenant grounded in the unique relationship of trust and friendship between God and Moses.

The intercession wins a concession. "My presence will go with you, and I will give you rest" (v 14). But the concession is personal;[21] it is directed personally to Moses, not to the people (cf. LXX). Moses' response is thus quite in order. The concession is not yet enough. And so he continues his negotiation. It should be noted, however, that v 15 is not limited to the personal appeal of the earlier section. It is an appeal for the people, cast in first person *plural* form. "If thy presence will not go with me, do not bring *us* up from this place." (The LXX reads a first person singular form. But the change violates the development of Moses' argument.) Indeed, the appeal focuses on the presence of God *for the people* as the crucial, distinctive quality that defines the people. Without the presence, there is no people. But it also focuses on the bond between Moses and his people. Without that bond, there is no leader. "For how shall it be known that I have found favor in thy sight, *I and thy people*? Is it not in thy going with *us* so that we are distinct. *I and thy people*, from all other people that are upon the face of the earth?" (v 16).

The concession and following exchange of dialogue in vv 17–23 again complicate the picture. In v 17a the goal of the intercession is appar-

---

20. Ibid., 594, which develops a different position. But see the comments on 595.
21. So ibid., 594. See also James Muilenburg, "The Intercession of the Covenant Mediator (Exodus 33:1a, 12–17)," *Words and Meanings* (ed. Peter Ackroyd and Barnabas Lindars; Cambridge: Cambridge University, 1968) 159–81.

ently reached. And the reason for the concession is the favor Moses holds in the eyes of God (v 17b). But that point was never at issue. The point of the intercession is to return the people to favor. And the text apparently refuses to establish a relationship which must depend on continued grace mediated through the favor Moses has always enjoyed. Thus v 18 carries a new appeal: "I pray thee, show me thy glory." The new concession establishes the name before Moses. And the name carries with it the surety of God's presence. That element is fundamental for the covenant between people and God. Traditional images define this new demonstration of presence, however.[22] The allusion to God's gracious and merciful character recalls the word play from Exod 3:14, again an element in the promise of presence. The description of God passing by Moses recalls the scene with Elijah in 1 Kgs 19:11–14. And again, the point is that God establishes intimacy with his own.

Chap. 34 continues the narration directly. The covenant will be reformulated as the first one. And a narrative account of the theophany promised in chap. 33 brings Moses' work to fruition. The tables of stone are restored. Yahweh appears, and his name is proclaimed. But even yet Moses is not satisfied. The covenant is not yet fully established with the people. This point is perhaps implied in the stipulation for Moses to come to God alone (34:2–3). And in the stipulation the unique office of Moses can be seen. But the point is also present in the proclamation of the name. In a traditional formulation, God's mercy and grace move to the fore. But v 7b has the counter pole. The guilty are still guilty. The renewed intercession in vv 8–9 is thus comprehensible. Moses' appeal for the people is now explicit and unambiguous: 1) presence of God, 2) forgiveness, and 3) renewed covenant. Moreover, here as in the other intercession the basis for the appeal is the favor Moses holds personally in the eyes of God. But his identification with his people lays that favor on the line. "Go in the midst of *us* . . . pardon *our* iniquity and *our* sin . . . take *us* for thy inheritance" (v 9).

The result of the intercession is also unambiguous. The covenant will be established. And the announcement focuses on the people. In v 10, God speaks: "I make a covenant. Before all your [sing.] people I will do marvels, such as have not been wrought in all the earth or in any nation; and all the people among whom you are shall see the work of the

22. See Childs, *Exodus*, 595–96.

Lord; for it is a terrible thing that I will do with you [sing.]." And then follows the stipulation of the covenant, with an appropriate conclusion in vv 27–28. The goal of the intercession has now been achieved.

The concluding panel, vv 29–35, must be placed in the context of the intercession motif, even though the intercession itself is no longer a part of the narration. The verses connect somewhat roughly with the context. One would expect some notation that the stipulations of the covenant were accepted by the people. That element occurs, at least in symbolic form, in chap. 35. Those who were willing contributed to the tabernacle as Yahweh commanded. But not in 34. The conclusion to chap. 34, then, sacrifices completion of the narrative line in order to focus on Moses as the one who intercedes.

The shining face, in 34:29–30, highlights Moses' unique position. It is possible, on the basis of the reference to the veil in vv 33–34, to suggest that a cultic mask, a symbol of the office, lies behind the panel.[23] However, the crucial point of the text is not to explain the origin of a mask. Rather the image highlights the symbolic quality of Moses' stature and authority. The veil that must cover Moses' shining face does so, as has long been noted, when he is not functioning in his official capacity.[24] The shining face is itself the symbol of the authority the man holds.

Hab 3:4 describes a similar pattern of images, with the veil (a different word but apparently a similar image) functioning to emphasize the glory of God while rendering the glory of God, otherwise so completely awesome, tolerable.[25] In the case of Moses, the symbol derives from his close association with God. Thus, it appears first when Moses returns from the mountain, a characteristic which Moses himself is not aware of. And the description is similar to one that depicts God's own glory (so Hab 3:4). But it is not sufficient to interpret the phenomenon simply as derived glory, as the glory of God reflected in his face. Rather, the symbol points specifically to the authority Moses holds before God

---

23. A. Jirku, "Die Gesichtsmaske des Mose," *ZDPV* 67 (1944–45) 43.

24. Childs, *Exodus*, 610.

25. Ibid., 619. See also Sasson, "Bovine Symbolism," 386–87. Sasson concludes: "In this . . . one single depiction of a horned Moses, symbolizing the old pagan faith being brought face to face with the God of the new creed, YHWH asserts his dominance. It is He who gives the orders. Moses does no more than present them to the people." The issue here is not, as Sasson suggests, the translation of the *crux interpretum* as "shiny" or "horned." The issue lies in evaluation of the term in what Sasson calls a metaphorical sense suggesting vanity, pride, force, dignity, and power.

and, incidentally, before the people. In Hab 3:4, the shining symbol refers clearly to the glory shining from the hands of God. And the veil covers his power. Moreover, the noun in Hab 3:4, to which the denominative verb in Exodus 34 is related, refers commonly to personal virtue, personal authority, and not to authority that simply reflects the glory of another party.[26]

In sum, the challenge to Moses' authority led to rejection of the people, a broken covenant. And it was only through Moses that the people are invited into a renewed covenant. The shining face finally countermands the challenge and affirms the authority of Moses before the people, indeed, his stature and favor before God. "Aaron and all the Israelites saw Moses, and behold the skin of his face shone. And they were afraid to come near him. . . . The Israelites saw the face of Moses, that the skin of the face of Moses shone. So he returned the veil on his face until he should go in. . . ."

INTERCESSION AND THE AUTHORITY OF THE LEADER

The tradition in Exodus 32–34 demonstrates the character and force of revolution. The people want a new leader. So their action crowns a new leader (a new god) and at the same time expels the old one. The action is decisive, the response of Moses and Yahweh equally decisive. An ambiguity in the call for obedience, however, comes sharply into focus when the relationship between Moses and Yahweh is examined. Moses behaves toward God in a manner that is not always obviously distinct from the revolutionary action of the people. This point is clear, not only in the accusatory question at the center of the intercession, not only in the repeated moves to negotiate the concessions he sought through his intercession, but also in the threats involving his own life, in his bold identification with his own people whom he himself recognized as rebels. Yet, the tradition carries no condemnation of Moses for such audacious behavior. On the contrary, Moses' revolutionary innovations

---

26. Sasson, "Bovine Symbolism," 386, discusses problems in the Habakkuk parallel. But to recognize difficulties in the text is not to dismiss easily the text as relevant evidence. Again, the issue is the metaphorical value of "horns" or "rays of light." In either case the text refers in some manner to the force, dignity, and power of God. Compare the transfiguration of Jesus whose face shines like the sun (Matt 17:1–7 and parallels). In some sense the shining face of Jesus is also a reflection of God's glory. But it is more; it shows an explicit intention to affirm Jesus' authority, coming after the question put to Peter, "Who do you say that I am?" (Matt 16:15) and closing with the affirmation, "This is my beloved son . . . listen to him" (Matt 17:5).

before God, his refusals to take the directive as it stood, are understood consistently as obedience and faithful loyalty.

Thus, an initial problem not only for interpreting the tradition but also for developing an ethical perspective of more general scope is to probe the difference between the two sides. The ambiguity in Exodus 32–34 suggests that the line between obedience and revolution can never be rigidly drawn. To do so reduces obedience to mechanical legalism. To the contrary, each new generation faces the necessity for determining where the line might be, and what loyalty to the right—or the left—side of the line should look like.[27]

But even more, Exodus 32–34 suggests not only that God attempts to persuade his rebellious people, but that Moses attempts to persuade God. And, moreover, he succeeds. He is not simply an instrument in the hands of an omnipotent God. Rather, he contributes along with God to the emerging present. This facet of the tradition is bound up in some manner with the pattern of divine promises in the tradition. Moses appeals for God to alter an announced intention on the basis of a prior promise. And so the intercession might be understood as the result of efforts on the part of any generation to depict the intentions of God, judged in the final analysis by the character of the promises that have endured throughout the generations. But that does not do justice to the central role of Moses as a leader of major magnitude. Persuasion depends on the trust enjoyed by the participating parties of a negotiation. Moses trusts God on the basis of the traditional promises. But God also trusts Moses. Thus, Moses stands in a significant position that opens the door for him to persuade God. Does the tradition not suggest very forcefully that God reveals himself as a king who wields the power to coerce or persuade, but also as a king who offers freedom to his subjects even to the point of being himself coerced or persuaded? Is it possible to understand, much less appropriate, the impact of that image in the representation of God's sovereignty as the sovereignty of a king?

The question is relevant, not only for the task of formulating concepts of God as King or the character of his persuasive lure, but also for the complementary task of formulating concepts of the subjects. What does the tradition suggest about the intercessor? Lawrence Dunlop has

27. The same point would apply to questions about the authority of scripture. To draw the line rigidly would reduce canonical status in the community to oppressive biblicism.

caught the force of the question: "Why should such and such a person be qualified to pray for others. . . ?"[28]

The tradition presents Moses as a creative innovator who defends his people at the risk of the favor he holds with God. The basis of the relationship is, to be sure, a mutual *trust*. And out of the assumptions established by the trust, God apparently takes the audacious intercession as the work of a loyal devotee, a loyal servant. But the qualification moves beyond mutual trust to the personal virtue of the man, the position of stature which he holds in the eyes of God. It is significant, then, that appeal to the favor Moses holds before God replaces an appeal to God's prior promises. Thus, Moses defends his people before God with the same loyalty to the people, the same courage and vigor apparent in his defense of the people before the Amalekites. Is not that stature and authority, that qualification or worth, a part of the pattern of traditions about Moses as heroic man?

The hermeneutical force of the observation, then, is that it is not necessary to divert that which is worthy and qualified from the man simply as reflected glory. It is possible to see the man as a primary agent in that real world. To live in full acceptance of that responsibility is the task of the loyal subject of the king, whether his response to the king is immediate support or opposition.

The heroic stature of Moses contributes, moreover, to the hermeneutical task posed to any subsequent generation by the tension inherent in an innovative action. How does any loyal subject of the king develop innovative programs without being dismissed as a heretic guilty of revolution? The image of the heroic servant of God establishes a context for making such choices in the demand of the moment. To be sure, the image is subjective. Its power to create such a context depends on the commitments of the generation struggling with the question. So Moses is obedient; the devotees of the calf cult are not. Jesus is the Christ for his disciples, a pretender for those who do not believe. Given the belief in the heroic figure, however, the power of the heroic image to create a context for making such decisions is strong. The point is not that the disciples do what Moses did, in simple imitation, but that the heroic figure instructs the faithful by the power of his stature. And decisions about revolution or obedience are made in the light of that instruction. Thus, each new generation recasts the Mosaic law. But for each genera-

28. Dunlop, *Intercessions of Moses*, 1.

tion the new law is a law that roots in the authority of Moses. Each recasting is undertaken out of loyalty to the image, loyalty to the stature and power of the figure. Such responsibility must be a part of what it would mean to believe in Moses (Exod 4:41; 14:41).

This perspective can be evaluated more adequately, perhaps, in the categories suggested by Lewis Ford. There is a sense in which the power of the heroic figure is the power of the past. And that facet in the tradition must always be there. But the power of the past can be destructive for the present. The laws of the hero can be frozen into hard and fast bonds. Indeed, the image of the hero itself can be frozen, so that rather than instructing each new generation, it reminds each generation of its shortcomings. Or, should the new set of people more or less succeed in matching the image, it may find itself robbed of any genuine vitality.

The context provided by the heroic figure, however, does not mean that the new generation lives in the past. Rather, it orients the new generation toward decisions to be established in the present.

> The locus of productive activity thereby shifts from the past causes to the present effect, which is active in virtue of its own power. The past causes determine the content of the present actuality, but only as this content is appropriated and unified by the present activity. . . . Our freedom lies in the power of the present to select and to organize that which we inherit from the past.[29]

The power of the present, which is already operative in the description of reality at the basis of the heroic tradition, feeds from the heroic tradition as a new present emerges.

But even more. The audacious quality of the hero's innovation, particularly as it assumes the form of intercession for the hero's people, suggests that the hero participates in the power of the future. Ford observes: "Through Jesus' faithful response to the Father, his human activity became the vehicle for divine activity, for Jesus' own power of the present allowed the divine power of the future to be fully effective."[30] In something of the same manner, Moses' faithful intercession for his people, as a part of his own power of the present, allows the divine power of the future to take its own shape. And the process, both from the promises of the past and from Moses' own stature and author-

29. So Ford, "Divine Power," 12.
30. Ibid.

ity, becomes fully effective in the present. It is, moreover, to such participation in the power of the future that Moses' disciples or Jesus' disciples are called. That call arises from the context created by the heroic tradition.

Mosaic authority may be understood, then, out of his participation in the power of God. This point may be already apparent in the narrative about the divine call. The call grounds Mosaic authority, both for Israel and for Egypt. It may be apparent in the signs. The demonstration of power in converting water to blood (not just blood-red water) or in the execution of rebels by the earth opening its mouth brings a coercive facet to his authority. The strength of that authority resides, then, in the power of God at the basis of his leadership. But the strength of Mosaic authority lies at least as much in his heroic identification with his people, in his protection and defense of them not only against hunger, thirst, and attacks from various enemies, but also against threats from God. We will obey Moses because he is *our* leader.

7. THE THEOLOGICAL SIGNIFICANCE OF CONTRADICTION WITHIN THE BOOK OF THE COVENANT

PAUL D. HANSON

DIVERSITY AND CONTRADICTION: THEOLOGICAL IMPASSE OR PORTAL TO DEEPER UNDERSTANDING?

Over the course of the last century, the contributions made by literary and form criticism to our understanding of the literature, history, and religion of Israel have been enormous. The legacy within the area of biblical theology is more problematical. The document which in former times could be utilized as one harmonious witness to the theology of the church had become a complex congeries of separate writings, reflecting divergent and often contradictory interpretations of historical facts and even diverse theological traditions. In the era of Wellhausen, the complexity on the diachronic plane was handled by a developmental schema in which the formulations of each new period of Israelite religion contributed to the gradual evolution of religious ideas. In the process the tension between old and new was an essential creative factor. Along with the emergence of the twin realizations that the prophets did not invent ethical concerns in Israel and that the second millennium in the ancient Near East was not nearly so religiously primitive as earlier scholars believed, detailed traditio-historical studies began further to complicate the picture by indicating that, even on the synchronic plane, diversity characterized the religious scene in Israel. Today we find ourselves heirs to a collection of diverging traditions, ideologies, theologoumena, and confessions: Baal metaphor/El metaphor; amphictyonic credo/royal ideology; Northern tradition/Southern tradition; Jerusalem cult/prophetic protest; Mushites/Zadokites; hierocrats/visionaries; wisdom tradition/ salvation-history tradition. Although not all of these dichotomies will prove their utility as accurate descriptions of the divergencies involved (for example, the Sinai/*Landnahme* dichotomy has been called into question by many), the complexity of traditions on the synchronic level, as well as on the diachronic level, is here to stay.

Thus far the dominant response to this aspect of the legacy of literary and form criticism has been one of crisis. The older theologies, and even the later generation of theologies which sought to reconstitute the discipline on the crest of neo-orthodoxy, have failed to give an adequate theological interpretation of the diversity and contradictions characterizing the relationship between various biblical documents and traditions. Although the increasing biblical illiteracy among moderns cannot be fully accounted for by this fact, it is not unrelated to the pair of options offered by biblical scholars: either a concept of verbal inspiration which postulates factual inerrancy and homogeneity of doctrine, or a concept of divergent literary documents which seems to exclude any notion of inspiration or biblical authority. Many find these options too limiting.

Perhaps the most creative effort to break this impasse has come from biblical scholars seeking to apply the Whiteheadian category of "process" to biblical theology. At least on the diachronic axis, contradiction thereby becomes one facet of the unfolding of a creative principle. The danger residing in this approach is the threat to the independent witness of the ancient writings themselves. In the service of a contemporary philosophical system, the biblical writings are studied for possible illustration of, and support for, the ideal of "process." That some of these attempts have not led to a heavy-handed misinterpretation of the ancient materials suggests that the concept of "process" indeed shares certain basic characteristics with biblical ideas of divine action and revelation. Methodologically, however, an approach is called for which is guided and controlled more directly by inner-biblical factors.

This approach will serve no useful end, however, if it becomes a modern form of naive biblicism, that is, if it predicates itself upon the axiom that all a biblical theology must do is repeat the words of scripture and the result will be a theological system adequate for the contemporary world.[1] The hermeneutical problem cannot so easily be bypassed.

1. Cf. the criticism which Langdon Gilkey directs at B. W. Anderson and G. E. Wright in "Cosmology, Ontology, and the Travail of Biblical Language," *JR* 41 (1961) 194–205.

Therefore it is broadly maintained that critical investigation must be carried out on two levels: 1) a critical-historical investigation seeking to understand the nature of the sources, including their ancient settings, functions, and meanings; 2) a critical, reflective exercise seeking to describe systematically the meaning and significance of the writings of the Bible for modern persons.

The strict separation of these two critical tasks has received emphasis in the past by influential writers.[2] This distinction can be overlooked only at the expense of a biblical interpretation which includes no safeguards against reading into the Bible purely modern ideas. But inordinate emphasis upon the separation has had one effect which is anything but salutary. As Brevard Childs has repeatedly observed, critical-historical scholarship has become capsulated within a methodology which has become incapable of handling the theological dimension of biblical texts. Although a huge gap separates us from the people of Israel, a basic common ground must not be lost sight of: they were human beings experiencing events not unrelated to events which occur within our lives.

This could easily lead to the basic postulate of historical positivism: the events of biblical times can be critically reconstructed only on the basis of analogy with contemporary experiences. Although analogy is a principle which is basic to our interpretation of ancient writings, it can be elevated to an absolute principle only at a tremendous price: loss of awareness that our modern experiences are partial (and in many demonstrable ways, severely truncated), and for that reason, unreliable as an absolute standard of human experience, not to mention of divine activity.

It seems essential to unbridle the imagination by allowing the ancient writings to speak for themselves, and to use the principle of contemporary analogy cautiously. However, the sharp distinction maintained by some between descriptive and hermeneutical functions of exegesis seems unsatisfactory when one comes upon instances where the biblical materials themselves contain clues to the modern hermeneutical problem. In this essay, therefore, the restraints and controls of critical descriptive methodology will be respected in the pursuit of the ancient meanings, settings, and functions of the materials studied, but the line separating

2. See especially the widely quoted article of K. Stendahl, "Biblical Theology, Contemporary," *IDB* I. 418–32.

descriptive and hermeneutical tasks will be left fluid where the biblical materials yield guidelines for the biblical theologian, or even the systematic theologian or ethicist.[3]

Believing as I do that a critical-historical method, properly understood and applied, is a tool serving to unlock the intrinsic meaning of biblical writings, and at the same time recognizing that such a method is partial and will be supplanted after a short generation by new methods, I shall seek to clarify how the critical investigation of the Book of the Covenant yields valuable clues to the theological significance of contradictions within biblical sources. Contradictions within the Bible fall into different categories, for example, factual data which contradict contemporary scientific theory (creation in Genesis 1), internal factual contradictions (Num 25:9/1 Cor 10:8), and internal theological-ethical contradictions. Our focus in this paper is exclusively on the last mentioned.

THE LITERARY STRUCTURE OF THE BOOK OF THE COVENANT

The starting point must be a description of the literary structure of the Book of the Covenant (Exod 20:22–23:33), for internal contradictions are usually the traces left within the documents of the long process of oral and literary transmission which culminated in the final version which we have received. An attempt to grasp the theological significance of such contradictions is destined for failure if it is not carried out in full awareness of this process.

The section 23:20–33, which itself is probably conflate, is widely recognized as the latest addition in the growth process culminating in the

3. We hope that the control which historical-critical methodology seeks to assure will not thereby be lost, for these guidelines must not involve the disguised importation of the jargon of some contemporary philosophical or theological system, nor can they be the repetition of shibboleths from the Bible. If any degree of objectivity is to be maintained they must be the results of inquiry into the theological implications of the intrinsic message of the biblical material itself, as clarified by the most adequate reconstruction of setting, function, and meaning which biblical scholarship is able to provide. In answer to the objection that this involves a mere substitution of a critical-historical method for a philosophical or theological system, it must be maintained that the critical-historical approach can be defended only as a method which seeks to clarify the meaning of the texts themselves. Where it does not do this, that is, where it either obscures the meaning or substitutes a meaning implicit within its presuppositions, it must be replaced. And it is certainly necessary for critical scholars to become less defensive in the face of criticism by scholars with a different approach who draw attention to the presuppositions (often hidden) in historical-critical methodology. At the same time, the historical-critical scholar must feel free to state his/her view that the harmonizing method of certain types of biblicism imports a modern category which the critical scholar finds lacking in the documents themselves: that of homogeneity of doctrine on both the diachronic and synchronic axes.

Book of the Covenant. Since it deals with the conquest of the land at a
point earlier than expected within the overall narrative, it was probably
already attached to the Book of the Covenant by the time that work was
introduced into the pentateuchal narrative.[4] Outside of this addition,
which bears the stamp of Deuteronomistic style, there is no trace of
influence from any period later than the League, either on the level of
language or custom. The position of some of the older literary critics
that certain of the parenetic features were added by Deuteronomistic
circles has been refuted by W. Beyerlin, who has demonstrated very
effectively that in the cases of affinities between the Book of the Covenant and Deuteronomy, the former consistently preserves the earlier
form.[5]

Although 20:22–23:19 is a literary unit which can be attributed as a
whole to the premonarchical period, it bears the marks of a rich antecedent history of development. The most obvious marks set the *mišpāṭîm*
section in 21:1–22:16 (RSV=22:17) off from the remainder: 1) 21:1
is a clear introduction to a collection of *mišpāṭîm* ("ordinances" or "case
laws"); 2) the form of the laws is consistently that of the typical case
law; 3) the entire section is free of parenetic expansion. These three
marks indicate that 21:1–22:16 (RSV=22:17) once existed independently of the larger unit 20:22–23:19.[6] Indeed, the facts that specific
connections with Israel's cult are lacking and that the covenantal theology permeating the rest of the Book of the Covenant is nowhere discernible combine with the recognition of numerous parallels with ancient
Near Eastern law codes in establishing the original setting of this section
in the adjudication of legal cases in the village gates during the League
period. This is not to declare that the *mišpāṭîm* were borrowed *en bloc*
by early Israelites from the Mesopotamians or Canaanites. The uniquely
Israelite ingredients indicate that the borrowing occurred within a community experience which added its own stamp to the formulation of case
law.[7]

4. M. Noth, *Exodus* (Philadelphia: Westminster, 1962) 174.
5. W. Beyerlin, "Die Paränese im Bundesbuch und ihre Herkunft," *Gottes Wort und
Gottes Land* (*Hertzberg Festschrift*, ed. H. G. Reventlow; Göttingen: Vandenhoeck
& Ruprecht, 1965) 9–29.
6. Within 21:1–22:16 (=RSV 22:17), the only secondary element is 21:12–17,
which shares with 22:18 (=RSV 22:19) a distinctive participial style.
7. For a detailed study of the similarities and differences characterizing the relationship between the *mišpāṭîm* and Mesopotamian parallels, see S. Paul, *Studies in the
Book of the Covenant in the Light of Cuneiform and Biblical Law* (VTSup 18; Leiden:
Brill, 1970) 43–98.

Turning to the remainder of the Book of the Covenant, we discover that the picture is even more complex. First, the homogeneity of form noted in the *mišpāṭim* is absent. The classical apodictic formulation in the second person singular imperative shares space with the participial form, and even with the mixed form in 23:4–5, which combines features of apodictic and casuistic law. With regard to content, these laws combine cultic legislation, such as the altar laws in 20:24–26, the cultic calendar in 23:10–19, and laws commanding exclusive worship of Yahweh (20:24 and 22:19 [=RSV 22:20]), with legislation regulating the social structures of the community. Finally, these various laws frequently include parenetic formulations which ground motivation for obedience in God's antecedent acts of deliverance (e.g., 22:20b [=RSV 22:21b]; 23:9b).

This array of divergent material raises the question of whether any unifying dimension is discernible in 20:22–26 + 22:17 (=RSV 22:18)–23:19 which yields recognition of a single early setting and function; or is it the product of an editor who swept together various materials having no organic unity? The essential evidence in favor of an original unified setting and function is the cultic and covenantal dimension which permeates this material as a whole, and which sets it in sharp contrast to 21:1–22:16 (=RSV 22:17). This essential point will be elaborated later.

EXAMPLES OF TENSION AND CONTRADICTION
WITHIN THE BOOK OF THE COVENANT

Even a cursory reading of the Book of the Covenant uncovers a pair of contrasting ethical positions which do not fit smoothly into one theological system, but which produce internal tension and contradiction. The offense is ameliorated somewhat through consultation with the commentaries which show that the inhumane qualities of many of the laws are in keeping with the social values characteristic of the period, as illustrated by the great law codes of the second millennium. Indeed, it is of some comfort to note that there is a distinct tendency within the case laws of the Book of the Covenant to enhance the humaneness.[8] Nevertheless, for the person who regards the Bible as scripture, the above considerations do not resolve the theological crux produced by the juxta-

8. Ibid., 40, *et passim.*

position of two classes of formulation, one predicated upon a discriminatory social idea betraying distinct lines of continuity with the prevailing
customs of the time, the other embodying a community ideal of equality
and compassion which challenges the prevailing structures of ancient
society. We shall enumerate each class.

Class I: 1) Slaves are property of their masters (21:1–11, 21, etc.).
2) Female slaves are denied the right to release after six years of service,
a right which applies only to male slaves (21:7). 3) Wife and children
are taken away from a husband/father being released if the wife had been
given to him by his master (21:4). 4) Women are property of their
fathers and later, if they marry, of their husbands (21:7; 22:15–16
[=RSV 22:16–17]; 21:22). 5) The fact that the intrinsic value of
human beings is related to their status as slave or free is indicated by the
laws stipulating more severe punishment for harm done to a free person
than to a slave (21:23–25; 21:26–27; 21:29–31; 21:32). 6) In the
three cultic festivals, only males are to appear before Yahweh (23:17).
Here, as always, it is essential to interpret the meaning of these laws
within their social setting and their historical period. For example, the
exclusion of women from cult participation may have stemmed from the
desire to prevent the recurrence of the debasing use of women as cult
prostitutes. Even when such care is exercised, however, laws presuppos-
ing slavery, accommodating to a view of women as chattel, and preserving distinctions in the relative worth of various classes of human persons
raise serious problems for the individual or community regarding the
Bible as scripture. But the problem is felt in its full seriousness only
when such laws are seen in relation to others which develop a vastly
different attitude vis-à-vis the socially underprivileged.

Class II: 1) "You shall not wrong a stranger or oppress him, for you
were strangers in the land of Egypt" (22:20 [=RSV 22:21]; similarly
23:9). 2) "You shall not afflict any widow or orphan. If you do afflict
them, and they cry out to me, I will surely hear their cry; and my wrath
will burn, and I will kill you with the sword, and your wives shall become
widows and your children fatherless" (22:21–23 [=RSV 22:22–24]).
3) "If you lend money to any of my people with you who is poor, you
shall not be to him as a creditor, and you shall not exact interest from
him. If ever you take your neighbor's garment in pledge, you shall
restore it to him before the sun goes down; for that is his only covering, it
is his mantle for his body; in what else shall he sleep? And if he cries to

me, I will hear, for I am compassionate" (22:24–26 [=RSV 22:25–27]). 4) "You shall not pervert the justice due to your poor in his suit" (23:6). 5) "For six years you shall sow your land and gather in its yield; but the seventh year you shall let it rest and lie fallow, that the poor of your people may eat" (23:10–11a^a"). 6) ". . . and what they leave, let the wild animals eat . . . on the seventh day you must abstain from work in order that your ox and your ass may rest" (23:11a^b, 12b^a).

The contrast between these laws and the aforementioned is dramatic: 1) A highly developed humaneness regulates relations with the elements of society which could be exploited and victimized by the powerful: the stranger, the widow and orphan, the debtor, the poor. Even the wild animals are to be protected from cruelty. Perhaps 23:5 should be understood under this latter category, since it reflects at least as much concern for the poor ass collapsed under its load as for the owner who is in danger of losing his beast of burden! 2) This class of laws receives repeated grounding in a central theological confession: the people of Israel were once *gērîm* in the land of Egypt, yet Yahweh delivered them: "you know the *nepeš* (the essential quality of existence) of the *gēr*, having yourselves been *gērîm* in the land of Egypt" (23:9b).

Accompanying these laws are a pair of commands which serve as the theological basis for class II: 1) "You shall not make gods of silver alongside of me nor shall you make for yourselves gods of gold" (20:23; cf. 22:19 [=RSV 22:20] and 23:13). 2) "You shall be men consecrated to me" (22:30a [=RSV 22:31a]. Sole worship of Yahweh, and being a holy people before Yahweh by acting in accord with his saving acts on their behalf in Egypt stand as a noteworthy theological pair, for they represent the theological center from which the community ideal of class II radiates.

LITERARY STRUCTURE AS EXPLANATION OF CONTRADICTIONS

Does the critical reconstruction of the oral and literary process underlying the Book of the Covenant (the second section above) satisfy the theological problems raised by the contradictory theological-ethical positions contrasted in the third section above? It is significant to note that the vast majority of instances of class I were found within the *mišpāṭîm* section, that is, as a part of the collection of case laws which reflected a history in village juridical praxis prior to its insertion into the Book of the Covenant. It is of further significance that all of the instances of class II occurred in that part of the Book of the Covenant which betrayed connections not with juridical practice "in the gates," but with the cult and its covenantal theology.

These observations might suggest that 20:22–26 + 22:17 (=RSV 22:18)–23:19 are theologically Yahwistic, whereas 21:1–22:16 (=RSV 22:17) are secular, thereby leading to the conclusion that the former are to be regarded as significant for biblical theology, the latter as falling outside the interest of the theologian. This conclusion would fail utterly to explain the facts that an influence from 21:1–22:16 upon other parts of the Book of the Covenant is apparent, and that the *mišpāṭim* section is in the present form of the Bible part of the Book of the Covenant, and a part of Yahweh's word to the people. Nor does it address the significance of the parenetic sections for the corpus in its present form.

The reconstruction of the oral and literary process generating the Book of the Covenant does not in itself adequately address the theological issues which the contradictions raise. Yet this reconstruction cannot simply be ignored.

A THEOLOGICAL INTERPRETATION OF CONTRADICTIONS

Three options are available to the biblical theologian in an attempt to treat the contradictory perspectives found in the Book of the Covenant. 1) He/she may follow the route of harmonization by emphasizing the tendency in the *mišpāṭim* toward a more humane posture than was typical of the great law codes of the second millennium, while overlooking the remaining inhumaneness upon which many of the laws are predicated, thereby lessening the tension between classes I and II. 2) He/she may allow the contradictions to stand without attempting to account for them in theological terms, being satisfied to recognize inconsistencies between divergent traditions. There is no question that this is the only honest option if the sources themselves do not point toward a theological explanation for the contradictions. 3) He/she may seek to ascertain whether the biblical writing itself bears clues to the theological significance of the contradiction; if it does, he/she would utilize such clues to the fullest possible degree to give a theological interpretation of the contradictions.

The critical reconstruction of the oral and literary process culminating in the present form of the Book of the Covenant affords such clues.

Option 2 is therefore unnecessary, option 1 is less than honest with the evidence, while option 3 recommends itself.

A primary focus on the core, recognized in 20:22–26 + 22:17 (=RSV 22:18)–23:19, reveals that it is the product of an organic growth process on the level of oral transmission. The stages which led to that basic collection, however, cannot be reconstructed. What we must begin with, therefore, is a collection which drew together various laws, some perhaps from the wilderness period, others from the early settlement, a collection nevertheless constituting an organic whole by virtue of a unified perspective: the covenantal confession of the early cult festival in which the disparate tribal elements celebrated their basis for unity. The setting of this collection in the central cult is suggested not only by the covenantal perspective permeating the whole, but by the specific features of the early cult ritual which one may extrapolate from texts like Deuteronomy 27 and Joshua 24: Yahweh's command for sole worship (20:23; cf. 22:19 [=RSV 22:20]; 23:13); 2) command to be persons holy to Yahweh (22:30 [=RSV 22:31]); 3) stipulation of the holy festivals (23:14–17); 4) other important stipulations (*passim*); 5) blessings (20:24b); 6) curses (22:22–23, 26b [=RSV 22:23–24, 27b]; 23:7b). In striking contrast to the *mišpāṭîm* section, these commands, stipulations, blessings, and curses are in the first person of the God Yahweh in his theophany in the cultic celebration.

This cultic structure is the framework within which the various legal materials of 20:22–26 + 22:17 (=RSV 22:18)–23:19 are set. This setting casts light on the intended function of this material: the various tribal groups, having entered the land (or having escaped the oppressive Canaanite social structures of the land), in the process of becoming sedentary and agrarian, begin to draw together guidelines for the ordering of their new life together. The materials are diverse, but they do not come together willy-nilly; they constitute an organic whole. We must inquire further into the reason why this is so.

The unity is not the product of a common source, for diverse materials stem from the customs (in part presettlement) of various tribes, legal practices (23:1–8), and even local taboos (20:25–26). The unity comes instead from a cultic process: these diverse materials coalesced at the point of the yearly festival when the tribes confessed their common faith in Yahweh. In being drawn toward Israel's religious center, these materials underwent a process of transformation in a covenantal relation-

ship between Yahweh and the people. Yahweh alone was to be wor-
shiped and the people were to be a holy nation before him. Moreover,
the stipulations defining that holiness received from the sacral context a
new quality and grounding: they were constructed as inferences drawn
from Yahweh's antecedent saving activity on Israel's behalf. Thus we
find in the core of the Book of the Covenant not only the central pair of
commands to worship Yahweh alone and to be holy persons to Yahweh,
but in addition a series of motive clauses which tie obedience of specific
commands to the central confession of the cult: when the Hebrews were
suffering the oppression of slavery in Egypt, Yahweh heard their cry with
compassion and acted mightily to deliver them. These motive clauses
are a vivid manifestation of the early molding of these laws within their
new worship setting, and give clear evidence of the effect which the cultic
matrix had upon legal practices in early Israel. Law was not a secular
matter nor was obedience an alien obligation; law was at the heart of
Israel's covenant with its God, and obedience was a response emanating
from Israel's central religious experience: "You shall not oppress a
stranger, for you know what it feels like to be a stranger, having yourselves been strangers in the land of Egypt" (23:9; translation of
B. Childs).[9]

Israel, like any new people, experienced the need to order life on the
basis of social structures appropriate to its experiences and ideals, and
this led to borrowing from neighboring cultures as well as to drawing
upon Hebrew tribal customs. But the need was not met in the usual,
ancient Near Eastern manner of introducing an institution of civil jurisprudence running independently of the cult, that is to say, as a separate,
secular phenomenon. Instead, the various legal materials were drawn
into the cult festivals themselves, thereby obliging those materials to
interact with and be transformed by the central confessions of the religious community. The result is the unique amalgamation of civil, moral,
and cultic prescriptions which we find in the core of the Book of the
Covenant. In the great law codes of Mesopotamia, such mixing did not
occur, for the three realms were not integrated. Civil law, as expressed
for example in the actual body of laws in the Codex Hammurabi, was a
strictly secular institution, having nothing to do with the cultic officials or
the deity. The priests, in turn, dealt with cultic regulations, but had no

9. Brevard S. Childs, *The Book of Exodus: A Critical Theological Commentary*
(Philadelphia: Westminster, 1974) 445.

part in civil proceedings.[10]   Thus, a unique innovation occurred in Israel: a legal collection was predicated upon worship of one God, and the aim of that collection was to establish persons holy before Yahweh. Covenant with the deity and all three orders of obligations were brought into relationship with each other in a new way, causing an interaction among the cultic, moral, and civil realms which would have far-reaching implications for the history of both religion and law.

The legal collection in 20:22–26 + 22:17 (=RSV 22:18)–23:19 thus betrays a lively dialectic within which a living confession acts upon legal materials drawn toward it.   In the face of such a finding, it is no longer sufficient for the interpreter to presuppose that he/she is dealing with a lapidary codex, the internal consistency of which should be maintained by harmonizing exegesis.   In the place of an immutable, timeless law is the dramatic unfolding of a view of God in relation to his creation, a process integrating disparate materials into one perspective encompassing cult, ethics, and civil statutes.

If this understanding of the character of the Book of the Covenant is correct, it would require changes in most commentaries and other forms of theological exposition.   For theological commentary cannot deal adequately with the book of Exodus if it concentrates on the uniqueness of the confessions of the *magnalia dei*, and only as a second thought and as a separate exercise studies the laws in search of origins in Mesopotamian, Hittite, Canaanite, or tribal sources.   Rather, an approach must be adopted which will be comprehensive enough to treat a process by which early Israel drew materials from various geographical *loci* and spheres of life, integrated them into an act of covenant celebration in the cult, and assimilated the most diverse materials to a dynamic of creativity and liberation centering on what God had done and was doing.   Such a theological interpretation will thereby expose the central creative force behind the process of the growth of tradition, and will seek to trace the various levels discernible in that process.   In the case of the core of the Book of the Covenant we find that central dynamic in the confession of the only true God who delivered an enslaved people from oppression to communal life in covenant with him.   This confession of antecedent gracious activity lays the foundation for the cultic, moral, and civil responses which would constitute that people as a holy nation (as sum-

10. S. Paul, *Studies*, 35–36.

marized in the preamble in Exod 19:3–6, which is a later stage of growth of the covenantal framework already found at the core of the Book of the Covenant).

According to this understanding, theological interpretation is dealing, not with a timeless law, the consistency of which must be defended, but with a process of an unfolding socio-religious ideal. Thus, internal tensions and contradictions will not be explained away as a threat to the literature's integrity (or, for that matter, as proof against inspiration), but will be explicated as carefully as possible as clues to that process of unfolding. The interpreter will inquire not only into the source of each law, but also into the relation of each part to the dynamic confessional center, dealing with parts which are fully assimilated to that center as well as with parts less assimilated or remaining largely untransformed, thereby compromising or even contradicting the creative, liberating thrust of the center.[11]

From this confessional center, which traditio-historical research shows to have been the crystallization point in the process of oral and literary growth, each part of a given level of legal material can be interpreted. Here we must limit ourselves to a mere sketch of examples from 20:22–26 + 22:17(=RSV 22:18)–23:19.

After the redactional link in 20:22 the unit is introduced with a statement of the central theological basis of the community: exclusive worship of Yahweh (20:23). This attracts to itself a set of stipulations dealing with altars and including material as central to the confession as the blessings of the covenant, and as peripheral as the types of building materials to be used in constructing the altar (20:24–26). There follows a triad of laws decreeing death for certain types of offenses which were regarded as so heinous as to incur devastating divine wrath amidst the people if not purged (22:17–19 [=RSV 22:18–20]).

Next appears a series of apodictic laws which are fully assimilated to the central confession of the covenant cult (22:20–26 [=RSV 22:21–27]). They, like the preceding, aim at avoiding destructive divine

---

11. The question can be asked whether the effort to describe the central dynamic underlying a level of tradition does not lay itself open to uncontrolled subjectivity in which the central dynamic becomes the critic's personal theology. While recognizing the seriousness of this problem, we would note that all interpretation seeks to order the material studied and will labor under the same danger; therefore, theological interpretation from a traditio-historical perspective recommends itself as a serious attempt to allow this identification of the central dynamic to be determined by the growth process manifested by the material itself.

wrath, and at safeguarding against the recurrence of the grievous experiences of the Hebrew slaves in Egypt. But this function is tied inextricably to the central religious experience of Israel through a series of motive clauses. The commands are once again in the form of the divine address of the cult. First, Yahweh commands that "you shall not wrong or oppress the stranger, for you were strangers in the land of Egypt." Secondly, a similar command relating to the widow and orphan is grounded in a self-description of the God who will hear the cry of the oppressed, and who will break out in terrible punishment against the offender. Thirdly, very humane laws are stipulated regulating interest-free lending and handling of items taken as security; they are grounded in a confession of the God who will respond to the wronged poor persons out of divine compassion. These laws bear witness to the dramatic transformation in legal and social structures effected by the covenant confession of the God who delivered Hebrew slaves from their oppression.

The remaining laws stem from the same communal effort to establish structures safeguarding a holy people before Yahweh by prohibiting activity which would incur divine wrath or which would reinitiate the oppressive experiences of the Egyptian period. In the former category fall the laws in 22:27–29 (=RSV 22:28–30), although special problems arise in connection with 22:28b (=RSV 22:29b) since the *prima facie* reading suggests child sacrifice. This is probably an instance of a law from the Canaanite environment which was tied to the widespread belief that divine wrath could be placated only by sacrifice of all first fruits, including firstborn sons (*sic*). Although this pagan custom itself was not yet assimilated to the central confession, its being set within the context of that confession created the tension within the tradition which gave rise to a radical transformation of the custom through the practice of redemption (Exod 13:13, 15; 34:20; Num 3:44–50; 18:15–16; cf. Genesis 22). As examples of laws devoted to safeguarding against the recurrence of the oppressive laws of the Egyptian period, we can cite 23:6, 9, 11, 12. Once again, obedience is grounded in the central confession of the early cult (23:9b).

It is striking how profoundly the legal material in this core section of the Book of the Covenant has been assimilated to the central confession of the cult. Laws originating in local taboos, in legal praxis, and in prophylactic rites have all been transformed by being related to a central

religious experience of the release of Hebrew slaves from their oppression.   The document emerges as a powerful exposition of a community
ideal of even-handed justice, humaneness, and compassion.   It bears
witness to an early attempt in Israel to recreate the same creative, liberating, and sustaining dynamic within the community as the Hebrews had
experienced in the foundational events which had constituted them as a
people.   Not that tensions are completely resolved.   Counter to the humane and even-handed tenor of an exodus confession and the laws assimilated thereto are the apparent command to sacrifice firstborn sons and
the failure to include women in the command to worship Yahweh in the
three yearly festivals.[12]   In these rare examples is seen evidence that
even in the core, the process of assimilation had not yet run its full
course.   Yet underway was the community whose oral tradition was being
transformed into this remarkable guide to a righteous and human corpor-
ate life as a people covenanted with Yahweh.

In addition to the process by which various legal materials were
melded into an organic whole around a central confession, the next
noteworthy stage of growth involved the insertion of the *mišpāṭîm* section
(21:1–22:16 [=RSV 22:17]) into the core.[13]   This literary critical
observation does not help one to decide the relative antiquity of the two
sections.   It merely indicates that the *mišpāṭîm* ("ordinances" or "case
laws") were taken from a setting other than the cultic setting which
produced 20:22–26 + 22:17 (=RSV 22:18)–23:19, and were spliced
into the latter.   We have already indicated that the setting of the *mišpāṭîm* was the premonarchical juridical procedure "in the gates" in which
the elders of a village would try persons guilty of civil offenses.   Within
that setting, the underlying function was the universal one of maintaining
social stability through a uniform handling of jurisprudence.   In the case
of the Hebrew tribes, the new sedentary life gave birth to new problems
in this realm, and the environment readily produced laws dealing with
such problems as injury inflicted by oxen, homicide, repayment for in-
juries done to one's slaves or wives, and damages to one's crops by
another's carelessness or malice.   The distinctness of this setting in con-

12. Although a nongeneric meaning for *'anšê* is attested in biblical Hebrew, its common meaning is "men."   If the latter is the meaning in 22:30 (=RSV 22:31), this
verse represents another instance of the latent sex discrimination of this stratum.
13. It is not necessary to rehearse here the literary evidence for establishing 21:1–
22:16 (=RSV 22:17) as an insertion, since that evidence can be found in the commentaries.   Attention can here be limited to the clear introduction in 21:1 and the
uniform casuistic form of the laws.

trast to the cultic setting of the core is evidenced by the total lack of reference to the cult, to its confession, or to Yahweh. Since two distinct functions characterized these two settings, the appearance of inconsistencies was inevitable, once the two corpora were fused. The function of establishing social stability by drawing heavily upon the laws of the environment could diverge sharply from the function of molding a community by a new ideal derived from the confession of a God who established a nation by delivering a group of oppressed slaves from their bondage. The former function had a decidedly conservative thrust and was tied to the status quo of the prevailing social order; the latter embodied a liberating dynamic which called such established structures into question.

In the first, oral stage of growth, materials were drawn from alien settings, but, as we have already observed, interaction with the confession led in large part to their transformation. Now, in this next *literary* stage of growth, the same theological process is to be detected, that is, another collection of legal material drawn from a context outside the central confessional experience of the cult is drawn toward that center. But a notable difference is to be detected as well: whereas the oral process by its very nature was able to transform the assimilated materials to the dynamic of the confession, the process of bringing *en bloc* a unit set in the more rigid form of a literary composition into relation with the central covenantal confession did not allow the same degree of melding to occur. The result was apparent, and is recorded in the third section above: a far greater number of tensions and contradictions between the legal materials and the central confession than was characteristic of the core in 20:22–26 + 22:17 (=RSV 22:18)–23:19.

Was this second stage in the attempt to assimilate all expressions of community guidelines to the central confessional ideal therefore abortive? First, the only alternative must be recognized: the two could have been allowed to develop separately, with the consequent competing of two ideals in Israel, one embodied in the cult, the other in the judicial system.[14] Instead of the development of a tension between *two* separate institutional forms, the insertion of the miّšpāṭîm into the Book of the Covenant manifests the attempt to draw the latter toward the central confession, that is, to internalize the tension within *one* institution. Here

14. This separation would have been in conformity with standard ancient Near Eastern practice; see S. Paul, *Studies, passim.*

the literary form was not so malleable as was the earlier oral material, but the significance of even juxtaposing the *mišpāṭîm* with the more confessional material must not be overlooked. Rather than two different ideals developing independently of each other in Israel, the two were brought into direct conflict with each other in one document. The resulting tension would expose the *mišpāṭîm* to the ideal inherent in the confession and the commands molded by that confession, thereby encouraging the dynamic process to continue whereby the humaneness, equity, and compassion inherent in the historical confession of deliverance from Egypt would exert an important influence on Israel's legal procedures.

The theological significance of the tension and conflict effected by this insertion is considerable: the examples of legal practices and social customs which either blatantly or subtly contradicted the ideal of community implied by the religious confession could not go unheeded when these examples resided in the same document which gave expression to that community ideal. The juxtaposition guaranteed that interpreters who refused to gloss over contradictions through a harmonizing exegesis would have to address the offense of the contradiction. Inevitably questions such as the following would arise: how could the God who is credited with delivering slaves from their bondage also be credited with promulgating within that free people slave laws continuous with social structures broken by the exodus events? How could the God who was moved to action by the cry of the afflicted widow or orphan treat women and children as property of the master or husband? How could the God who compassionately heard the groans of the oppressed creditor promulgate laws which differentiated between the relative worth of different classes of people, which denied female slaves the rights granted to male slaves, and which made worship a matter of male prerogative? The liberating dynamic which was recognized in the foundational events of exodus, wilderness, and conquest is kept alive amidst such tensions. Remaining inequities in the system are not allowed to rigidify into an immutable, timeless code, subservient to the prevailing social customs of the ancient world. In literary terms it is because the *mišpāṭîm* were not left to be preserved in isolation from cultic traditions, but were drawn into the Book of the Covenant, that the developing social system in Israel was touched by the central confession of the community, and exposed to the transforming power of that confession. The confession can thus be recognized as revelatory, as bearing witness to a salvatory power which was not confined to the important foundational events of Israel's history, but which lived on as a dynamic, whose inner power was transmitted through the entire process of transmission within the cult, and later in the narrative sources.[15]

Thus the tensions and conflicts between the core and the *mišpāṭim* testify to the character of biblical legal traditions as a dynamic process— underway, pressing on, but never coming to rest and fulfillment. Only an exegetical approach which fails to grasp this dynamic character of the tradition will attempt to force the entire Book of the Covenant into a homogeneous system delivered in one audition and intended to be an immutable norm for all time. If the process-character of the tradition *is* grasped, however, contradictions will not be blunted, but will be brought to full exposure as clues to the restless nature of a divine word which attacks oppression and inhumanity ever anew, even when expressions of that oppression and inhumanity remain embedded in the scriptural ve-hicles which have carried that word from its ancient origins on into the "latter times."

It is important that the student of the Bible oppose all attempts to gloss over contradictions growing out of the diversity of biblical tradi-tions. If properly interpreted, they will not create a theological impasse, but rather a portal to a deeper understanding of the living character of the Bible as Word of God. Even as in the life of the individual whose act of compassion so contradicts habitual modes of selfishness and dis-crimination as to challenge him or her to a new orientation, even as the community's usual habits of greed and intolerance are challenged by the testimony of the saint, even as the history of a whole decadent civiliza-tion was impregnated with new meaning by the life of One utterly given to the justice and compassion of God's Kingdom, so too the creative, liberating, and sustaining dynamic within a portion of scripture may

---

15. Powerful testimony to the transforming power inherent in the tension between the discriminatory practices of the *mišpāṭim* and the central confession is given by the book of Deuteronomy. For in the reformulation of Israelite law in that book, it is obvious that struggling with such tension has led to a new level of equity and humane-ness within biblical legal tradition. For example, the discriminatory distinction be-tween the male and female in the laws of release in Exod 21:2–11 is eliminated in Deut 15:12–18. In the laws concerning rape, seduction, and divorce in Deuteronomy 22, a heightened concern to give legal rights to women is apparent (cf. Deut 21:10–14). Also, in contrast to the Book of the Covenant's restriction of central cult participation to males, the book of Deuteronomy emphasizes that the cult is to em-brace "you and your son and your daughter, your manservant and your maidservant, the Levite, the sojourner, the fatherless, and the widow who are within your towns" (Deut 16:14).

contradict the very verbal and cultural vehicles in which it is contained, and break forth with a new power to transform existing structures.   That power should not be lost amidst well-intended, but dishonest harmonizing exposition.

The remaining stages of the literary history of the Book of the Covenant also testify to its living character.   At some point before it was placed into the larger pentateuchal narrative, 23:20–33 was added as a narrative conclusion.   The effect of this addition was to underscore the grounding of the legal material in the history of God's saving activity. Not only did the parenetic sections tie obedience to God's antecedent acts of deliverance, but God's protection was also anticipated in future events as well.   Within that future setting the relation among God's antecedent gracious activity, Israel's response in obedience or disobedience, and the resulting blessings or curses is described in ways similar to those found in the core of the Book of the Covenant.   And the central theme of worshiping Yahweh to the exclusion of all other gods is reiterated.   Thus we see that as the individual legal materials were assimilated to the central creedal tradition in the setting of the cult, later in the process of literary growth those legal materials were made a part of the *Heilsgeschichte* by way of the construction of a narrative conclusion.

The process of integrating the entire Book of the Covenant into the framework of the exodus-conquest narrative (and thereby further underpinning the relationship of the legal materials to the confessional tradition) was carried one stage further when it was placed within the broad narrative context of the Epic.   As a part of the foundational events leading from the exodus through the wilderness to Sinai and the conquest, the Book of the Covenant thus became a central part of God's redemptive activity.   Its position in the central confessional tradition was thereby assured, and safeguarded against any attempts to separate it out as a part of a different institution.   The tension between that central confession and the laws which the process of transmission had not completely assimilated to the exodus tradition thus became a legacy left to future generations.

THE BOOK OF THE COVENANT AND THE
THEOLOGICAL SIGNIFICANCE OF
CONTRADICTIONS WITHIN SCRIPTURE

We shall briefly suggest ways in which contemporary believers may reflect on the implications of our study.   In this context, a prophet like

Amos may be a guide, insofar as he gives a vivid example of an interpreter of antecedent tradition who does not slavishly apply the laws of
the Book of the Covenant in a casuistic-legalistic fashion, but captures
the liberation dynamic which permeated that book, and utilizes it as the
foundation stone of his prophecy.[16]

Indeed, this living relationship to the biblical traditions seems to characterize biblical writers in general. Consider, for example, how Second
Isaiah could build upon the creation and exodus traditions, and yet, in
drawing out the creative and liberating implications of those traditions,
boldly proclaim: "Remember not the former things, nor consider the
things of old. Behold, I am doing a new thing; now it springs forth, do
you not perceive it?" (Isa 43:18–19). Or consider the antitheses of
the Sermon on the Mount. It seems like a retreat to a rigid and unbibli-
cal methodology therefore—just to cite two examples—to apply 1 Cor
11:10 or Exod 23:17 legalistically to our contemporary situation.
These laws must rather be interpreted within the context of an internal
dynamic which comes to expression in Exodus in the redemption of
Hebrew slaves from oppressive structures, and in the Epistles when Paul
speaks of a faith within which "there is neither Jew nor Greek, there is
neither slave nor free, there is neither male nor female; for you are all
one in Christ Jesus" (Gal 3:28). Biblical theology must recognize an
internal tension within the biblical documents which reveals a dynamic
which reaches far beyond a given writer's environment. This must be
allowed to stand in sharp clarity, even where it contradicts other ingredients which stand as reminders that the writer in question is also an
authentic member of his/her particular world and time.

Within the Book of the Covenant, therefore, one must recognize a
creative, egalitarian, and liberating dynamic which transcends the social
vehicles within which it is carried.[17] It is this dynamic which challenged
the prevailing mythopoeic "orthodoxy" presided over by guardians of the
status quo, kings and priests. From this unfolding dynamic emerged a
challenge to injustice, inhumaneness, and idolatry wherever they occurred, even when they remained lodged at the heart of Israel's religious
institutions. Within that process, the stages recorded within the Bible
are historically foundational, and therefore authoritative in a unique
sense. Yet to freeze any portion of scripture into an immutable theolog-

16. E.g., Amos 2:6–7 (cf. 8:6)/Exod 22:21–27; Amos 2:8/Exod 22:25–26 (cf.
Deut 24:11–13); Amos 5:11/Exod 22:25.
17. See P. Hanson, "Masculine Metaphors for God and Sex-discrimination in the
Old Testament," *The Ecumenical Review* 27 (1975) 316–24.

ical or ethical system would run counter to the dynamic unfolding within scripture itself. Rather, it is a dynamic which must be viewed as continuing to unfold within our own experience as well and in a steady movement toward the eschatological Kingdom which is a part of God's plan for creation.

It is from the desire to appropriate and reapply that dynamic out of the conviction that it is nothing less than the revelation of God's activity in the world, and from the will to participate in the unfolding of that Kingdom, that the type of biblical-theological interpretation which we have been describing must be carried on. In relation to any specific text, this does not constitute an invitation to intuitive exegesis. Rather through the tools of critical scholarship the central confession of a biblical tradition is to be discerned, the relation of various parts of a particular text to that central confession is to be assessed, and the relation of that confession to the unfolding dynamic of scripture and subsequent tradition as a whole is to be interpreted.

The application of this approach to the Book of the Covenant uncovered contradictions between a creative, liberating, sustaining dynamic growing out of Yahweh's earliest dealings with a slave people and laws regulating slavery and based upon stratified views of human worth. These contradictions were interpreted within their setting, and their theological implications were carefully considered. Viewed thus, the contradictions themselves become an incisive witness to a power within Israel's experience which even its sacred traditions are unable to encompass or control. The formulations of divine will thus become agents pointing beyond themselves. And the tensions inherent within those formulations prevent the tradition from coming to rest; although laws predicated upon discrimination could stand alongside the dynamic confession for centuries, even millennia, before causing an explosion of higher consciousness, ultimately the power residing in that tension would attack those social customs and laws which remained unassimilated to the revealed nature of the compassionate God who hears the cry of the oppressed.

We are still today witnessing classes of oppressed people who are searching our scriptures and pointing to the contradictions between a dynamic which is creative, liberating, and life-giving, and certain laws which participate in the discriminatory customs of their time of composition. As students of biblical tradition, we must not defend the consistency of scripture through harmonizing exegesis, but explicate the contradictions where they are found as objectively and honestly as possible, and allow them to demonstrate for us anew the "in-process" nature of our tradition. It should be neither a source of embarrassment nor surprise to realize that it often takes a long time for social structures to "catch up" with the ground-breaking confessions which believers hold to be revelatory of divine will. We recognize, for example, how black theology has stimulated new reflection along these lines. Similarly, women who recognize in our social and ecclesiastical structures discriminatory regulations sanctioned by the Book of the Covenant bear witness to the same type of contradiction and tension. They assume a prophetic posture in our community when they insist that the liberating dynamic at the confessional heart of the Book of the Covenant, to which many of the laws of the Book of the Covenant had only begun to assimilate, be cut loose from time-conditioned structures so as to infuse all structures and institutions with the humaneness, equity, devotion, and compassion of the God who is able to reveal his will and nature to a people because they "know what it feels like to be a stranger."

Does this view of the theological significance of certain contradictions within biblical material undermine biblical authority? The question is a vastly broad and important one which cannot be covered here. We do feel, however, that it does not undermine the notion of authority, but redefines it. What has commonly been construed as an authority characterized by immutability is redefined as an authority encountered in scripture—as in contemporary life—which is dynamic, living, unfolding. The ultimate referent is God, who is confessed as a creative, liberating, sustaining Agent who is deeply involved in all of creation, and whose activity—and by inference from that activity, whose nature and will—is recorded in a unique way in scripture. Is this redefinition a new form of rationalistic idolatry? The charge cannot be dismissed lightly, for any effort to define the character of the ineffable God participates in idolatry. But the dogmatic position which claims that scripture is a monolithic, immutable record of God's will is also the product of reasonable human reconstruction. It does not seem unreasonable, therefore, to challenge that position in an effort to better understand the inexhaustible richness of our scriptural heritage.

8. THE RENEWED AUTHORITY OF OLD TESTAMENT WISDOM FOR CONTEMPORARY FAITH

WAYNE SIBLEY TOWNER

One of the problems confronting contemporary religious faith was already old when it confronted the writers of the OT. It is the problem of discerning the role which God plays in human history and in individual experience. Are the insurance companies correct in calling certain events "acts of God"? Is his hand really visible in great deliverances of history? Does God actually intervene in natural or historical sequences to punish wrongdoers, reward the righteous, heal the sick, give directions to those who seek a sign? In short, is God the direct cause of any of the events that impinge upon people's lives?

Vast numbers of the inhabitants of the twentieth century have a simple answer for all these questions: No. Modern physical and social science, philosophy, even theology have provided such adequate explanations for at least the proximate causes of all kinds of events that very many people, religious believers included, no longer sense any immediacy of divine activity in the things that go on around them.

The fact is that most of us have consciously or unconsciously adopted what can only be called a "secular" way of accounting for human experiences. This is a mode of explanation for why things happen the way they do which neither requires nor postulates any immediate divine causality in events.[1] As believers and theologians we will, of course, affirm that all events whatever occur within the overarching reach of God's hegemony; indeed, we will affirm that the human participants in

---

1. For a typology of recent definitions of the term "secularization" I have found particularly helpful the essay by Larry Shiner, "The Meanings of Secularization," in J. F. Childress and D. P. Harned, eds., *Secularization and the Protestant Prospect* (Philadelphia: Westminster, 1970) 30–42. In my essay I shall use the term "secular" in the restricted, almost technical sense given above, i.e., devoid of any sense or assumption of immediate divine causality. (The quotation marks with which I enclose it throughout the essay are intended to remind the reader of the fact.)

these events may very well be motivated in their actions by a burning sense of divine guidance. But the events themselves will be interpreted within the secularly explicable nexus of cause-and-effect.

But the issue of divine causality remains acute for contemporary faith, nonetheless. This is the case partly because traditional religious language, from the idioms of popular piety right through the Bible itself, has always been shot through with expressions of the conviction that God is an active participant in the things that happen to people in this world. In this respect the English expression, "God willing," is of a piece with the ancient biblical adage, "Are not two sparrows sold for a penny? And not one of them will fall to the ground without your Father's will" (Matt 10:29). To abandon this deeply rooted way of accounting for events in favor of a "secular" mode is to create a crisis of authority for believers. The question has become urgent: Is there no scriptural warrant for interpreting events in a way that is desacralized, nontheonomous, essentially "secular"—the very way in which most of us do in fact interpret them?

A number of biblical interpreters have recently been sensing that there are indeed such warrants, and that one such locus of authority is to be found precisely in the wisdom materials of the OT. One reason is that, on the face of it, wisdom literature has a strongly secular flavor. The extensive survey of human realia in the book of Proverbs, the vast deep exploration of the problem of suffering and the justice of God in Job, and the reflective despair over the adequacy of earlier dogmatic formulations in Ecclesiastes, all speak one way or another to the plight of the human being attempting autonomously to make sense out of experience. The same flavor pervades other blocks of material now often identified with the work of wisdom circles in Israel, especially Genesis 37, 39–50 (the Joseph story); 2 Samuel 9–20 through 1 Kings 1–2 (the so-called Succession Narrative); the wisdom psalms; the first six chapters of Daniel; and, of course, the apocryphal wisdom books of Ben Sira and the Wisdom of Solomon.[2]

With these materials as the evidence, OT wisdom can perhaps best be defined as—to use von Rad's sentence—"practical knowledge of the laws

---

2. The recent effort by R. N. Whybray to provide an objective semantic basis for identifying given corpora of OT materials with an ongoing wisdom tradition looks promising. Whybray has no difficulty identifying at least the canonical materials cited here with such a tradition. See his *The Intellectual Tradition in the Old Testament* (BZAW 135; Berlin: Walter de Gruyter, 1974) 154.

of life and of the world, based upon experience."[3]   One might add that "wisdom operates without the necessity of a synthesis,"[4] but in quite an unsystematic and pragmatic way seeks to make cogent points about particular human experiences—be they sacred or profane—which will win the assent of the reader.

Obviously, a definition this broad implies a unity within the materials being surveyed which may not be particularly apparent or even likely within a literary corpus as chronologically and formally diverse as this.[5] Nevertheless, the commentators which I here survey assume a fundamental harmony of purpose in OT wisdom similar to that which I have just identified; so, therefore, shall I.   These commentators generally assume that late wisdom differs from the earlier tradition mostly in that it narrows and deepens the exploration of a few key theological issues.   So, for the purposes of this study, shall I.   With these clarifications, I turn now to a review of the recent work to the end of answering the question "In the view of contemporary commentators, do the wisdom materials of the OT open out into an affirmation of a significant and valid place for a 'secular' way of accounting for human experience, even within the context of religious commitment?"

I

One of the roots of the contemporary discussion of the dialogue between OT wisdom and this "secular" way of interpreting experience was the 1955 essay by Klaus Koch, "Gibt es ein Vergeltungsdogma in Alten Testament?"[6]   As the title indicates, this study addresses the problem of the biblical motif of divine retribution.   As that motif is usually expressed in the OT, it appears to be the utter antithesis of any kind of secular outlook.   With direct and visible interventions, God rewards those who obey him and punishes those who disobey him.

---

3. Gerhard von Rad, *Old Testament Theology* (2 vols.; New York: Harper & Row, 1962–65) 1. 418.

4. Walter J. Harrelson, "Wisdom and Pastoral Theology," *Andover-Newton Quarterly* n.s. 7 (1966) 10.

5. In fact, von Rad's definition has been criticized along these very lines by J. L. Crenshaw, "Method in Determining Wisdom Influence upon 'Historical' Literature," *JBL* 88 (1969) 129–42, especially 131–32.

6. Klaus Koch, "Gibt es ein Vergeltungsdogma in Alten Testament?" *ZTK* 52 (1955) 1–42.   This essay is reprinted together with responses and additional studies by F. Horst, H. Gese, W. Preiser, J. Scharbert et al., in K. Koch, ed., *Um das Prinzip der Vergeltung in Religion und Recht des Alten Testaments* (Darmstadt: Wissenschaftliche Buchgesellschaft, 1972).

Koch finds the wisdom approach to this problem very different, however. He begins with such texts as Prov 26:27–28:

> He who digs a pit will fall into it,
>   and a stone will come back upon him who starts it rolling.
> A lying tongue hates its victims,
>   and a flattering mouth works ruin.

Koch argues that the OT wisdom tradition speaks frequently of requital for evil but does not insist that this requital is inflicted by God. In these texts, the evil deed seems to bring about its own unhappy consequence almost as a law of nature. Koch finds in Proverbs no predetermined code of rewards and punishments, no doctrine of divine retribution; rather, the relation of deed and result is more like that of seed and harvest. Human acts can correctly be called "destiny-producing deeds." The same principle applies to the wisdom psalms and much more broadly in the OT, according to Koch.

A second major source for the current discussion of the affinity of OT wisdom to a "secluar" way of interpreting events is the chapter of Gerhard von Rad's *Old Testament Theology* entitled "Israel before Yahweh."[7] In section five, "Israel's Wisdom Deriving from Experience," von Rad shows that the task of wisdom is to perceive laws and orders in nature, and then to objectify these perceptions in language. Initially, the goal was not to articulate a single set of principles or a natural law governing all experience; rather, the gnomic sayings of the "older human and empirical wisdom" sought only to preserve insights into aspects of experience in the hope that those insights will prove useful to others in achieving an elementary mastery of life. Total mastery of life was not aspired to, much less any control over Yahweh's mysterious command of events. Even the "artistic" wisdom cultivated in royal circles for the education of persons of high degree reckoned with the fact that the individual must be aware of ". . . the point where in his action and in the expansion of his ego a man comes up against the mysterious limits set by God."[8]

Von Rad specifically denies that the older wisdom literature of the OT expresses a "secularized and emancipated piety."[9] The cultic sphere, for example—that important realm of experience in which Yahweh is

---

7. Von Rad, *Theology*, 1. 355–459.
8. Ibid., 433.
9. Ibid., 434.

praised and petitioned and offered sacrifices—is in no way delimited by wisdom's search for the natural orders and struggles for the mastery of life. Furthermore, although wisdom from beginning to end reckons that deeds are intrinsically "destiny-producing," wisdom also readily acknowledges that human decisions also please or displease Yahweh (e.g., Prov 11:1, 20; 15:8, 9, 26). Proverbs such as 16:9; 19:21; 20:24; 21:2, 30–31; 26:2, make clear that Yahweh is a "limiting" and "incalculable" factor in experience.

Nevertheless, von Rad also discerns what might now be called a "secular" outlook in the wisdom materials of the OT. In an unlikely way, this emerges in later wisdom, especially Proverbs 1–9, precisely when the tradition gropes toward a unifying theological principle. That effort culminates in the presentation of the hypostatized figure of Dame Wisdom, the firstborn of all creatures, the architect of creation, the mediator of revelation from God to man.[10] Von Rad's assessment of this development is ultimately a negative one. As creation becomes more and more the legitimation of the divine claim upon the individual and the source of revelation itself, the concepts of cult, saving history, and the people of God diminish in significance. "Wisdom's call to men to follow her, her invitation to life, is uttered out in secular life, quite apart from the sacral."[11] But with the demise of signs and divine interventions and cultic sureties, Yahweh's action becomes increasingly hidden and remote. The way is clear for the skepticism and despair of Ecclesiastes, which, in the *Theology*, at least, von Rad seems to regard as evidence of the ultimate failure of wisdom's effort to comprehend and master experience

---

10. Cf. Prov 3:13–18; 4:4–9; 8:1–31; 9:1–6; Sir 14:20–27; 24:1–34; Wis 6:12–16; 7:22b–8:1 (also 8:2–16).

11. Von Rad, *Theology*, 1. 452. Von Rad's interpretation of personified Wisdom has some of the qualities of a *tour de force*. By his reckoning, the introduction of hypostatized Wisdom in the later phases of the canonical sapiential tradition represents a movement *away from* the humanistic empiricism of the older tradition and *toward* theology. However, because this figure of Wisdom also addresses the world without reference to cult, covenant, or sacred history, the movement can also be seen as a turn toward a naturalism ultimately destructive of theology.

Von Rad takes what appears to be a more positive view of the Speaking Creation, personified Wisdom, in his chapter "The Self-Revelation of Creation" in *Wisdom in Israel* (Nashville: Abingdon, 1972), 144–76. He argues that the picture of Wisdom as the architect of creation in Prov 8:22–31 is only a fuller statement of what the older Wisdom intended to say, and that the intimate, personal address of personified Wisdom to the individual rests on a firmly Israelite basis. W. Zimmerli, in reviewing this section of von Rad's book ("Die Weisheit Israels. Zu einem Buch von Gerhard von Rad," *EvT* 31 [1971] 680–95) wonders whether all affirmations of Yahweh's

and to shoulder responsibility for events in the world within a limited but recognizable sphere of human autonomy.

The next source of the current discussion of the relation of wisdom to a "secular" interpretation of experience is the 1962 article by Walther Zimmerli on "The Place and Limit of the Wisdom in the Framework of the Old Testament Theology."[12] Building in part upon von Rad's work, Zimmerli also draws upon current research into Egyptian wisdom with its stress upon the divine *ma'at* (truth, world order) to underscore the contention that OT "wisdom thinks resolutely within the framework of a theology of creation."[13] This assessment of the significance of creation and world order as the basis upon which wisdom builds its program is much more positive than was von Rad's. As Zimmerli puts it, "We have to put the question whether there is a human right to go out to master the world. The Torah answers this question by its recital of the creation. Explicitly, it is stated that man's going out is not against God's will. God authorizes man's going out by his own word and blessing."[14] Unlike the Egyptian *ma'at*, Israel's wisdom knows a type of obedience which has an affinity not to universal and fixed rules, but ". . . a peculiar affinity to God's command. Even if there is no simple identification of the commandment of the covenant and the rule of wisdom, the older wisdom cannot overlook the revealed will of God."[15] And yet the teacher of wisdom is not a lawgiver but rather a counselor whose advice to the student or to the king is couched in maxims which freely combine observations drawn from study of the created world with insights drawn from the will of God expressed in covenant law.

In sum, Zimmerli perceives in the OT wisdom tradition both the sum-

---

personal relationship with his people whatever must depend not only upon the witness of creation, but also upon Israel's historical encounter with the Yahweh who is Lord of all creation.

I shall offer no further assessment of the impact of hypostatized Wisdom upon the question of the biblical warrant for offering "secular" interpretations of experience, largely because the writers whose work I am reviewing do not pursue the matter in this direction.

12. Walther Zimmerli, "The Place and Limit of the Wisdom in the Framework of the Old Testament Theology," *SJT* 17 (1964) 146–58. First published as "Ort und Grenze der Weisheit im Rahmen der alttestamentlichen Theologie," *Les Sagesses du Proche-Orient ancien. Colloque de Strasbourg, mai, 1962* (Paris: Presses Universitaires de France, 1963). Reprinted in Zimmerli's collected essays, *Gottes Offenbarung* (Munich: C. Kaiser, 1963) 300–15.

13. Ibid., 148.

14. Ibid., 152.

15. Ibid.

mons to the mastery of the world, flowing from creation theology, and
the summons to obedience, flowing from covenant theology. Human
beings are given scope for responsible autonomous action, but God's
right to direct the whole movement of history is never impinged upon.
Without actually addressing directly the question being explored in this
essay, Zimmerli in this way outlines a biblical version of what can be
described as a "secular" interpretation of experience exercised within a
theological framework. It is the conscious and mature assumption of
responsibility for the consequences of human decisions, exercised by persons who also have the wisdom to know that God is free to move in
hidden ways to maintain the orders of the world and to implement his
will for his children.

Roland Murphy's 1969 article on "The Interpretation of Old Testament Wisdom Literature"[16] is of relevance to this discussion. Murphy
suggests that "we must move into theological anthropology if we are to
do justice to the wisdom literature."[17] He explains what he means by
"theological anthropology" by quoting Karl Rahner: "Man is represented
as a being without equal in his world, so truly personal as to be God's
partner, for whom everything else by the will of the Creator—and therefore its own *real* nature—is merely environment."[18] Man is at stage
center in OT wisdom literature. Yet Murphy, like Zimmerli and von
Rad before him, emphasizes that this literature is also very clear about
the limitations of human mastery of experience. For him, as for so
many other interpreters, Prov 21:30–31 is a key to proper understanding:

> No wisdom, no understanding, no counsel,
>   can avail against the LORD.
> The horse is made ready for the day of battle,
>   but the victory belongs to the LORD.

Murphy puts it this way: "This stress on experience must also be measured against the affirmation of the wisdom tradition that wisdom is from
God; he 'gives' it."[19]

16. Roland Murphy, "The Interpretation of Old Testament Wisdom Literature," *Int*
23 (1969) 289–301. I find this article more revealing of his personal assessment of
wisdom than his comments in "Assumptions and Problems in Old Testament Wisdom
Research" *CBQ* 29 (1967) 407–18.
17. Murphy, "The Interpretation of Old Testament Literature," 292.
18. Ibid., n. 11.
19. Ibid., 293.

At about the same time that Murphy was writing the above mentioned study, John Priest was discovering the presence of "Humanism, Skepticism, and Pessimism in Israel."[20]   What Priest calls "humanism" is closely akin to the anthropocentric outlook discovered in the wisdom materials by the previous interpreters.   "Humanism not only focuses its interest on man; it also displays confidence in—or at least reliance on—man's capacity to confront human life and cope with its problems."[21] Furthermore, for Priest such humanism in ancient Israel's context is seminal for a variety of literary genres and themes.   Priest argues that in fact historiography and even theological writing in Israel, above all the work of the Yahwist, spring from a prior "humanistic" impulse.   In sum, for Priest, "Hebrew theology is seen as necessarily posterior to Hebrew humanism."[22]   Although he does not spell out in any detail the hermeneutical implications of such a position, Priest does admit that for himself, "theology . . . begins with the conviction that the most searching questions about man in the totality of his relationships emerge from below—the anthropological or sociological—and then move to the above —the theological."[23]

Precisely to guard against attributing primacy either to the secular or the theonomous aspects of OT wisdom is a task undertaken by Gerhard von Rad in his last book, *Wisdom in Israel*.[24]   For the most part this book elaborates positions already taken in the *Theology*; however, by devoting an entire volume to the place and content of the wisdom tradition, von Rad testifies to the upward revision among scholars of the

---

20. John Priest, "Humanism, Skepticism, and Pessimism in Israel," *JAAR* 36 (1968) 311–26.

21. Ibid., 313.

22. Ibid., 317.   Priest draws support for his thesis from von Rad's study "The Joseph Narrative and Ancient Wisdom," *The Problem of the Hexateuch and Other Essays* (New York: McGraw-Hill, 1966) 292–300.   Von Rad's proposal that the portrayal of Joseph as the ideal wise man in Genesis 37, 39–50 reflects a *Sitz im Leben* in wisdom circles at the Jerusalem court in the time of the united monarchy has been subjected to a searching critique by J. L. Crenshaw, "Method."   George W. Coats recently responded to Crenshaw's article in defense of at least the heart of von Rad's position in "The Joseph Story and Ancient Wisdom: A Reappraisal," *CBQ* 35 (1973) 285–97.   This debate is an important one and is by no means yet complete.   However, for the purposes of this essay I am not obliged to enter into it.   The issue of where to locate the *Sitz im Leben* of wisdom writing in ancient Israel neither adds to nor detracts from the contention that that tradition in its present canonical form contains within it elements of a "secular" mode of accounting for human experiences.

23. Priest, "Humanism, Skepticism, and Pessimism in Israel," 326.

24. See above, note 11.

significance of this material within the canon. The only substantive development which I can detect between von Rad's two major treatments of wisdom is the weight which, in the later book, he places upon the tendency toward desacralization or "secularization" (his word) evident in the OT wisdom tradition from its very earliest phases.

Drawing upon his earlier studies, von Rad argues that in the early monarchical period Israel experienced a rapid decline in what Buber once described as "pan-sacralism," and an equally rapid discovery of man as the subject of reflection. The contrast can be demonstrated strikingly by comparing 1 Samuel 13–14, representing the older pan-sacral faith, with the Succession Narrative, possibly written only a generation later. In contrast to pan-sacralism, the later text recognizes "a relative determinism inherent in events and also . . . the recognition of a relative value inherent in worldly things [life, property, honor, etc.]."[25] But did this newer view whittle away at faith in Yahweh's overall power? Not one whit. This is possible because, for Israel, Yahweh's word and act are just as real a part of everyday life as are other events. In fact, for those who can perceive correctly, Yahweh's word and act underlie and comprehend all experience. Herein lies the meaning of the common phrase, "The fear of the LORD, that is wisdom" (Job 28:28; cf. Prov 1:7; 9:10; 15:33; Ps 111:10). Von Rad's hermeneutic turns on this point: the apparent secularity of the wisdom of the OT proves to be a complex phenomenon not at all similar to modern secularism.

It is not to be supposed, however, that the connection between Yahweh's overriding order and the phenomena of experience is without ambiguity. Although the ultimate ground of the orders and laws perceived in the created world is Yahweh's will, his activity in the world is a depth which contains both darkness and light. "Man," observes von Rad, in one of the most frequently cited statements in the book, "is always wholly in the world, and he must always deal only with Yahweh."[26] In a less dialectical observation Professor von Rad quotes the key text Prov 21:31—"The horse is made ready for the day of battle, but victory belongs to the LORD"—to support the claim that "its aim is . . . to put a stop to the erroneous concept that a guarantee of success was to be found simply in practising human wisdom and in making preparations. Man

25. Von Rad, *Wisdom*, 59.
26. Ibid., 95.

must always keep himself open to the activity of God, an activity which completely escapes all calculation. . . ."[27]

Von Rad thus finds wisdom constantly pulled between the two poles of natural versus revealed truth, or norms derived from experience versus limitations experienced at the mysterious edge of knowledge. The quest for good and evil is pragmatic as is every other quest by the wise man. " 'Good' is that which does good; 'evil' is that which causes harm."[28] A man is righteous who fulfills the claims and expectations placed upon him by the community. There is no place for moral heroism in all of this—the wise man simply gets right with the orders. The orders are Yahweh's; however, they are only ambiguously discernible in specific situations.

Von Rad's dialectical approach leaves him with the rather awkward notion that wisdom writers had always to look at phenomena in two ways. Nearly every event, and certainly experience as a whole, had to be affirmed at once to be discreet and calculable, and at the same time influenced by the divine "accompaniment" of all events. Some such dual interpretation of experience was the price Israel's wise had to pay for their radical monism: there could ultimately be no source of events except Yahweh. His presence was always a dynamic factor within the whole environment of people, and yet was always perceived only in hiddenness. The phenomenon can be illustrated by comparing the beloved passage Prov 21:31:

> The horse is made ready for the day of battle,
> but victory belongs to the LORD. . . .

with another reflection on the same matter, Prov 24:6:

> . . . by wise guidance you can wage your war,
> and in abundance of counselors there is victory.

Von Rad sums up the problem of the double vision toward all events by observing that OT wisdom really knows no guiding idea or rational rule, but only the common goal of wresting from experience some way of warding off the incalculable and chaotic. "The phenomena [themselves] are never objectified; they are always conceived only from the point of view of their relationship to the man in each particular case."[29]

27. Ibid., 101.
28. Ibid., 77.
29. Ibid., 311.

The last major contributor to the discussion, at least as far as this essay is concerned, is Walter Brueggemann. Between 1968–72, Brueggemann wrote a series of essays and a book which deal with the matter of the dialogue between OT wisdom and modern "secular" interpretations of experience. Many of the themes to be spelled out through this entire corpus are articulated already in one of the early essays which, like so many of the other contributions to this entire discussion, appeared in *Interpretation*. This was the 1970 article entitled, "Scripture and the Ecumenical Life-Style."[30] Revealing immediately his deep indebtedness both to von Rad and to Zimmerli, Brueggemann also takes a more radical position than either of them.

The "ecumenical life-style" as he understands it is rooted in what he calls the "creation-wisdom" approach and seeks dialogue among people and between humanity and the world. It is the antithesis of the much more common triumphalism of religion, which is rooted in the conviction that God intervenes in history to save his chosen people and promote his cause. The faith of the wise, according to Brueggemann, is a faith which sees life's goal as a healthy community living in *šālôm*. This is possible when the community is wise enough not to devalue this earth and this time in favor of some other earth and time. "The teaching of the wise in Israel leads to the affirmation that this is the world for which we are intended and we had better invest here. . . . Our destiny is wrapped up in this ambiguous time and place, and here we must work out our faith and our personhood."[31] The wise know that experience is reliable, although they also recognize the orders which cannot be transgressed. Brueggemann acknowledges wisdom's emphasis upon the limits of knowledge pointed out by von Rad, but he believes that the ultimate concern of these writers lies in a different direction. For him, the wise seek above all to teach the community not to err by failing to live right up to the limit of the knowable. The crucial claim by Brueggemann on behalf of the wisdom world view is that Genesis 1 and Psalm 8 (both of which he identifies with the larger scope of the wisdom impulse in Israel) make clear that God has turned the world over to man to run and that he holds mankind accountable for that world. To leave the operation of the world to God is not, therefore, an act of faith. "It is an

---

30. Walter Brueggemann, "Scripture and the Eccumenical Life-Style," *Int* 24 (1970) 3–19.
31. Ibid., 10.

abdication from the task which he has entrusted to us."[32]   In all, then, the crucial questions raised by OT wisdom are about humanity, not about God.   The human individual is put at the center and is trusted. Key words in the resultant view of the human role are "responsibility" and "adulthood."   Clearly the hermeneutical appropriation from wisdom implied here draws a straight line from what Brueggemann perceives to be the essential outlook of OT wisdom to an enlightened "secular" approach to the interpretation of experience.   There is very little need for analogy-building or translation in moving from the one to the other. Wisdom already in its own form and context embodies the best of what we might call modern "secular" insight.

In a December 1970 article entitled, "The Triumphalist Tendency in Exegetical History,"[33] Brueggemann modifies this position somewhat. The problem is not the tension between the event as secular reality and the divinely established framework within which events take place, but rather in the matter of the "inbreaking" of God.   The trouble with the recital of the acts of God from the side of the *heilsgeschichtlich* approach was that it always had to stress this inbreaking.   A theology of creation and blessing, which is the theology fundamental to wisdom literature, stressed not interventions, but a God who ordains and guarantees and upholds.   The Succession Narrative, representative of an early wisdom outlook, already provides such a model.[34]   In the Succession Narrative, the relation of the king to God "exists primarily in the realization that God's graciousness provides a context of support and freedom in which the man is trusted to live his own life. . . .   [It suggests] that the initiative and responsibility for shaping human life have now passed into human hands not as modes usurped from Yahweh, but deliberately and willingly granted by him."[35]

Brueggemann's exploration of the relation of OT wisdom to contem-

32. Ibid., 13.

33. Walter Brueggemann, "The Triumphalist Tendency in Exegetical History," *JAAR* 38 (1970) 367–80.

34. Brueggemann gains support for this argument from R. N. Whybray, *The Succession Narrative* (SBT 9; 2d series; London: SCM, 1968)—a book which has been subjected to the same critique as that directed to von Rad's article on the Joseph cycle by J. L. Crenshaw, "Method."   See above, note 22.

35. Brueggemann, "Triumphalist Tendency," 372.   In yet another article on the subject ("On Trust and Freedom.   A Study of Faith in the Succession Narrative," *Int* 26 [1972] 3–19), Brueggemann follows von Rad in shifting additional stress to the perception in older wisdom of Yahweh's presence and underpinning of events. "[Yahweh] is much more the *creator of the context* for human freedom and responsibility that a *disruptor of events*" (18).

porary "secular" interpretation of experience reaches its culmination in his book *In Man We Trust: The Neglected Side of Biblical Faith.*[36]   In this somewhat underestimated volume, which Roland Murphy describes as "instructive and challenging biblical theology," Brueggemann draws together the ideas which have been explored in the preceding articles. The picture of David given in the Succession Narrative is the picture of one who is operating out of the essentially "secular" orientation.   This is "the practical orientation of a man concerned with the shaping of history, moving toward a future which can be shaped but not predicted, which can be received but not manipulated."   In such a world, "God is to be worshipped, but things have now lost their divinity; therefore, the king has new freedom in disposing of them."[37]   Brueggemann now becomes very explicit in dealing with the "Theology of the Secular."   He says, "Wisdom teaching is profoundly secular in that it presents life and history as a human enterprise."[38]

II

Before offering some concluding observations of my own, I wish to summarize the chief points of this emerging discussion of the biblical and theological warrant that OT wisdom literature provides for a "secular" interpretation of experience.

1. Commentators find in the corpus of OT wisdom literature and related texts an affirmation of an aspect of human experience which concerns itself with human responsibility for the well-being of the world and the community, exercised within a sphere of free autonomy.

2. The roots of this viewpoint within the OT wisdom are thought by many to lie in the desacralization of creation and the trend toward humanism which took place at the Jerusalem court of the united Israelite monarchy.   Be that as it may, the viewpoint is present in the "older" wisdom, as well as in the later strata.

3. There is a deep and intrinsic link between wisdom and creation theology in the OT.   The world is not only the theater of mankind's redemption, as salvation history would have it, but is also the environment in which mankind's self-emancipation and kingly rule take place.

---

36. Walter Brueggemann, *In Man We Trust: The Neglected Side of Biblical Faith* (Richmond: John Knox, 1972).

37. Ibid., 66.

38. Ibid., 82.

The link between creation theology and wisdom is discerned not only at the point of their common origins in Israel's literary history, but also in the constant concern in wisdom with those fixed orders within the created world which are perceived as limitations upon human knowledge.

4. Two major motifs run through OT wisdom literature from beginning to end. First, people have a major and legitimate place for their own decision-making within the created world. It is this exercise of autonomy that looks to the modern interpreters like our own "secular" experience. Second, however, there is also a limit to that scope of decision-making and autonomy. Yahweh is still the creator and sustainer of the world, and his transcendence is the basis of the orders against which an individual and people must measure themselves. It is to this limitation that Israel points when it says, "The fear of the LORD, that is wisdom" (Job 28:28).

5. The desacralized view represented by wisdom remains a permanent theological option for Israel. The ahistoricality of wisdom literature, which, in the heyday of the "God who acts" era, was regarded as its weakness and inferiority, seems now more and more to be regarded as its strength.

6. It must be pointed out that no clear solution has yet been achieved for a number of matters bearing upon the subject of OT wisdom. The problem with what to do with retributional theology remains alive. Everybody trades upon Koch's attempt to reduce the concept, especially in the wisdom literature, to the inevitable outworking of "destiny-producing [human] deeds." But Koch's essay can be criticized as too schematic, too willing to overlook the admittedly infrequent but nonetheless significant instances in wisdom materials in which Yahweh is presented as poised to intervene for good or ill (e.g., "take delight in the LORD, and he will give you the desires of your heart. Commit your way to the LORD; trust in him, and he will act," Ps 37:4–5). This is a crucial point for the entire discussion, for should the Koch thesis fall one would be hard pressed to argue that wisdom excludes Yahweh from an active retributive involvement in a range of experiences which modern interpreters would tend to interpret "secularly."

This problem points to an even larger area of uncertainty. There is still no generally agreed-upon view of how autonomous and theonomous factors relate to any particular event. Von Rad seems to feel that each event is perceived at least potentially in two different ways simultaneously by the wisdom writers themselves. It is von Rad above all who uses the term "mystery" in describing the intersection of these two ways of looking at events. But even if one allows for the providential hegemony of God over all creation, was it then and is it now possible to discern both divine and mundane proximate causes for the same event?

III

Human dignity is best protected by theology if the latter affirms both the freedom of humans to act responsibly, and also our distinct limitation in the matter of what we can know. Both of these affirmations are essential, because they are realistic. What I would hope for is the achievement of a biblically warranted, theologically validated affirmation of our "secular" interpretation of experience comprehended within a theological framework built upon the doctrine of creation as the good handiwork of a creator who remains also the sustainer and the ultimate redeemer of the world.

OT wisdom appears to provide prime support for such affirmations. Hermeneutics depends, after all, on the establishment of analogies; and the analogies are there. For OT wisdom there was a sphere of human autonomy surrounded by limits which were also described as the divinely established orders. Our analogue to this model will look the same, with the exception that the sphere of human autonomy will be greatly enlarged as we are able to describe far more extensive segments of experience in terms of various sequences of cause-and-effect. The particular events of history are not divine irruptions, as a *heilsgeschichtlich* view would have it, but products of historical sequences which include elements of inevitability, chance, and even piety.

As part of our refusal to view events theonomously, we shall have to eliminate the notion of divine retribution from any interpretation of events, at least insofar as retribution implies direct intervention. As spelled out by Koch, the link between the "destiny-producing deed" and its consequences can, with some reservations, be affirmed; a similar formulation can certainly be used to describe the modern secular experience of social causation. Thus it will still be possible to say, "As a man sows, so shall he also reap." For us, however, this understanding of "retribution" cannot be lifted out of the enlarged secular sphere of cause-and-effect, or imply the direct agency of God in the matter.

The conclusion of it all, then, is this. Contemporary faith confronts a crisis of authority when it confronts the determination of modern people to interpret the events of their experience "secularly," without assuming any immediate divine causality. And yet within the canon of the Bible, particularly in the wisdom literature of the OT, warrant is to be found for affirming the basic premise of this "secular" interpretation of events— namely, that individuals are free to make decisions and shape their destinies within the large sphere of human responsibility. The Bible certainly does not authorize us to pretend there are no limits to this sphere of responsibility, much less to deny the providential hegemony of God over the whole of creation. However, the fact that we have canonical authority to interpret the events of our experience in the nonsacral, "secular" way in which we do can help overcome the core of this crisis of authority. Finally, the canon of the Bible provides an important opening for constructive dialogue with those who reject faith altogether because they can never finally discover the hand of God in the things which happen to them.

9. A STYLISTIC STUDY OF THE PRIESTLY CREATION STORY

Bernhard W. Anderson

Discussions of the biblical canon have to take into consideration not only the final literary shape of particular texts or of canonical units (e.g., the Pentateuch) but also the prehistory which preceded the literary conclusion. To use a well-known figure of speech, the texts must be understood in a dimension of depth, not just on a flat surface, "superficially."[1] Yet not all biblical texts provide a clear basis for reconstructing previous literary or traditio-historical *stages* which must be taken into account by the interpreter. Indeed, in some cases the meaning of the text is to be found by examining in depth the literary structure of the text itself. A case in point is the Priestly creation story with which the Pentateuch opens. The purpose of this essay is to explore the present literary form of the story, especially the word-event structure that is intrinsic to the narrative.

I

Ever since the publication of Gunkel's monumental commentary on Genesis, the first edition of which appeared at the turn of the twentieth century,[2] scholars have had to take with increasing seriousness the interrelationship of form and content in biblical literature. Before writing his commentary, Gunkel had issued his pioneering study, *Schöpfung und Chaos in Urzeit und Endzeit* (1895), a thematic study occasioned by the archaeological discovery of Mesopotamian literary remains at the ancient Babylonian capital of Nineveh. In this work Gunkel shows that the

1. This figure appears in Gerhard von Rad, *Genesis* (2d ed.; Philadelphia: Westminster, 1972) 23, and is employed effectively by Brevard S. Childs in *The Book of Exodus: A Critical Theological Commentary* (Philadelphia: Westminster, 1974).
2. Hermann Gunkel's commentary on Genesis first appeared in the series *Handkommentar zum Alten Testament* (Göttingen: Vandenhoeck & Ruprecht, 1901). The third edition appeared in 1910 and the fourth through the sixth (1964) editions were reprints.

motif of the mythical battle between the creator-god and the opposing powers of chaos can be traced through various types of biblical literature, from the opening of the book of Genesis to the Apocalypse of John. But in his Genesis commentary, as Jay Wilcoxen has rightly observed, Gunkel's attention shifted from the *Stoffe* (Gunkel's preferred term for traditional materials) to the *Gattungen* (literary genres) in which traditional matter was formulated and transmitted.[3] Since the literary genres arose out of folk materials and were shaped in the creative oral period, it is the task of the interpreter, according to Gunkel, to go behind the present text and to investigate the original formulation of the material in its *Sitz im Leben* (this has come to be known as form criticism). Furthermore, the interpreter's task is to consider how original formulations underwent an evolution, a *Literaturgeschichte*, which finally resulted in the received text (this came to be known as traditio-historical investigation.)

The Priestly creation story provides an excellent example of the inseparable relation of form and content. All commentators, even conservatives like Benno Jacob and Umberto Cassuto, recognize that the story incorporates traditional materials, including the chaos motif. The question is the degree to which traditional materials have been homogenized in the present account which compresses eight creative acts into six "days of work." Gunkel's thinking about this matter seems to have shifted. In his monograph on "Creation and Chaos" he was primarily concerned to show that the creation story rests on an ancient mythical tradition, ultimately Babylonian in origin. In his Genesis commentary, however, he maintained that the Priestly Writer was dependent upon a *Vorlage* which he reworked heavily (*"sehr stark"*).[4] It was his judgment, however, that the revision was so thoroughgoing that it is no longer possible to recover the content and wording of the original.

Other scholars were not so restrained in their attempts to reconstruct the prehistory of the text. At the beginning of the twentieth century two scholars, Stade and Schwally, independently proposed that the present creation story is the end-result of the blending of two accounts, one dealing with God making the world and the other with creation by God's

---

3. Jay A. Wilcoxen, "Narrative," *Old Testament Form Criticism* (ed. John H. Hayes; San Antonio: Trinity University, 1974) 58–59.

4. Gunkel, *Genesis* (3d ed.; 1910) 119–20. He lists eight "traces of an older *Vorlage*," in addition to the sequence of creative events.

word.[5]   Years later Gerhard von Rad attempted to buttress this view with a literary analysis of the Priestly Writing in which he posited two identifiable strands (P^A and P^B) and, in the case of Genesis 1, a *Tatbericht* (P^A) and a *Befehlsbericht* (P^B).[6] The attempt to separate out *literary* sources has not been successful. Martin Noth, in his *Ueberlieferungsgeschichte des Pentateuch*, rejects this purely literary approach, although he admits that, from the standpoint of the history of traditions, there is a discernible tension between *Tatbericht* and *Wortbericht*.[7]

In recent years this traditio-historical approach has provided the opportunity for the discussion to take a new turn, along the lines of a supplementary hypothesis. Werner Schmidt maintains that the nucleus of the story is a stratum of tradition which was closely akin to other ancient Near Eastern texts, notably the Babylonian *Enuma elish*. Superimposed on this old level of tradition is a later interpretive expansion which sets forth a more sophisticated theological view. In his judgment, the present text is the end result of a traditio-historical development, in the course of which the old *Tatbericht*, with its emphasis on creation by making, was reinterpreted to stress creation by fiat, thereby giving the final story the tone of a *Wortbericht*.[8] This traditio-historical analysis is carried one stage further by P. A. H. de Boer, who finds *three* tradition-strata in the story: 1) a myth portraying God as a divine "handicrafts-man," like the divine Potter in prophetical sayings; 2) a myth portraying God as the Divine King who made heaven and earth (as in some of the psalms), and 3) various supplements by late priestly writers who sought to systematize received traditions.[9]

---

5. Bernhard Stade, *Biblische Theologie des Alten Testaments* (Tübingen: J. C. B. Mohr, 1905) 1. 349: Friedrich Schwally, "Die biblischen Schöpfungsberichte," *Archiv für Religionswissenschaft* 9 (1906) 159–75.

6. Gerhard von Rad, *Die Priesterschrift im Hexateuch* (BWANT 65; Stuttgart: Kohlhammer, 1934) 11–18, 167–71; see his synoptic outline, 190–91. In his *Genesis*, he is more cautious about reconstructing "the long road in the history of tradition which lies behind the present form of this account of creation," but he still speaks (64) about earlier and later versions (creation by act and creation by word).

7. Martin Noth, *A History of Pentateuchal Traditions* (Englewood Cliffs, N.J.: Prentice-Hall, 1972) from the 1948 German edition, 10–12, 235. For a trenchant criticism of von Rad's theory of the duality of literary sources in the Priestly Writing, see Paul Humbert, "Die literarische Zweiheit des Priester-Codex in der Genesis," *ZAW* 58 (1940–41) 30–57, especially 30–35 on the creation story.

8. Werner H. Schmidt, *Die Schöpfungsgeschichte der Priesterschrift* (WMANT 17; Neukirchen-Vluyn: Neukirchener, 1964). See 160–63 for his reconstruction of "the oldest stage of the tradition."

9. P. A. H. de Boer, *Fatherhood and Motherhood in Israelite and Judean Piety* (Leiden: Brill, 1974) 47–48, 49–51. He maintains that at the earliest level of

It is not my intention to deny the use of traditional *materials* in the creation story. The question is whether the text provides evidence of a tradition-historical evolution whose stages are still evident and which, to some degree, must be considered by the interpreter; or whether, alternatively, the story is a meticulously wrought composition in which form and content are indissolubly united. The latter, in my opinion, is the case. In this essay I am returning, though in a restricted sense, to Gunkel's view that the composer of the story, while drawing upon traditional motifs, has so completely reworked the materials by casting them into his own literary form that it is impossible to recover an earlier *Vorlage*. It is my thesis that a stylistic study of the shape of the text itself, rather than explorations into its presumed prehistory, will throw light on various theological matters, such as the translation of the opening sentence (1:1), the alternating descriptions of God as Maker and Creator, and the preeminent role of man on the earth.

II

Careful study of the Hebrew text of the creation story discloses many rhetorical features which cannot be examined within the limitations of this essay: examples of verbal assonance, chiastic arrangement, the strategic positioning and collocation of words, among others. Here our attention will focus on the overall form of the story which displays throughout a striking literary symmetry and integrity.

1. *The Formulaic Pattern.* The first thing that strikes one is that the story as a whole is structured in a sequence of literary "panels" or paragraphs, each of which is governed by a divine command and its execution.[10] Creation takes place, not by word-events, but by word-fulfillment events. For some reason, Sean McEvenue, in his study of Priestly narrative style, does not deal with this phenomenon in the Priestly creation story; but he has provided ample evidence that the command-execution sequence, which is characteristic of narrative art generally, was a distinctive feature of Priestly style, notably in the laws of Sinai (Ex-

---

tradition, God and Goddess were co-participators in the creation of humankind (Gen 1:26).

10. See especially the excellent commentary by Claus Westermann, *Genesis* (BK 1/1; Neukirchen-Vluyn: Neukirchener, 1966–74) 111–30. Westermann analyzes the component formal elements of "the structure of the command."

odus 25–31) which Moses faithfully executes (Exodus 35–40).[11]
The connection between word and deed is emphasized by repeating
verbally the content of the command, though with some variations. In
the flood story, for instance, we find the command formula, "then God
said to Noah" (*wayyō'mer 'ĕlōhîm lĕnōaḥ*, 6:13) and the corresponding
obedience formula, "And Noah did according to everything that God
commanded him, so he did" (*wayya'aś nōaḥ kĕkōl 'ăśer ṣiwwā 'ōtô
'ĕlōhîm kēn 'āśāh*, 6:22). The stylistic connection between command
and execution, or word and fulfillment, is found in both the old Epic
flood tradition and its priestly recension, and in both cases repetition is
characteristic of narrative style.

In the creation story God is the one who both announces and fulfills
his word. With this qualification, which puts the story in a different
category from those dealing with the obedience of Noah or Moses, each
of the panels displays a command-execution sequence. Reduced to a
minimum, the formulaic elements of the pattern are: 1) a declarative
formula, "then God said" (*wayyō'mer 'ĕlōhîm*); 2) a command which,
with the possible exception of the heavenly council implied in 1:26, was
addressed to no one, since no other being was present to participate in
the creation; 3) execution of the command, usually introduced by the
formula, "and so it happened" (*wayyĕhî kēn*);[12] and 4) finally a formula
of divine approbation which indicates the perfect correspondence between the command and its execution.[13] This pattern, of course, is not
followed inflexibly. The *wayyĕhî kēn* formula is conspicuously absent in
the first panel, perhaps because light was conceived to be an instantaneous flash, like lightning, out of uncreated darkness; moreover, the formula is lacking between vv 26 and 27, where we would expect it, and is
found instead in v 31, probably because of the expansion of the story to
make room for a special divine blessing upon man (v 28) and a formal
grant of food (vv 29–30).[14] Furthermore, at three points the pattern
is expanded with the motif of naming (vv 5, 8, 10). And in v 22 we find

---

11. Sean E. McEvenue, *The Narrative Style of the Priestly Writer* (AnBib 50; Rome:
Biblical Institute, 1971).

12. Following LXX, this formula probably should be transposed from the end of v 7
to the end of v 6, corresponding to the sequence in vv 9, 11, 15, 24. Also in v 20,
following LXX, the formula probably should be restored.

13. The formula of approbation probably belongs at the end of v 8, as in LXX,
following the creation of the celestial vault. In every other case God responds to an
act of creation with a word of approval.

14. See Humbert, "Zweiheit . . . ," 31–32.

a blessing upon marine and flying creatures which, in its linguistic formulation, is akin to the blessing given to man (1:28). These and other deviations,[15] however, do not disturb the fundamental D-C-E-A literary pattern: Declarative Formula, Command, Execution, Approbation.

Once these stylistic features are taken seriously, important consequences for exegesis follow. In the first place, from a stylistic viewpoint there is no reason to suppose that the declarative formula (*wayyō'mer 'ĕlōhîm*) of v 3a is the apodosis of a temporal clause, whose protasis begins with v 1. Some translators, arguing that grammatically v 1 may be taken as either an independent sentence or a dependent temporal clause, attempt to resolve the problem by appealing to other texts, biblical or extra-biblical. But when the text is viewed in terms of its own internal structure, there is clear reason to believe that the declarative formula in v 3a functions in the same manner as it does elsewhere in the creation story: as a discrete introduction to a following creative word-act.

In the second place, from a stylistic point of view the command-execution structure is intrinsic to the narrative, apparently from the time of its literary formulation. The repetition in the execution provides no basis for positing duplications which, in turn, justify attempts to reconstruct an *Urtext* or an *Urstadium der Tradition*.[16] It is noteworthy that Werner Schmidt, while admitting that the *"Urtext"* can no longer be recovered with certainty, finds traces of the supposedly early *Tatbericht* precisely at those points where the divine command is executed (vv 4b, 7, 9 [LXX], 12a, 16–17a, 21, 25). Inconsistently, he makes an exception in the case of the creation of man (vv 26–27a), at which point the reconstructed early level of tradition contained both a cohortative command ("Let us make . . .") and its execution ("And God created . . .").[17] This traditio-historical analysis, in my judgment, finds the feeblest support from an appeal to the difference between the verbs of making (*'āśāh*) and creating (*bārā'*). Significantly, the episode of the creation

15. In the first panel, the divine approbation comes immediately after the creation of light, not after the separation of light and darkness, lest it be suggested that God also approved the darkness of chaos.

16. Westermann, who is sensitive to the depth-dimension of the text but is even more impressed with the stylistic features of the present text, observes: "Therefore, one coarsens the text when he wants to divide Genesis 1 into a 'deed account' and a 'word account,' the 'word account' never existed as such, and the 'deed account' cannot be reconstructed" (*Genesis*, 120).

17. Schmidt *Schöpfungsgeschichte*, 161; see also 127–49. Von Rad's literary analysis (see above, note 6) also cuts into the command-execution sequence.

of man begins with the command, "let us make" (*na'áseh*) and the execution of the command is reported by saying, "So, God created . . ." (*wayyibrā'*). It is arbitrary to change the second verb to *"machte,"* as does Schmidt, for the sake of a hypothesis. The prophet Second Isaiah, an approximate contemporary of the so-called Priestly Writer, used these verbs interchangeably, even within the compass of a single sentence (43:7).[18]   And a psalmist, speaking out of Israel's cultic tradition, could exclaim:

> By the word of the LORD the heavens were made [*na'āsû*],
> and by the breath of his mouth all their array!
> . . . .
> For he spoke and it happened,
> he commanded and it occurred! (Ps 33:6, 9)

The tension between "creating" and "making," between creative word and creative deed, in the creation story has been grossly exaggerated. In any case, the narrative style of the story, with its essential connection between command and execution, provides no basis for supposing that the text is the end-product of a literary or traditio-historical evolution in which *Tatbericht* and *Wortbericht* were finally united.   Theologically, the statement that God is the Maker and that God is the Creator are not different at all.

2. *The Twofold Movement.* Let us turn now to another major stylistic feature of the creation story. The creative drama falls into two parts, each of which comes to its own climax. The first section (vv 3–13), that is, the first triad of days, consists of four creative word-deeds, with two at the climax; and correspondingly, the second section (vv 14–31), or the second triad of days, consists of four creative word-deeds, with two at the climax. In the past, commentators have been troubled by this scheme which compresses eight acts of creation into the confines of a six-day work-week and which introduces a theological tension between God's effortless, instantaneous creation and the extension of his creation over a period of time, at the end of which he "ceased" from all of his work (cf. Exod 31:15 [P]: "on the seventh day he rested, and was refreshed."). What we regard as problematic, however, may not have troubled the composer of the text. It is noteworthy that some scholars (e.g., Schmidt) believe that the calendar scheme belongs to the latest

18. See the table of creation verbs used by Second Isaiah, in B. W. Anderson, *Creation versus Chaos* (New York: Association, 1967) 124–26.

phase of the history of the tradition; but von Rad, who also attempted to separate out an early *Tatbericht* and a later *Befehlsbericht,* came to the conclusion that the motif of God's "resting" (*šābat*) from his "work" (*mĕlā'kâ*) belongs to the oldest version. "We reckon it to be an important result," he wrote, "that the seven-day scheme, though it finally conforms to the material in small degree, nevertheless does not represent literarily a late reworking but is firmly anchored in the oldest ascertainable form of Genesis 1."[19] At this point we face again the issue of the interrelationship of form and content, which should be considered anew from the standpoint of stylistic study.

So much attention has been given to the possible prehistory of the creation story that one thing has not received sufficient attention: the story in its present form is structured in parallel sections[20] so as to portray a twofold movement from heaven to earth, thereby elucidating the theme stated in the superscription to the whole: "In the beginning God created the heaven and the earth." The narrator's focus on the earth is indicated at the outset in v 2, which serves as the immediate preface to the creative drama proper. The prefatory portrayal of chaos opens with an express interest in *the earth*, which stands in an emphatic position: "Now, the earth was once a chaotic waste . . ." (*wĕhā'āreṣ hāyĕtā tōhû wābōhû*). Accordingly, in the two triads of days there is a double movement from the cosmic realm to the earth—from heaven, to waters, to earth; and the terrestrial focus is evident at the climax point of each section (that is, the third and sixth days), where in each case two creative events pertain to *the earth*.

Let us see how this double movement occurs. The presuppositions for the unfolding drama of creation are given in the portrayal of primeval chaos in the prefatory v 2. The chaotic waste (*tōhû wābōhû*, a hendiadys), which constitutes the background of God's creative activity, has two characteristics: primeval, uncreated darkness, and watery depth over which an awesome wind was sweeping.[21] Darkness (*ḥōšek*) and water

---

19. Von Rad, *Die Priesterschrift*, 17.

20. Scholars have long emphasized the twofold division and have perceived correlations between the two series: first and fourth days (light//luminaries), second and fifth (firmament separating the waters//birds and water creatures); third and sixth (dry land + vegetation//land animals + Man). "Dieser Parallelismus springt in die Augen," observed Franz Delitzsch; and he insisted that the correspondence remains even if one supposes that there was an older eight-act account without the division into days. See his *Genesis* (Leipzig: Dörffling und Franke, 1887) 45–46.

21. Compare this "wind of Elohim" with "the wind of Yahweh" mentioned in Isa

(*mayîm*) are the two chaos motifs that figure in the ensuing drama.

In the first panel (first day), which opens with the declarative formula, "Then God said," the Creator caused light to burst forth in the uncreated darkness. This *Urlicht*, for which there is no anticipation in the prefatory portrayal of chaos, was not permitted to become a twilight, a suffused mixture of light and darkness; for God *separated* created light and uncreated darkness into their proper spheres, naming the one Day and the other Night. In the second panel (second day) the narrator turns to the other dimension of primeval chaos; the watery abyss. Executing his own command, God made a celestial vault to *separate* the upper waters from the lower waters. God named the vault Heaven (*šāmayîm*), although nothing is said about the cosmic realm, for instance, the number of heavens or the location of the Creator's heavenly palace in or above the cosmic ocean (cf. Ps 8:2). In the third panel (first part of the third day) the narrator's vision descends to the lower waters, the remnant of primeval watery chaos. At God's executive command, the waters were accumulated into a bounded location (a third act of *separation*) and the submerged "dry land" (*yabbāšâ*) became visible.[22] The accumulated waters were named Seas (*yammîm*) and the *yabbāšâ* was named Earth (*'ereṣ*). Nothing further is said about the lower waters at this point: this matter is picked up again in the second section, vv 20–23. In the fourth panel (second part of the third day), which is paired with the third panel, the narrator turns specifically to the *yabbāšâ*, named Earth, which at God's command produced vegetation. The greening of the earth is emphasized by using an assonant verb and noun (*tadšē'/deše'*); and the earth's fecundity is stressed by using the maternal verb *wattôṣē'* ("and the earth brought forth"), a verb which is recapitulated at the climactic point of the second part of the story, as we shall see. Thus the paired third and fourth panels, which deal with the earth and its fertility, constitute a climax point in the unfolding drama of creation.

The second part of the story (vv 14–31) follows essentially the same movement: heaven—waters—earth. The fifth panel (fourth day) begins by recapitulating, though in a modified sense, the motif of cosmic light that was introduced at the first (v 3). At the same time, attention turns

---

40:7, the hot wind from the desert which is likewise not creative but signalizes death and chaos.

22. LXX preserves the verbal repetition of the command which is appropriate in the context of execution: *wayyiqqāwû hammayîm mittaḥat haššāmayîm 'el miqwêhem wattērā' hayyabbāšâ*).

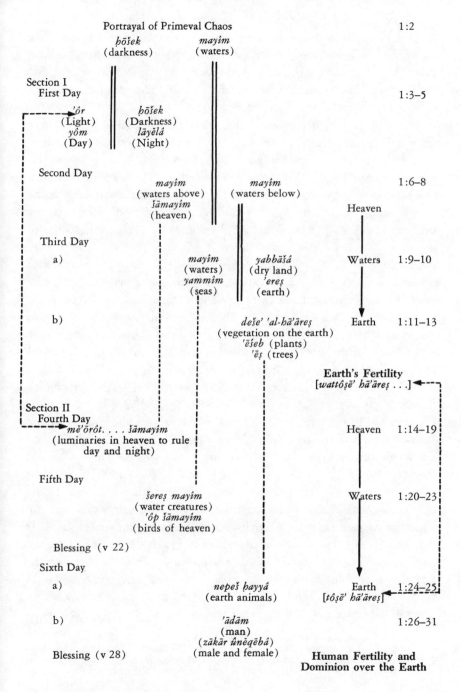

to heaven, specifically, the celestial vault (*rāqîa' haššāmayîm*) mentioned previously in vv 6–8. Executing his own command, God made the luminaries (*mĕ'ōrōt*) and placed them in the celestial expanse to perform functions which are given in chiastic reversal of the command itself: to shed light on the earth, to govern the day and the night (i.e., to mark times), and "to separate" (*lĕhabdîl*) the light and the darkness *from an earthly standpoint* (in contrast to the separation referred to in v 4). In the sixth panel (fifth day) the drama moves from the *šāmayîm* ("heaven") to the *mayîm* ("waters") which previously had been accumulated and named *yammîm* ("seas, lakes"). Fulfilling his own word, God created swarms of marine creatures, including monsters of the deep. Interestingly, the flying creatures, although they soar over the earth and beneath the celestial vault, are in some sense associated with the waters. Indeed, some construe v 20 to mean that the waters were commanded to "bring forth" not only fish but birds as well,[23] although it is doubtful that the Masoretic Text implies this. The first appearance of *nepeš ḥayyâ* (biological life in contrast to organic life) is accompanied by a special blessing (v 22). Finally, in the paired seventh and eighth panels (sixth day) the story returns once again to the earth. Just as the two sections of the story are bracketed together at their beginnings with the motif of heavenly light, so at their respective climax points, a link is made by repeating the maternal verb *tôṣē'* (cf. 1:12). God commanded the earth (v 24) to "bring forth" (*tôṣē' hā'āreṣ*) living beings (*nepeš ḥayyâ*); and in the execution sentence, which repeats the content of the command, it is stated that God "made" them (v 25). The eighth and concluding panel deals with the preeminent *nepeš ḥayyâ* (living being), man, consisting of "male and female" (*zākār ûnĕqēbâ*). The close affinity of this earth creature with the land animals is indicated not only by the pairing of these two creative acts, as in the former pair dealing with the earth (third day), but by the subsequent announcement that man shares the same table with the animals (vv 29–30). At its second climax, however, the story shows that man is more than an earth animal. Created in the image of God, man is related to the sphere of God's cosmic administration by virtue of a decree announced in the heavenly council and hence is God's representative on earth. No blessing is given

23. See LXX: '*Exagagetō ta hudata herpeta psuchōn zōsōn kai peteina petomena epi tēs gēs.* . . . The modern translation of the Jewish Torah (Philadelphia: Jewish Publication Society, 1962) translates MT: "Let the waters bring forth swarms of living creatures, and birds that fly above the earth across the expanse of the sky."

to the animals. The blessing is reserved for man who is empowered to be fertile, multiply, and exercise dominion over the earth.[24]

In summary, the creation story discloses an overall literary design, based on a double movement, in two triads of days, from heaven, to waters, to earth. At both of the climactic points the earth is the focus of concern. The twin panels at the climax of the first section emphasize the earth's fertility which is released at God's command. And the twin panels at the climax of the second part once again emphasize the earth, but above all God's supreme creature, man, to whom is granted fertility and dominion over the earth.

III

So far we have considered the main body of the creation story. The unity of the story is further strengthened by the *inclusio* which relates the end of the story to its beginning. Echoing the superscription of 1:1, the epilogue (2:1–3) opens with an epitomizing statement that "the heaven and the earth in their whole array were completed." The text, especially in 2:2, seems heavy and therefore some literary critics have suspected doublets which indicate different sources.

> God completed on the seventh day his work that he made;
> He ceased on the seventh day from all the work that he made.

Here, however, the narrator emphasizes the *seventh* day by means of complementary positive and negative statements. Picking up the previous verb (*wayyĕkullû*) at the end of 2:1, though modulating it from the passive to the active (*wayyĕkal*), he states positively that God brought his work to completion; and, with rhetorical balance, he states negatively that God ceased from the work that he made. This balancing of the positive and the negative, as Paul Humbert has observed, is continued in the next line which speaks about the blessing of the seventh day and also about its removal from the profane sphere, that is, its sanctification.[25] Thus positive and negative statements complement each other, and the epilogue is rounded off with a motive clause, introduced by the particle *kî* ("for"):

24. See further my essay, "Human Dominion over Nature," *The Bible and Contemporary Thought* (ed. Miriam Ward, R. S. M; Somerville, Mass.: Greeno, Hadden & Co., 1975) 27–45.
25. Humbert, "Zweiheit . . . ," 34.

God blessed the seventh day and declared it holy;
for *(kî)* on it God ceased from all the work
that he creatively made.

The final words, *'ăšer bārā' 'ĕlōhîm la'ăśôt* (literally: "which God created to make") are difficult to render smoothly into English. The sensitive reader of the Hebrew, however, will sense that the clause echoes the *bārā' 'ĕlōhîm* of the superscription (1:1) and at the same time recalls the usage of both verbs, *bārā* and *'āśāh*, in the main body of the story.[26] Thus the conclusion, forming an *inclusio* with the opening statement, rounds off and completes the whole. Cassuto's attempt to defend the integrity of the creation story on the basis of numerical harmony (e.g., the mystic significance of the number seven: thirty-five references to *'ĕlōhîm* = 7 × 5; twenty-one occurrences of *'ereṣ* = 7 × 3; etc.) is clearly a *tour de force*; yet in dealing with the concluding verse of the creation story he has displayed a sound sensitivity to literary style. He writes:

> Just as the prologue announces at the outset the main subject-matter of the account that follows, so the epilogue looks back and epitomizes within the limits of one short sentence the content of the preceding narrative, reawakening in the heart of the reader, by means of this synthesis inherent in its words, the sentiments that were aroused within him in the course of his reading.[27]

It is striking that Gerhard von Rad, though advocating a different view of the tradition-history of the creation story, moves toward a similar conclusion. The opening verse of Genesis 1, he says, is "the summary statement of everything that is unfolded step by step in the following verses."[28]

One final matter deserves consideration. It is often said that the Priestly creation story extends from Gen. 1:1 through 2:4a. This declaration assumes that the *tôlĕdôt* formula in 2:4a ("These are the generations of the heaven and the earth when they were created" [*bĕhibbārĕ-'ām*]) belongs essentially to the creation story, either as its misplaced introduction or, as most recent interpreters believe, as its summary conclusion. This view, however, is not consonant with the usage of the

---

26. *'āśāh* is used in vv 7, 16, 25, 26, 31; *bārā'* in vv 21, 27. No sharp distinction can be made between the usage of these verbs. Notice that the epilogue (2:2) even stresses the verb *'āśāh* by using it twice in one sentence.

27. Umberto Cassuto, *Genesis* (Jerusalem: Magnes, 1944), 1. 70. This stylistic feature is also stressed by Benno Jacob in his *Genesis* (Berlin: Schocken, 1934) 68.

28. Von Rad, *Genesis*, 49.

tôlĕdôt formula elsewhere in the Priestly Work. It is noteworthy that the Priestly Writer/Editor uses the formula five times to organize his presentation of the primeval history and five times in the patriarchal history, and in every instance, as Frank Cross has shown, it is a superscription to what follows.[29] The rubric in 2:4a is no exception to the general rule. The formula is a superscription to what follows, that is, the paradise story which the Priestly Writer/Editor appropriated from old Epic tradition to supplement and enrich his historical presentation, one that leads through the succession of the generations to Noah and eventually to the patriarchal history. It is not accurate to say that the creation story extends from 1:1–2:4a. The proper conclusion is found in 2:3 which, as an *inclusio*, corresponds with 1:1.

This observation of the structure of the Priestly Work (the final form of the Tetrateuch or Pentateuch) has important theological implications. Properly speaking, the creation story, according to the Priestly scheme, is not really part of the primeval history (*Urgeschichte*), which begins with the portrayal of human history in the genealogies and narratives from Gen 2:4a and on. Rather, the creation story is the preface to the primeval history. It sets the stage, and provides the theological and anthropological presuppositions for the ensuing story (world history, patriarchal history, folk history) which, in its received edition, comes from the hand of the Priestly Writer/Editor. In the Priestly presentation, then, creation is not the beginning of history. It is proto-historical, for it lies in the realm of mystery which belongs properly and exclusively to God, as Job was reminded (Job 38:4–7). Thus the pentateuchal story of redemption, in which Israel has a special role, is grounded in the prior affirmation of faith that God is the Creator. This theological accent is also found in the prophecy of Second Isaiah, an approximate contemporary of the Priestly Writer, who announced to Israel that hope for the redemption of Israel and of the nations of the world is grounded in faith in God as Creator (e.g., Isa 40:12–31).

To summarize: A stylistic study of the creation story yields dissatisfaction with the widely accepted hypothesis that the present shape of the text is the end-result of literary or traditio-historical stages in which *Tatbericht* and *Wortbericht* were conflated and harmonized. It is clear

29. Frank M. Cross, "The Priestly Work," *Canaanite Myth and Hebrew Epic* (Cambridge: Harvard University, 1973), 293–325, especially 301–5.

that the composer of the story has made use of traditional material; but form and content are so inseparably united that attempts to reconstruct a prehistory of the text, and to derive theological judgments from that presumed evolution, are not fruitful. When viewed stylistically, the story is a unified and symmetrical whole, whose meaning is disclosed in the internal structure of the narrative itself, with its word-event pattern. Furthermore, the theological meaning of the story is also disclosed by considering its *function* in the larger narrative whole which we have received from the hand of the Priestly Writer.

10. *"I WILL NOT CAUSE IT TO RETURN" IN AMOS 1 AND 2*

ROLF P. KNIERIM

There has never been agreement among exegetes on the meaning of the suffixed object pronoun *-nû*, connected with *šûb* (hi), in Amos' prophetic poem against the nations.[1] While many of the earlier proposals have now been abandoned[2] and a certain consensus is emerging, we are, nevertheless, confronted to this day with a number of diverse interpretations. A review of the most significant of them shall be our first task.

I

H. W. Wolff[3] has argued that in each of the eight strophes, the suffix *-nû* means "it," and that in the general announcement *lō' 'ăšîbennû* ("I will not cause *it* to return"), the pronoun points to the specific word of judgment, pronounced subsequently.[4] The suffixed object pronoun refers to a *word about to be spoken*, and with regard to that word, Yahweh announces in advance that he will not revoke it.[5] Wolff sees this "statement of irrevocability" as both explained and motivated by Amos' experience which is related in the cycle of his visions:[6] Yahweh, having

[I am greatly indebted to Ms. Judy Orr and Mr. Michael Floyd, research associates at the Institute for Antiquity and Christianity, Claremont Graduate School, for valuable assistance in the preparation of the manuscript of this essay.]

1. Amos 1:3, 6, 9, 11, 13; 2:1, 4, 6.

2. For a discussion of former proposals, see W. R. Harper, *Amos and Hosea* (ICC; Edinburgh: T & T Clark, 1905) 16–17. H. W. Wolff, *Dodekapropheton 2: Joel, Amos* (BKAT 14/2; Neukirchen-Vluyn: Neukirchener, 1967) 160, 184–87. W. Rudolph, *Joel-Amos-Obadja-Jonah* (KAT 13/2; Gütersloh: Gütersloher Gerd Mohn, 1971) 129–30.

3. Wolff, *Amos*, 168, 169, 186.

4. Amos 1:4–5, 7–8, 10, 12, 14–15; 2:2–3, 5, 13–16.

5. Wolff calls this announcement die "Unwiderruflichkeitsansage." *Amos*, 166, 168. So also S. Paul: "the absolute irrevocability of the divine decision," in his "A Concatenous Literary Pattern," *JBL* 90 (1971) 401.

6. Wolff, *Amos*, 184, 187.

twice revoked his intention of judgment as a result of Amos' intercession (7:3, 6), finally let Amos know that he would no longer forgive (7:8b; 8:2b; 9:4b). This change in Yahweh's decision from forgiveness to nonforgiveness became the basis for the statement of irrevocability in Amos 1 and 2.

Wolff's thesis, a typical example of contextual exegesis, is intriguing. Even so, it leaves us with a number of questions and objections. The thesis of a causal relationship between the cycle of visions and the poem against the nations is doubtful.[7] The differences in both poems are as great as the similarities. In particular, the vision cycle is concerned with Israel only in contrast with the poem against the nations. Moreover, even if such a causal relationship between the two poems should exist, it is not clear why the vision cycle should explain and motivate the stereotyped formula *lō' 'ăšîbennû* as Wolff understands it. Certainly the phrase *lō'-'ôsîp 'ôd 'ăbôr lô* ("I will never again pass by them"), which is repeated in the vision cycle (7:8b; 8:2b), has a passing similarity with the catch-phrase of the poem against the nations, "I will not cause it to return." In both, Yahweh states his refusal to do anything favorable in the future or from now on. In every other respect, however, the two phrases are different. The verbs denote dissimilar types of action. Yahweh himself "passes by" in one case, and he "causes something to return" in the other case. Also, as already noted, the recipients of the action are distinctly different groups, Israel in one case and the nations in the other. Finally, although the phrases have a similar grammatical construction—first-person negative imperfect—they are actually antithetical expressions. In one case the negative connotes "no longer," and it indicates a change in Yahweh's attitude: he will no longer forbear punishment. In the other case the negative connotes "definitely not," and it indicates Yahweh's refusal to change his attitude: he will not waiver in carrying out the punishment he has unleashed. And if the suffix *-nû* in Amos 1 and 2 cannot refer to the words of judgment in the vision cycle, the interpretation of the suffix as "word [of judgment]" cannot be substantiated from the vision cycle.[8]

---

7. J. Lindblom (*Prophecy in Ancient Israel* [Oxford: Blackwell, 1962] 239–42), sees them in relationship but in reverse order.

8. Wolff is imprecise when he says: "Die stereotype Ansage, dass Jahwe sein *Wort* nicht zurückwendet (1:3–2:6), findet eine einleuchtende Erklärung in der Folge der Visionen; denn die beiden ersten Berichten von einer Rücknahme der Unheils*drohung* (7:3–6) die späteren nicht mehr" (emphasis mine). *Amos*, 184. What Yahweh takes back is a *vision* granted to Amos, but not his own *word*!

Can this interpretation be sustained, however, from the immediate context in which our formula occurs? One would have to assume that within the quoted Yahweh speech (e.g., Amos 1:3a^b–5b^a), the object "it" of the general threat "I will not cause *it* to return" refers to the specific threat *spoken* in vv 4 and 5, but not the threatened event. While announcing the destruction of the house of Hazael, Yahweh would be concerned with the irrevocability of his own announcement, but not with the unavoidability of the announced destruction. In other words, each of the strophes in the poem against the nations would be dictated by two different concerns: Yahweh's word in the general threat and the content of the announcement in the subsequent specific threat. Such an interpretation from the immediate context is not impossible, but it is certainly not the only possible one. The alternative would be to understand the stereotyped phrase "I will not cause it to return" as parallel with the equally stereotyped phrase "and I will send fire" (e.g., 1:4a). In this case, the object "it" in the general threat would be paralleled by the object "fire" in the opening of the specific threat. It would then mean the unavoidability of the destructive event, but not the irrevocability of Yahweh's announcement itself. This exegesis is equally viable, especially if one understands the form *wĕšillaḥtî* (e.g., v 4a) as an explication of *lō' 'ăšîbennû*. Hence, a decision cannot be reached on the basis of the immediate context alone. It will have to include an examination of the connection of the suffix-pronoun with the verb *šûb*.

Traditionally one has referred to *lō' 'ăšîbennāh* in Num 23:20b.[9] Using this phrase, Balaam says that he "will not cause the blessing to return" which he is going to pronounce. Here, the object "it" (in fem. suffix) refers to the blessing, that is, to a *word*-event. To this extent, Num 23:20b could throw light on Amos 1 and 2. However, Balaam's word stands in a context totally concerned with his *blessing* or *cursing*, with the question upon whose commission he is going to *speak*, and whether or not he is going to *revoke* a *spoken* blessing or turn back a blessing commissioned by God (Num 23:20a). In this text, the phrase "I cannot revoke it" is singularly determined by its context. It cannot be taken as formulaic, that is, as saying the same thing wherever it occurs regardless of its context. This must be said apart from the fact that Numbers 23 has to do with blessing, and Amos 1 and 2 with announce-

---

9. So also Wolff, *Amos*, 187.

ments of judgment, and that the subject of the action (or non-action) is
the prophet in the former case and Yahweh himself in the latter. The
nonformulaic character of the phrase in Num 23:20b includes also the
object pronoun -*nāh*, "it," which means a *word*-event only because of its
context, and not because of a supposed fixed connection with the verb
šûb apart from this context. This conclusion is important because it
prevents us from automatically substituting the meaning of the suffix in
Num 23:20b for that of the suffix in Amos 1 and 2, and then proceeding
on this basis to a comparison with passages such as Isa 45:23 and 55:11
in which the root *šûb* is connected with the subject or object *dābār*.

  Num 23:20b does not prove that the object pronoun "it" in Amos 1
and 2 means a "word." The same is true for Isa 45:23 and 55:11. As
in Numbers 23, the phrase "it shall not return" in Isa 45:23 is explicitly
defined by the context: "By myself I have *sworn*, from my *mouth* has
gone forth in righteousness a *word* that shall not return." The same goes
for Isa 55:10–11: "For as the rain and the snow come down from
heaven . . . , so shall my *word* be that goes forth from my *mouth*; it shall
not return to me empty, but it shall accomplish that which I purpose, and
prosper in the thing for which I sent it." Aside from the fact that in
Isaiah 55, a return of the word is implied, both passages use the word *šûb*
in the context of an explicit discussion of the effects of the *word* of
Yahweh. In Amos 1 and 2, however, this context is not only absent, but
the phrase *lō' 'ăšîbennû* seems to stand in a different context altogether.

  W. Rudolph[10] is in agreement with Wolff and others to the extent that
he, too, says that the suffix points to "the following." But beyond this
statement, Rudolph seems to be saying three different things at the same
time. When saying that *hēšîb* "bedeutet widerrufen, zurücknehmen,
rückgängig machen wie Num 23:20; Jes 43:13; Esth 8:5, 8," he pre-
determines the interpretation of the suffix in the sense of a *word*-event.
But then, he turns around and says that "das Suffix geht aufs Folgende,
auf die drohende Strafe." By choosing the German expression "drohende Strafe" instead of, for example, "Strafdrohung" or "Androhung
von Strafe," the suffix is now interpreted as anticipating the catastrophe
itself which will not be called back, rather than Yahweh's word announcing it. Finally, when saying that "das scheinbar beziehungslove <es>
ist absichtlich geheimnisvoll zur Erhöhung der Spannung: <es>, was

10. Rudolph, *Amos*, 129, 130.

denn? höret weiter!" Rudolph explains the object "it" from the psychology of rhetoric, as used to heighten the listener's suspense and attention to the following. In this sense, however, the question just what that "following" element is, whether that which will not be caused to return is Yahweh's word or the announced catastrophe, becomes irrelevant. We should, nevertheless, like to know which of the three proposals is preferable, if any of them at all.[11]

D. L. Christensen has proposed a different reading of the original text in which the -*nû* is a sort of ballast variant over against the various names of the previous colon which varied in length.[12] The verb is emended to a qal form ("I will not turn back") with a variety of possible endings instead of a suffix. This proposal is not convincing. It has no support from any textual tradition. Christensen would have to reconstruct variations in the verb form from strophe to strophe in accordance with his assumed metrical balance. This he does not do, quite apart from the question of what weight the argument of metrical balance can have in this instance.[13] His reconstruction does not make the problem of reading the whole line any easier. We see no reason to remove the suffix from the original text form.

Rarely mentioned, but interesting nevertheless, is the proposal by V. Maag.[14] He considers the phrase *lō' 'ăšîbennû* together with older formulaic phrases used by Amos as allusions to the Day of Yahweh. The suffix -*nû* in our phrase would then refer to the Day of Yahweh which is about to come and which Yahweh will not hold or call back. Maag's proposal is highly suggestive inasmuch as the object "it" may indeed be something related to or connected with the Day of Yahweh without being identical with it. But its identification with the Day is highly improbable. In most of the references for the "Day of Yahweh"

---

11. W. L. Holladay, without discussing our problem extensively, is less ambiguous in his proposal, also tentative: "presumably [punishment]," in *The Root Šûbh in the Old Testament* (Leiden: Brill, 1958) 102. Cf. also RSV at Amos 1:3: "I will not revoke the punishment."

12. D. L. Christensen, *Transformations of the War Oracle in Old Testament Prophecy* (HDR 3; Scholars Press: Missoula, Montana, 1975) 59, 62.

13. Christensen himself is methodologically ambiguous as to the weight of poetic structures when emphasizing, on the one hand, uniformity of some elements in structure (e.g., ibid., 69) while stressing, on the other hand, the point that "there is no *a priori* reason for making the OAN tradition here as banal and monotonous in structural form as many commentators have assumed it to be" (67).

14. V. Maag, *Text, Wortschatz und Begriffswelt des Buches Amos* (Leiden: Brill, 1951) 240, 245–47.

(thirty-one out of forty-seven), "the Day" is the subject of such statements as "it comes" or "it is near." Furthermore, Yahweh is never the
subject of a statement about the Day of Yahweh. He neither causes it to
come, sends it, or prevents it from coming. Finally, the expression "the
Day of Yahweh" is never connected with the root *šûb* or with any other
verb which might describe the Day of Yahweh as something which he
sends out or withdraws. The phrase in Amos 1 and 2 would be the only
linguistic evidence of this kind.

A critical reservation must finally be noted against the interpretation of
the suffix as "punishment"[15] or "judgment." These interpretations
imply that "it" refers to the coming catastrophes as punishments sent by
Yahweh. Rather than referring descriptively to the events as such, "it"
would refer to the *nature* of Yahweh's action. It would be a qualifying
rather than a descriptive statement. Before accepting this proposal, we
would have to answer one question: Which of the Hebrew words for
"punishment" or "judgment" does the -*nû* stand for? That is, what term
fits into the semantic field which forms the background of our poem?
Moreover, any attempt to substantiate this proposal on substantive
grounds would have to show exegetically the *conceptual* background
within which Yahweh can be understood as having made a "judgment"
or as having unleashed a "punishment" which he is not going to "cause
to return." Until such exegesis is done, proposals of reading "punishment" for -*nû* only betray, at best, our own theological predilections. At
worst they show us at a loss when it comes to a precise exegetical grasp
of the problem.

II

Before proposing an alternative to the positions discussed so far, we
should make a few general observations.

1. The consistent, formulaic connection of the suffix with the verb
throughout the entire poem (eight times) makes it highly probable that
the suffix had a distinct meaning, and not an ambiguous one. This
probability is statistically supported by the fact that all the third person
singular suffix-pronouns, masculine or feminine, connected with *qal* or
hif forms of the root *šûb*—more than thirty—refer to a distinct object
and never have an ambiguous meaning.

15. Cf. Holladay, *Šûbh* 102; RSV; in part Rudolph, *Amos*, and others.

2. The fact that the exact meaning of the suffix is not explicitly defined in the poem or by Amos does not at all mean that its connotation was nonexistent or purposely ambiguous. It can very well mean that no explanation was needed because Amos could presuppose general familiarity with such a formulation. Therefore, one can assume that Amos is expressing himself within a traditional paradigm of diction. We shall investigate whether the formula *lō' 'ăšîbennû* can be located in such a tradition.[16]

3. The structure of the strophes, at least their logical structure, deserves special attention.[17] Except for Amos 2:6–16, the structure of the strophes follows this pattern:

  I. Messenger formula: "Thus says Yahweh"
 II. Word of judgment
    A. Expressed formally or generally
      1. Formal/general motivation: "For the three. . ."
      2. Formal/general announcement: "I will not cause it to return"
    B. Expressed substantively or specifically
      1. Specific motivation: "Because they have threshed. . ."
      2. Specific announcement: "So I will send fire. . ."
III. Concluding messenger formula

The main body, II, the word of judgment consists of two types of statements, a formal or general one (A), and a substantive or specific one (B). Each of these types consists in itself of a motivation followed by an announcement. Our formula *lō' 'ăšîbennû* is the formal/general announcement following the motivation in the formally expressed word of judgment. This very logical structure of the strophes of the poem (a quite frequent phenomenon in Hebrew literature) suggests that the statements of the different parts explain one another. As each type of announcement (the main statement in both parts) has its basis in the preceding motivation, so do the general and the specific motivations or announcement complement one another. This means that our formula *lō' 'ăšîbennû* must be seen as related to the equally stereotyped *wĕšillaḥtî*

16. V. Maag, *Amos*, 245 n. 3 points in the right direction when saying that *"lō' 'ăšîbennû* ist feste Formel, die mit bekanntem eschatologischem Inhalt erfüllt gewesen sein muss."
17. It has been correctly discussed by Wolff, *Amos*, 164–69; Rudolph, *Amos*, 130–31; whereas Christensen offers a different interpretation in *War Oracle*, 65–69.

'ēš "And I will send fire,"[18] and as interpreted from that phrase in a twofold way. First, a negative action ("I will not cause . . . to return") is complemented by a positive action ("I will send out . . ."); secondly, the object "it" of the negative action may in one way or another be interpreted by the word "fire" in the positive action.

This observation of the interrelationship between the elements of the word of judgment suggests that the special announcement unfolds or interprets exactly, perhaps even literally, what the formal announcement presupposes: that Yahweh will send something (fire) against the nations after that something goes forth from him, something which he has decided not to cause to return to himself. To be sure, our suffix-pronoun cannot refer to this fire itself since Hebrew 'ēš is feminine. Such an identical meaning in both announcements is not, however, necessitated by their parallelism. What is suggested by this parallelism is a possible phrase complementing the phrase "to send fire," derived from a semantic context common to both.

4. It is necessary to discuss briefly the problem of translating the verb šûb in the context of Amos 1 and 2. The list of proposals is extensive including, for example, "to put back in position," "to replace," "to restore," "to give back, to pay back, to repay," "to answer," "to revoke," "to withdraw."[19]   Inasmuch as these are to be taken seriously, each must depend on a specific interpretation of the suffix.[20] But as long as the suffix is not defined, every semantic translation of šûb is unsubstantiated. In such a situation, it seems best for the time being to render the phrase on its etymological basis and translate it "to cause to return." And just this translation shows yet another basis for comparison with the formulation in the specific announcement: There is a parallel between the negation of "return" and the verb šlḥ, "to send."

III

We are now prepared to propose the thesis that the term to which Amos is referring is 'ap, "anger." Although the tradition of Yahweh's anger is very broad in the OT and expressed in a semantic field consisting

---

18. Amos 1:4, 7, 10, 12; 2:2, 5. To these one must add 1:14: *wěhiṣṣattî 'ēš* = I will kindle a fire.

19. Cf. Holladay, *Šûbh*, 87–105; Harper, *Amos*, 16–17.

20. Wolff, *Amos*, 160, says correctly: "Die Übersetzung von Šûb hi. hängt von der Deutung des Suffixes ab."

of at least ten different roots,[21] examination of all the possibilities shows
that '*ap* is the most likely term to which Amos refers. '*ap* is connected
twenty-three times with *šûb* (qal) and seven times with *šûb* (hif). The
difference between the qal and hif is insignificant. Both forms are used
interchangeably in positive or negative statements, and in genres such as
thanksgiving or communal complaint,[22] report,[23] announcement,[24] call
to penitence or justification.[25] However, texts such as Ps 85:4; Isa
12:1; Hos 14:5; Jer 4:8; and Exod 32:12 also prove that the connection
of the two words is formulaic in public liturgies, in oracles, or in intercessions. This is confirmed by Jer 2:35 where Jeremiah quotes the people's
use of the traditional formula: "I am innocent because his anger has
turned away from me." Jeremiah, however, argues that the people have
illegitimately concluded that they are innocent. The variety of grammatical forms in which the formula occurs does not thereby affect its
idiomatic character since this variety depends on the different contexts.

However, it is important to note that the formula occurs in three
different groups of statements: in positive statements about the return of
Yahweh's anger (eight times); in negative statements saying that Yahweh's anger does not or will not return (eleven times); and conditional
statements (eleven times). In three out of eight cases of group one,[26]
the return of Yahweh's anger is caused by the return of the people to him
(by purification, confession of sin, and humbling of themselves). Additional evidence comes from Jer 2:35, for in this passage the people are
accused of arguing falsely that Yahweh's anger has returned even though
they have not returned to him. The matter becomes clearer in group
three where in eight out of eleven references[27] the return of Yahweh's
anger is explicitly made dependent on the people's purification, re-

---

21. The most important words about God's anger are: '*ap* (about 170 times), *ḥēmāh*
(about 90 times), *ḥārôn* (39 times), '*ebrāh* (24 times), *qeṣep* (26 times), *za'am*
(22 times). '*ebrāh* and *ḥēmāh* are feminine; *za'am* and *qeṣep* are not connected with
šûb; and *ḥārôn*, especially the verb *ḥārāh* (53 times) is mostly connected with '*ap*.
On the other hand, *za'am* is connected with *šāpak* (Ezek 21:36; 22:31; Zeph 3:8;
Ps 69:25; and with *šālaḥ* (Ps 78:49).
22. Isa 12:1; Ps 85:4.
23. Josh 7:26; Ps 78:38; 2 Kgs 23:26; 2 Chr 12:12.
24. Isa 5:25; 9:11, 16, 20; 10:4; 66:15; Jer 23:20; 30:24.
25. Num 25:4; Deut 13:18; Ezra 10:14.
26. Hos 14:2 and 3; Josh 7:26; 2 Chr 12:12.
27. Exod 32:12; Num 25:4; Deut 13:18; Jonah 3:9; Dan 9:16; Ezra 10:14; 2 Chr
29:10; 30:8.

pentance, or intercession.[28]   The case is clinched in the negative statements of group two which are prophetic announcements of judgment motivated by the people's failure to return to Yahweh.[29]

To this evidence one must add some observations about the semantic field in which the formula occurs.   Together with many of our references and uncounted others are phrases such as "the anger of Yahweh burned against" (*ḥārāh*[30] or *bō'ēr*[31]), is "poured out" (*nittak*),[32] is "sent out" (*šālaḥ*),[33] "shut out" (*šāpak*),[34] "comes" (*bô'*),[35] to mention only the most important ones.

There is an interesting differentiation within the semantic field, however.   As far as the phraseology expressing the *outbreak* of Yahweh's anger is concerned, there is a wide variety of expressions even though the formula *ḥārāh 'ap* is used in the vast majority of cases (fifty-three times).   When we look at the phraseology expressing the *turning away* of Yahweh's anger, the picture is quite different.   As far as I have been able to see, there is the phrase *šûb 'ap* (twenty-eight times concerning Yahweh), with only three exceptions.[36]   Last, but not least: the language of Yahweh's anger is often connected with terms like "smoke" (*'āšān*)[37] and "fire" (*'ēš*).[38]

IV

We can draw some conclusions.

1. Both linguistically and conceptually the OT knew of a pattern according to which the anger of Yahweh arises or burns, is sent out, returns

28. Gen 27:45; Prov 24:18; and Job 14:13 reflect different contexts.
29. Isa 5:25; 9:11, 16, 20; Jer 23:20. Cf. R. Fey, *Amos und Jesaja* (WMANT 12; Neukirchen-Vluyn: Neukirchener, 1963) 83–100, especially 101.
30. Exod 32:11; Num 25:2; Josh 7:1; Isa 5:25; 9:19; Jer 23:19; Ps 78:31; 2 Chr 12:8.
31. Isa 30:27; Ps 2:12.
32. Jer 7:20; 42:18; 44:6.
33. Ps 78:49; Ezek 7:3; Job 20:23.
34. Lam 4:11; Zeph 3:8; Isa 42:25.
35. Zeph 2:2; Jer 49:37.
36. Ps 37:8 (*ḥerep mē'ap* = refrain from anger; and *'azōb ḥēmāh* = forsake wrath); Deut 29:22 (*ḥāpak* = turn).
37. Deut 29:19; 2 Sam 22:9; Isa 65:5; Ps 18:9; 74:1; 78:21, 31.
38. Deut 32:22; Isa 5:24, 25; 9:17, 18; 66:15; Jer 15:14; 17:4; 23:19, 20; 30:23, 24.   Cf. also E. Johnson, *AGK, Theologisches Wörterbuch zum Alten Testament* (ed. G. J. Botterweck and H. Ringgren; Stuttgart-Berlin-Köln-Mainz: Kohlhammer, 1971) 1. 376–386, especially 385, 386.

or does not return, the last ones predicated on the condition of whether or not the people return to Yahweh. This pattern was so strong that it has been expressed in formulaic phraseology, the most consistent form of which was the word connection *šûb 'ap*. Even though most of our references belong to a later time, the basic pattern and parts of its formulaic elements were doubtlessly old, well known, and shaped at least by the eighth century B.C.[39]

2. The problem of the original setting in life of the concept and its language, and the problem of the (possibly) various settings of the different types of phrases can only be touched upon here. The clarification of these problems would require a much more extensive and detailed study, especially traditio-historical in character, than can be afforded here.

In any case, the word connection *šûb 'ap* occurs early in nontheological narrative language, in a positive formulation (Gen 27:45; cf. Prov 29:8). The most articulate positive formulations about the return of Yahweh's anger, however, occur in the context of texts typically related to cultic events, language, or traditions.[40]

Some of the conditional statements are also rooted in language reflecting a cultic background.[41] In such contexts, the phrase for the *return* of Yahweh's anger has its most distinctive setting whereas, on the other hand, the phraseology about the *rise* or outbreak of his anger is not used in contexts reflecting a cultic background. The reason for this phraseological division is obviously that the burning of Yahweh's anger is experienced in natural or historical catastrophes (such as drought or war), whereas its "return" is experienced through the mediation of reconciliatory cultic events (such as the return of the people to Yahweh).

At this point, the negative formulations enter our discussion. They presuppose that the people did not return to Yahweh so that Yahweh causes his anger not to return. The negative announcement arises out of the recognition that penitence, purification, and the return to Yahweh had not taken place. At this point the question can be left open as to whether this recognition was genuinely part of, and took place in cultic events. The negative phraseology may have been as much intrinsic to

---

39. Exod 32:12 (E); Num 25:4 (J); Hos 14:5; the Isaiah references; Gen 27:45 (J/E), and perhaps Prov 24:18; 29:8.
40. Isa 12:1; Hos 14:5; Ps 85:4; Jer 2:35.
41. Exod 32:12; Num 25:14; Dan 9:16; Ezra 10:14.

cultic patterns as the positive or conditional phraseology. Alternatively, the older prophets may have independently formulated the negative phraseology by changing traditional, positive liturgical oracles into negative announcements of judgment. To be sure, the negative statements occur only in prophetic or prophetically influenced traditions. This might well indicate that those prophets were the first actually to state that Yahweh would not turn away his anger, or would not cause it to return, because there had been no return to him.

3. A comparison between the phrase *lō' 'ăšîbennû* in its context in Amos 1 and 2, and the word connection *šûb 'ap* in its various forms and its conceptual background is called for. We have earlier assumed that Amos most probably refers to a well-known traditional formula with an unambiguous meaning when consistently using the suffix pronoun "it" in connection with the Yahweh announcements "I will not cause . . . to return." Since these announcements are formulated negatively, they appear to be antipodes within the total conceptual framework around the accusatory phrase "Yet you did not return to me" in Amos 4:6–11.[42] Furthermore, they are the formal complement to the special announcement in the same strophes introduced by the phrase "I will send fire." All this suggests that Amos' message of judgment upon Israel was more significantly influenced by the concept of Yahweh's anger than has been recognized so far. This also seems to be true for his poem against the nations. The hypothesis would then be allowed that the suffix pronoun *-nû* in *lō' 'ăšîbennû* refers to *'ap* (or *ḥărôn 'ap*). Given the relationship between the general and the specific announcement in each strophe, the gist of the poem against the nations would be this: Because Yahweh's anger is burning, has been going forth, and because he has decided not to retract it, he will hurl fire against the nations. The phrase *šûb 'ap* was generally known as a distinctive expression for the withdrawal of Yahweh's judgment, that is, his punitive action. And exactly this non-withdrawal of his judgment is the focus of the general or formal part of the message in Amos 1 and 2.

Isaiah, after having used the phrase *ḥārāh 'ap* (Isa 5:25), employs the full formula *šûb 'ap* in a similar context: his announcement of the con-

---

42. This inference must be drawn even though the authenticity of that passage has been disputed, e.g., by Wolff, *Amos*, 250–54. Compare, however, the defense by Rudolph, *Amos*, 172–75.

tinuing judgment.[43]   Jeremiah, too, makes use of this tradition (Jer 4:8; 23:20).

There is a certain problem with our hypothesis in that $lō'$ '$ăšîbennû$ appears in announcements of Yahweh's irrevocable anger against the nations whereas the mainstream of the phraseology concerned with the return or non-return of his anger is found in traditions concerned with Israel.   The thrust of our conclusions points to a solution in the general direction of the so-called Holy War or Divine Warrior traditions on the one hand, and in the general direction of the Day of Yahweh tradition on the other hand.   The idea of Yahweh's anger burning against Israel's enemies was related to both traditions.   What has been observed is that Amos uses both in order to announce Yahweh's opposition even against Israel itself.[44]   It seems that along with this internationalization of the tradition went another internationalization: the extension of a tradition about the return of Yahweh's anger, perhaps specifically at home in cultic language, to a message not only affecting Israel but also the nations, because of their unusually brutal actions.   This, Yahweh will no longer forgive.

Finally, a tribute must be paid to a practically forgotten interpretation of our text which has seemed to me all along the most preferable.   In following a hypothesis of Vater from 1810, Harper said in 1905—not without some ambiguity—that the pronoun -$nû$ "probably refers to the anger of Yahweh."[45]

---

43. Cf., e.g., Isa 9:18: "Through the wrath ($'ebrāh$) of the LORD of hosts the land is burned ($ne'tam$), and the people are like fuel for the fire."
44. Cf. Maag, *Amos*, 246–51.   Christensen, *War Oracle*, 69–72.
45. Harper, *Amos*, 16.

INDEXES

[Prepared by Mr. Norbert Pusch, Wissenschaftlicher Angestellter im Alttestamentlichen Seminar der Universität Hamburg]

INDEX OF SCRIPTURE REFERENCES

INDEX OF AUTHORS